FIFTH ROW CENTER

FIFTH ROW CENTER

BENEDICT NIGHTINGALE

A CRITIC'S YEAR ON AND OFF BROADWAY

BOOKS

792

N 564 f

Library of Congress Cataloging-in-Publication Data
Nightingale, Benedict, 1939–
Fifth row center.

Includes index.
1. Nightingale, Benedict, 1939– . 2. Critics—
United States—Biography. 3. Theater—Reviews.
1. Title   *Criticism*
PN1708.N5A34   1986   792'.092'4   [B]   85-40740
ISBN 0-8129-1248-9

Manufactured in the United States of America
9 8 7 6 5 4 3 2
First Edition

For my wife and children,
who tolerated a year of separation,
punctuated by pond-hopping.

FIFTH ROW CENTER

September

A long, deep, ear-splintering blast, something between a foghorn and the Trump of Doom, woke me up in the middle of last night. Either I was on an ocean liner in dangerous waters, or I was in the city that boasts the noisiest fire trucks in the world. The bed didn't seem to be rocking and rolling, the window was a bit large and square for a porthole, and the big black shape vaguely discernible outside looked more like a building than an iceberg or a North Sea oil rig, so the first of those alternatives began to feel rather unlikely. Yes, that was right. I was in New York—wasn't I?

My disorientation and doubt weren't altogether surprising. It had all happened pretty quickly. There I was, in the middle of what we British think of as summer, going about my business as a critic, broadcaster, sometime university teacher, and whatever, when the phone rang, and on the other end was Bob Berkvist, who edits the Sunday *New York Times*'s arts and leisure section, telling me to be very, very calm. "I should sit down if I were you," he suggested. This struck me as somewhat odd advice to receive out of the blue from 3,000 miles away, and my first reaction was to assume I had made some ghastly error in one of the reviews of London theater I'd lately sent him. I was about to discover the punishment for having confused Ian McKellen with Alec McCowen, or Alec McCowen with Michael MacOwen, or Michael MacOwen with Geraldine McEwan—but, no, that grave, kindly voice appeared to be offering something that sounded remarkably like

3

a job. What about coming to New York for a year to fill the slot Walter Kerr was about to vacate as Sunday theater critic? And now here I am, a month or so later, starting my first prolonged visit to the great American Oz for, oh, it must be twenty years.

Yes, it was 1963 when I settled in Greenwich Village after a year on a postgraduate scholarship at the University of Pennsylvania. Down there in Philadelphia I'd had as high a time as anyone could in Philadelphia in the early sixties. I'd filled my days not working, and getting to know the fellow student who was to become, and remain, my wife. That busy regimen did, it's true, leave little pause for trips out of town, but out of town I did from time to time go, mainly to what struck my country-cousin mind as the most exhilarating place human ingenuity had yet invented. Beside sedate old Philly, let alone London, New York seemed refreshingly hectic, brash, cluttered, garish, alive. I liked everything about it, from the rude money changers at Horn and Hardart's to the chess hustlers in Washington Square to the special smell that came steaming up into the streets from that inscrutable subway system. If someone had mugged me, I would probably have thanked him for the experience and made an appointment for a repeat attack.

So I took a sublet on Bank Street and immersed myself in it all. I and my wife-to-be bought paperbacks at midnight in Sheridan Square, solemnly followed Dylan Thomas's footsteps to the White Horse Inn, and had the odd bite at the Hip Bagel, where men with beads and gold earrings congregated for coffee and conversation. We heard Thelonius Monk play, and Lenny Bruce incoherently rail against racism. We went to the theater, too, but not often, not a lot. Even then Broadway seemed expensive, not least to someone struggling artificially to prolong the natural life of his student grant.

Still, we kept abreast as best we could of the burgeoning career of Edward Albee, then the great new hope of the Amer-

ican theater. We saw Arthur Kopit's *Oh Dad, Poor Dad,
Mamma's Hung You in the Closet and I'm Feelin' So Sad,*
which boasted Hermione Gingold as the lady owner of several
pet piranha fish, some Venus flytraps, the corpse of her late
husband, and a spectacularly repressed son. It directed a
series of exotic snooks and teasing salaams at maternal voracity and seemed to me then, and indeed seems to me now,
to be as lively a treatment of that subject as the modern theater
has produced. And then, of course, there was off-Broadway,
or the beginnings of it, most strikingly represented by something called the Living Theater. We saw its production of
Kenneth Brown's *The Brig* and marveled at the terrible precision with which it re-created the persnickety rituals of a
particularly punishing marine prison.

It had to end, of course. Back to Britain I went, and into
journalism, starting as a staffer on the *Guardian* and, because
of my lifelong fascination with the subject, finding myself writing more and more about the theater, theater events, theater
people. I became the paper's northern drama critic, based in
Manchester, where its head office still was. The city itself, an
important theatrical center earlier in the century, was in cultural decline; but plays and musicals still passed through on
their way to London, and there was still a decent repertory
company there, as there was in Liverpool, Sheffield, Nottingham, Stoke-on-Trent, and several other of those old,
moldering industrial towns.

It was a taxing job because the managements weren't as
considerate to critics as their softer London counterparts.
First nights started at seven-thirty or eight, not a moment
earlier, and since the *Guardian* deadline was eleven, that
meant that reviews had to be hastily scribbled at the back of
the orchestra, in phone booths, in pubs, anywhere one could
find. I remember trying desperately to make sense of the world
premiere of Harold Pinter's *Homecoming* in a hotel lounge,
surrounded by respectable men and women harrumphing and

hallooing in dismay at its apparent immorality. I remember finishing a review of Büchner's *Danton's Death* in the middle of a fight that had broken out between rival gangs in the waiting room at Liverpool Lime Street station. And then there was always a phone to find and the most notorious copy takers in England to cope with at the other end. Once I reviewed a dramatic adaptation of Lloyd C. Douglas's biblical novel called, throughout, *The Lobe*. But that was nothing to the afflictions of my London counterpart, who discovered over breakfast that the previous night he'd seen an opera titled *Doris Goodenough* and, another time, enjoyed a production of *The Merchant of Venice* whose protagonist was one Skylark.

Increasingly the job seemed to make greater demands on the nerves than on the critical faculties, and I moved to London, became a free-lance, and ended up writing a more leisurely theater column for the weekly *New Statesman*, among other things. People tell me it's an enjoyable life, and so I suppose it is if you hanker to leave home just as everyone else is returning, battle your way in all weathers to theaters in all sorts of arcane places, and night after night after night pursue an inevitably ill-rewarded search for the masterly production, the fresh and original play. That probably sounds ungrateful, since my decade and a half as a London critic has brought me fine new work by Harold Pinter, Tom Stoppard, Alan Ayckbourn, Simon Gray, David Storey, et al. and wonderful performances by Laurence Olivier, John Gielgud, Ralph Richardson, Ian McKellen, Peggy Ashcroft, Vanessa Redgrave, Diana Rigg, and many another. But one does inevitably have to endure a fair amount of desert before slaking one's thirst in such oases. On bad nights, as I have driven through the rain to worthy events in Whitechapel or Battersea, it's seemed to me that it's lucky I love the theater, or I'd have come to hate the theater.

Still, New York should provide a respite from the British rut, if that's what it's become. Just being here is a stimulus

because my visits since that frolicsome time in 1963 have been
so lamentably infrequent that what was once familiar now
seems strange and what was strange has become stranger still.
How many more big slick office buildings can be crammed
into the avenues around Grand Central, and how much more
tawdry can the area around Times Square become? To travel
from the east end of Forty-second Street to the west, which
one used to do by shuttle train but must now do in a sort of
subterranean action painting on wheels, is more than ever like
passing from Alphaville to a blend of Rio, Calcutta, and hell.
And why do people keep sidling up and hissing, "Smoke,
smoke?" into my ear?

Some things seem swankier; some, tackier. Here's the Trump
Tower, which is indeed exotic enough to trump anything, starting with the Hanging Gardens of Babylon, and yet here are
streets whose alternate ruts and bulges suggest they've been
attacked by zealots with sledgehammers, then mended on
roughly the same principle as pinning the tail on the donkey,
by blindfolded partygoers with buckets of tar. Unsurprisingly
the taxis buck and rear their way across town, demanding
considerable skill and patience of drivers who, so it seems to
me, have become politer and more affable, less like the surly
mug shots on their dashboards than they used to be. Perhaps
they've transferred some of their more negative feelings to the
street signs, which have become edgy, feisty, and all those
other things New Yorkers once took perverse pride in being
themselves: LITTERING IS FILTHY AND SELFISH, SO DON'T DO IT;
DON'T EVEN THINK OF PARKING HERE. And who or what is this
gridlock that I'm so bluntly enjoined to shun?

Not that the old feistiness and hysteria have altogether been
eradicated from the human population. Two initial vignettes.
A bohemian-looking figure shambles into my local laundry,
asks how much it costs to clean a shirt, and, not liking the
answer, exits with a wail of "You're not going to drive me out
of the city." "That guy's got problems," announced the man

behind the counter. "*I* got problems," he added in an indignant, proprietorial way, as if he and only he were entitled to possess anything so special as a problem. Again. A svelte gentleman in a white smock entered a bar and began collecting for what appeared to be the Black Muslim cause. "You're trying to destroy me," the owner half yelled, half gobbled. "This is the end for me. I can't go on. I'm being *killed*." The Black Muslim gravely bowed and wordlessly withdrew.

Will some of the same odd and unpredictable energy find its way onto the New York stage? I wonder. Will the American theater alternately unsettle and overpower me, like those bumpy streets and beetling buildings? Will the drama reflect the preposterous variety, the fun and the danger, of this city? Will it give me the emotional and intellectual shaking up I feel I need as I settle deeper into jaded middle-age? That's what I'm hoping, though I have to add that the omens aren't yet all that good. The schedule of coming events with which I've been presented at *The Times* seems distinctly thin, off-Broadway as well as on it.

Back home I'm used to going to the theater three, four, five times a week and still finding myself out of touch with happenings on the fringe and out of town. And when I left London, the month ahead looked pretty busy. The Royal Shakespeare Company was due to open two new plays, revivals of work by Jonson and Bulgakov, and Shakespeare's *Measure for Measure* and *The Tempest,* with Derek Jacobi as Prospero. At the National Theater we were promised the premiere of David Mamet's *Glengarry Glen Ross,* and elsewhere strongly cast productions of Anton Chekhov, Clifford Odets, John Vanbrugh, Tennessee Williams, and Sam Shepard, along with three or four interesting-sounding new plays.

Now, some of these things will obviously be more rewarding than others, but on most or even all of them I could, I think, base what I'm asked to contribute to *The Times,* a weekly "review-essay." That means finding something strong enough

in itself, and interesting enough in its wider issues, to allow
me to burble on for 1,300, 1,500, even 1,800 words. It's the
sort of space and freedom I've always craved; but a worry
began to niggle at the back of my mind when Bob Berkvist
and Frank Rich, my colleague on the daily *Times*, went through
the theater schedule with me. "It's slow," said Bob. "I've
never known it this slow," added Frank. We couldn't for the
life of us see more than half a dozen things worth much more
than a sniff in the next five or six weeks.

Could the situation I and my colleagues seem often to face
in Britain—too few inches for too many productions—actually be reversed here? Could the American theater prove
too parsimonious for the ample maw of my *Times* column?
Could—but enough of nervous speculation. My jet lag has
responded to two days' careful nursing. It's time to get out
there and start discovering what's really going on.

What a letdown. The production of *Uncle Vanya* in the East
Village looked very beguiling on paper. How could it be otherwise, with Chekhov the author, Andrei Serban the director,
and La Mama the host? But all went strangely awry.

The La Mama Experimental Theater Club was founded way
back in 1961, to give new writers their heads and, as it turned
out, actors back their bodies. It became known for visual and
verbal daring and a style of performance that sometimes approached the acrobatic. That was where the grotesque doll
people of Jean-Claude Van Itallie's *America Hurrah* ripped
apart their motel bedroom in 1965. That was where the young
soldiers of Megan Terry's *Viet Rock* killed and were killed a
year later. Sam Shepard, Leonard Melfi, Lanford Wilson—
all were associated with La Mama in the days when its name
became internationally synonymous with what was artistically
(and indeed politically) radical, the sixties and early seventies.
And when Andrei Serban came to the United States from
Eastern Europe in 1970, that was where he first went to work

and when he eventually produced a famous trilogy consisting of *The Trojan Women, Medea,* and *Electra.*

Serban's prime quality seems to me a magnificent chutzpah. He clearly had it when he launched his career by presenting *Julius Caesar* as a kabuki play in Rumania, of all well-drilled nations. He certainly had lost none of it when he brought that same *Trojan Women* to the Edinburgh Festival eight years ago. It was an unforgettable occasion. Up there, Helen was being ritually humiliated with offal; over there, a bare-breasted Cassandra was dancing with lighted torches; and all around, anonymous females seemed to be clicking, snarling, barking, gutterally hiccuping, and letting slip the odd sentence in Aztec, Mayan, and even Ancient Greek. It was less Euripides, you felt, then a field report presented by some sensationally avant-garde anthropology institute, but it undeniably had imaginative clout.

Serban's *Cherry Orchard* in 1977 I didn't see. I'm told that Meryl Streep all but stole the show as an extravagantly clumsy maid and that the proceedings were, on the whole, rather too knockabout. Chekhov was never well served on stage by the kind of droopy traditionalism that led D. H. Lawrence to dismiss him as "Willy Wetleg," but he did write comedies, not farces. Serban's production evidently went in the right direction, only too far. What kind of balance would his *Vanya* achieve?

Well, signs and symptoms of Serban's chutzpah were plentiful enough. You could see them in the set itself, a vast wooden folly designed (so it seemed) by a megalomaniac with a love of walkways leading only to stairways, stairways ending in cute little cul-de-sacs with room for one chair alone, and other such architectural prankishness. You could see some of that same chutzpah in the eccentricities of performance. Why did James Cahill's stately Professor Serebryakov suddenly goose his young wife, cackling with senile glee as he did so? Why did Mohammed Ghaffari's Waffles look and sound more like

a mountain bandit, an exotic Robin Hood of the Urals, than
the shambling hanger-on Chekhov actually created? What made
it necessary for Frances Conroy's Sonia to run several lengths
of the set, rather as if Serebryakov's house were a gymnasium,
before slumping to her knees in stark and (in spite of everything) not implausible pain? For what good reason did
F. Murray Abraham's Astrov burble with laughter when he
had something particularly bleak to say, such as "I don't even
like people any more, I haven't loved anyone in a long time?"
Above all, why did Joseph Chaikin's trudging, defeated Vanya
react to the professor's outrageous suggestion that the estate
be sold by stepping quietly over him, perching on his knee,
canoodling with him, and smiling his way through the line
"This is incredible, I can't believe what is happening"?

Let's pause there. It *was* incredible. I couldn't believe what
was happening either. Is that the way anyone ever behaved
at the most cataclysmic moment in his life? Or is it the way
certain directors, hell-bent on novelty, like to pretend people
behave? When the professor angrily riposted with "Make him
move to the village," it seemed almost redundant. Mr. Chaikin
seemed still to be doing experimental exercises in a rehearsal
room somewhere off Lafayette Street. One could say the same
about the oddities of performance around him. They smacked
more of the theater of surprise than of life.

It goes without saying that those looking for Chekhov will
find much of Serban's production misconceived. Apart from
anything else, a play about emotional claustrophobia, people
getting on each other's nerves and up each other's noses, is
ill served by so large an acting area. The performers were
obliged to shout intimacies across its empty acres. At times
you felt they'd do better to communicate by megaphone, semaphore, or maybe carrier pigeon. Serban has apparently in-
timated that the set needs to be this size because Vanya and
his relatives live in a big, mazelike mansion, but that is strange
logic, for it would mean that *Henry IV*, which traverses Eng-

land, could never be performed in anything smaller than Yankee Stadium. He would surely have been truer to the mood of Chekhov's play if he'd set it in a sauna, or maybe an oven. He would have been truer still if he'd forgotten all such external trickery and encouraged his actors to give good, rich performances, instead of the two-dimensional ones mostly to be seen at La Mama.

Still, truth to Chekhov may not be the only criterion of success in this particular instance. Many people will presumably be coming to the theater in search of Serban's imagination, not that of some nineteenth-century Russian. What of them? What of the sort of audience that would positively relish megaphones, semaphore flags, actors disguised as carrier pigeons, and similar invention? They, I suspect, will find even Serban's perversity halfhearted. They will wonder why he was content to play the odd game with Chekhov instead of thoroughly reconstructing him, as he reconstructed Euripides and, later, Aeschylus. The production is marooned midway between Serban and Chekhov, chutzpah and reality. It neither astonishes very greatly nor lives very much.

Two final memories. At the climax of his row with the professor, Vanya must go offstage, get a revolver, and fire it twice at the old man, both times missing. His frantic reentry is one of the most marvelous moments in drama, agonizing yet hilarious, embracing both despair and, if the actor knows his job, a rueful recognition of the folly of that despair. You might even say that it is the point at which tragicomedy, that most twentieth century of forms, makes its definitive reappearance after two and a half centuries in the theatrical closet. Well, it was never going to be easy for poor Mr. Chaikin. First of all, he had elected to play Vanya as a man almost past feeling, a sad sack three-quarters of the way to becoming one of the walking dead. Secondly, there was that fatuous, atmosphere-destroying scene on the professor's lap. Chaikin had no chance of working himself into what was really required, an ecstasy of envy, anger, and murderous clownishness. It was as if an old, dilapidated teddy bear were behind that trigger: Pooh as hit man.

Then there was the ending. For no reason I could discern, Miss Conroy's Sonia had opened the play by reading us her closing lines about God taking pity on herself and Vanya. Now she spoke them again, this time in their proper place, and she and Chaikin proceeded to busy themselves, as they had to, with the long-neglected household accounts. But from where I sat I could see that there was no lead in their pencils. They scribbled frantically away, as if miming the word "write" in a game of charades, and left no mark at all on the paper. For a production that, in spite of its eccentricities, was aiming to be realistic, this seemed odd—and somehow significant. The performers had doodled and squiggled their way through the play, and it, too, had been left more or less untouched.

I'm told that *La Cage aux Folles* is the season's first hit. As far as I can see, it is the season's first and only anything whatsoever. Nothing at all has opened on Broadway since its arrival last August, and remarkably little is planned. Half the thirty-eight functioning theaters are presently dark, though you would not know it from their fronts, some of which are festooned with bits and pieces of shows that closed weeks, if not months, ago. Someone naïve enough to believe what he sees might suppose Edward Albee's *Man Who Had Three Arms*, Arthur Miller's *View from the Bridge*, and the musical *Merlin*, among others, still to be in town. Is the idea to make the casual passerby think that theaterland is bustling with eager activity? If so, it seems remarkably misconceived. Once you've rumbled the disguise, you're only too likely to conclude precisely the opposite. The presence of all those vast multicolored tombstones only emphasizes the extent to which Broadway is, in fact, a cemetery.

The bright lettering outside the Palace Theater is no grave-yard gloss, though. *Cage* is not merely a hit, but a megahit, almost invisible behind its own rapidly accumulating mythology. You know the sort of story. People standing in line for weeks, then being told by a smiling box-office manager that there are no seats to be had this millennium. Scalpers asking and getting several times the already outrageous prices printed on the tickets. The odd theatergoer arriving in a cab with a grandmother, in hopes of selling the old lady for enough cash to put down as an advance on an orchestra seat. Is there such a thing as a rare cliché? That would seem best to describe the kind of publicity—not uncommon in more theatrically prosperous times, but these days so very difficult to justify—currently surrounding this, the first musical I've seen since my arrival in America.

The trouble with success is the expectations it creates. When you can't see a theater's brickwork for posters proclaiming "I was knocked half-senseless with delight"—roughly the case at the Palace—you'll be disappointed if the show inside doesn't send you back out dazedly giggling on a stretcher. It sometimes seems to me that the best service I can do those about to see a show I like is to tell them it's awful, frightful. That way the demands they bring to it may be more modest; their chance of enjoyment, rather greater. It would, I suppose, cause problems if one tried to introduce this idea in a regular critical column or if a producer plastered his theater with extracts from such a column. A show bragging that it was "one of the deadliest ever" might have trouble attracting customers in the first place. But once in, they might enjoy themselves more.

This is a digression and not a digression. I am no more immune than any other reader from the effects of enthusiasm within my own profession, and the combination of critical hype and public relations ado sent me into the Palace ready to be disappointed by anything short of a collaboration between Stephen Sondheim and Johann Strauss. *Cage aux Folles* wasn't that. There were times when I caught myself wondering if it was even a collaboration between Jerry Herman and Jerry Herman, though that was the name credited with both music and lyrics. His songs for *Hello, Dolly!* and *Mame* struck me as more memorable. So, yes, I was disappointed, as, rightly or wrongly, I sensed some of those around me were, too. Had we any right to be?

As everyone will by now know, the show concerns the efforts of a young man to prevent his putative in-laws from discovering that his father owns a transvestite nightclub and that the beaming lady who passes as his mother is actually its principal drag queen. But it must be broken to Albin, as this last character is called, that his "son" wants him to stay away from his engagement party. That is the main business of the first act and very drawn-out it is. It's not until the second that we get the big confrontation between suburbia and Sodom, and, as it turns out, it isn't funny enough to justify all its preparation and our waiting. It falls a bit flat, maybe even more so because of the frantic overacting that accompanies much of it. There is nothing more depressing than watching good performers mug, flaunt, and generally strain to extract laughter from a text whose innate humor it becomes only too apparent they don't trust.

There is, in fact, a curious lack of professionalism beneath the highly, almost ostentatiously professional surface of *Cage.* Harvey Fierstein's book is neither particularly well shaped nor especially well written, and Arthur Laurents's cast can be gratuitously silly. Against that must be set some strikingly staged numbers, beginning with one that allows the nightclub's collection of exotic human butterflies to display first their female finery, then their tenor and bass voices: "We are what we are. . . ." Against that, too, has to be credited the performance of George Hearn, whose Albin has dignity and wit, warmth and vulnerability, and a trace of self-mockery—never directed at homosexuality per se, I should add, only at the character's emotional extravagance. As I watched him practice masculine poses in preparation for what turns out to be an abortive transformation into his son's hearty Uncle Al, his big guileless face crumpling in dismay at the unnaturalness of all this heterosexuality, I found myself thinking of the havoc certain British actors of my acquaintance might wreak on that scene—or, for that matter, on the show as a whole when it makes the inevitable move to London.

A slight shove one way, and it could become horribly mawkish instead of what it actually is, ordinarily sentimental. A push the other way, and it could become nudging and winking, an exercise in vulgarity and embarrassment. That neither of these things happens at the Palace argues, I suppose, a degree of integrity in everyone involved. Though the show's success must be partly due to the frisson generated by a "shocking" subject—that male "Hannah from Hamburg" swaggering about in leather, cracking his whip—its aim would not appear entirely to be to titillate. Those responsible do try to suggest not merely that people have an absolute right to their own sexual predilections but that homosexuals may make more devoted couples and even better parents than many or most heterosexuals. That wouldn't exactly be a searing insight in a novel or a straight play: for a big Broadway musical, it has the merit of novelty, and maybe more than that. *Cage* could be a lot better. It could also be a lot worse.

Another frustrating evening at La Mama, but this time for different reasons. There was no problem writing about Serban or Chekhov or the curious hybrid that resulted from that implausible coupling. But how am I supposed to base an entire essay about Sam Shepard on the two fragments of his I saw last night, *Superstitions* and *Sad Lament of Pecos Bill on the Eve of Killing His Wife*? One might as well try to describe a Gothic mansion after inspecting a couple of bricks. Still, that's what my masters at *The Times* have decided they want, and that's what I hope to give them.

American drama hasn't done too well on the world's markets in recent years. In Britain we've seen a little David Rabe, a bit of Thomas Babe, some Lanford Wilson, less Mamet than we would have wished, and the odd snippet of Beth Henley, A. R. Gurney, Jr., and others. But only one American export has arrived with regularity and been received with consistent respect, and that, of course, is Sam Shepard. Part of the reason is presumably that he actually lived in London for some of the seventies, raising and racing greyhounds, minding his own business, discovering how very completely he was an American, and giving the odd play directly to British theaters. *The Tooth of Crime*, that wonderfully imaginative battle to the death between two rock stars, was first performed by the Open Space. In fact, we Londoners have seen most of his major works over the years: *La Turista*, *The Unseen Hand*, *Geography for a Horse Dreamer*, *The Curse of the Starving Class*, *Buried Child*, and, at the National Theater in 1981, *True West*.

But isn't it still rather odd that so distinctively, some would say exclusively, American a playwright should prove so relatively popular abroad? A more convincing explanation may paradoxically be found in that very distinctiveness, that apparent exclusiveness. After all, many Europeans find America quite as fascinatingly exotic as many Americans find Europe. There are plenty of Londoners, Amsterdamers, and Stockholmers who would like nothing better than to go slumming in Shepard's wide-open spaces, with their run-down motels and supercharged autos, their drifters and gamesters and musicians and crooks, their dust and sand and good arable earth, and the strange, slouching idiom of their inhabitants. Not many dramatists manage to create a landscape so vivid and complete that you can see it, hear it, smell it. Shepard has cumulatively done just that.

Well, yes. But the real reason for Shepard's high standing surely goes beyond that. The geography of the best of his plays is American, and more than American. *True West*, for instance, may occur in a world where some men gamble on fighting dogs in no-hope hamlets in the Mojave Desert and others on the likely success of bad movies in cozy Californian suburbs, but somewhere beneath its American surface it's as international as Beckett's *Endgame*, and in some of the same ways. It's about a tame brother who yearns to be wild, a wild brother who sees how useful it is to be tame, and the failure of each to escape the limitations of what he is and has become. It's about the longings of the head and the longings of the heart and the seeming impossibility of reconciling the two, at least in our generation. "I think we're split in a much more devastating way than psychology can ever reveal," Shepard has said. "It's not so cute, not some little thing we can get over. It's something we've got to live with."

That could be the epigraph of a good deal of the century's literature and much of the drama of recent years. Indeed, you could say that Shepard's brothers are the Far West counterparts of Beckett's Clov and Hamm: troubled mind and hungry body, each incomplete in itself, each obliged to depend on the other, each condemned to mutual incomprehension, resentment, and hostility. The last thing we see in the play is the two of them murderously circling each other in silhouette, to the baying of coyotes offstage. That's a memorable enough image of family fragmentation, long one of Shepard's obsessions; it's surely also meant to sum up, in appropriately stark terms, the civil war being waged inside most of us much of the time.

Fool for Love, which I caught and admired the other night, is no less pungently American and no less entertainingly international. It's set in the peeling heart of Shepard country. All we actually see, it's true, is a drearily furnished motel bedroom, but it takes no great effort to imagine the hot, worn tarmac outside, the pickup truck parked on it, the perpendicular scrub disappearing into the distance, the anonymous little towns beyond. Yet that western wilderness turns out to be the setting for a tribute to the unruliness of love that would be readily understood in any time or clime.

When Shepard was rehearsing the production at the Circle Repertory Theater, he apparently kept telling his leading performers, "That's fine, but take it further, take it still further," and one can see why. *Fool for Love* persistently caps one piece of emotional testimony with another and then another. Here's a woman alternately raging and clutching at a man who turns out to be her half brother and is himself hardly less fixated on her. Then out of the darkness comes a glare of lights, a screech of brakes, the bang of a shotgun, a crash of glass: his ex-mistress, so it seems, making her jealousy and anger rather drastically felt. And then we have one of the longest and most riveting of Shepard's celebrated monologues, this time describing the bigamous loves of the couple's father and his two wives' abject and finally suicidal obsession with him. As with *True West*, I found myself thinking of Beckett, particularly of the tag he himself applied to *Waiting for Godot: Nec te nec sine te* ("Neither with you nor without you"). The two brothers cannot, you feel, successfully live together or apart. No more can the lovers of this play, ultradestructive though their twin passion seems to be. It's another tale of unwilling interdependence, but darker, uglier, and more powerful than its predecessor, *True West* itself.

Indeed, astonishingly powerful. The script says the play is to be performed "relentlessly, without a break," and so it is. The stage directions ask the leading lady to utter "agonizing mournful wails" and require her very body to "weep," and there's hardly a part of Kathy Whitton Baker, larynx to fists to knees, that doesn't hurl itself into the task of obeying them. Shepard certainly flirts with melodrama. Given all the howling, banging on walls, and distraught falling to the floor, you could perhaps accuse him of taking flirtation three-quarters of the way to consummation. Yet somehow the play remains inviolate, vibrant, true. The comparison with Beckett is actually pretty inadequate because for him love is no more than a momentary flicker on Krapp's tape recorder, sex a drear ritual distantly remembered by the characters of *Play*, trapped in their funeral urns. For Shepard, love and sex are blazingly real and immediate, for better or worse—or, rather, for better *and* worse. There were times when it seemed to me that in *Fool for Love* we had an American *Phèdre* on our hands.

But the play has been around for some weeks. What opened last night was decidedly more flimsy. *Pecos Bill*, though receiving its New York premiere now, was Shepard's contribution to the Bicentennial, and as backhanded a tribute as you'd expect from a writer who tends to see America itself as a blend of the garish and the forlorn, the brazen and the desolate. It is a gaudy little cantata, in which the outlaw of the title, arriving onstage on a battered wicker scorpion, boasts of tearing down mountains, strangling tornadoes, and personally digging the Rio Grande, only to end in querulous bewilderment: "Why is we forsaken, lost in shame, forgotten?"

Still, it's a suggestive little piece. It contrasts the swank and glitter of the myth with the bleakness of America now, as much of Shepard's work does. It also, and perhaps more interestingly, reminds us of what is and always was squalid in that myth. This is surely the answer to those critics who have accused Shepard of mindless nostalgia for the Old Frontier. He dreams, like the suburban brother in *True West*, of release and liberty and being at one with the American wilderness. But he also knows how anachronistic is the figure cut by the brother who has actually lived in that wildness and how crude many of his predecessors actually were. The legendary Morphan Brothers, resurrected in contemporary suburbia in the course of *The Unseen Hand*, scratched an uneasy, precarious living from robbing trains. Pecos Bill was a swaggering loudmouth whose grand Homeric achievement was killing his wife.

Superstitions is more impressive, yet less important, consisting (as it mostly does) of monologue culled from the scattered reverie Shepard recently published as *Motel Chronicles*. If you've read that, you've seen this. If you've read that, you've seen *more* than this, since this concentrates on one aspect of the book only: dreads and fixations and compulsions and morbid, predawn fantasies. You try not to imagine how the chain saw will kick back and cut off your hand, and you just can't stop. You go out to empty the garbage, and suddenly you're thinking of the nuclear holocaust, and how you don't know it's coming until it melts you because you haven't a radio or a good friend to call you. You find yourself arranging your boots in a certain order, or putting your betting tickets in certain pockets, or walking in front of an unwanted lover's door in certain patterns. If she doesn't see you, you'll exorcise her, but if she does, you'll die.

What have these snippets to do with Shepard and his work more generally? Well, they describe obsessional behavior, and obsessional behavior is a foredoomed attempt to establish or reestablish some power over the environment around you and, of course, over yourself. It is desperate magic, born of insecurity and helplessness, betokening a terrible want of confidence not only in your significance but in your very identity. Fragmentary *Superstitions* may be. Absurd it may be to base on it very sweeping generalizations. But it gives you a glimpse into the haunted shanty of Shepard's imagination and hence into the minds of that legion of the lost, his dramatic characters. Whether or not he believes the Old West, the old values, the old possibilities amounted to too much—the implication is they didn't—Shepard knows they've long since irretrievably disappeared. In their place there's what a character in *Curse of the Starving Class* sums up as "cement pilings, prefab walls, zombie architecture owned by invisible zombies, built by zombies for the use and convenience of other zombies." Who can sustain any sense of worth in such a world? Who can find fulfillment in a country given over to moneymen and real estate swindlers, like those who ruin and selectively slaughter the dilapidated family at the center of the same play? Who can feel at home in Azusa in *The Unseen Hand*, a deadly amalgam of Safeway shopping centers and basketball games and "everything from A to Z in the USA," or in the Hollywood of *Angel City*, a place rather high-handedly evoked by green ooze and fanged men with green skin?

There's no escape from it all, no sanctuary to which you can even temporarily retreat. That would appear to be the bleak conclusion of Shepard's *Family Trilogy: The Curse of the Starving Class, Buried Child, True West*. Out there in Norman Rockwell country one parent is drunkenly smashing in the door, the other is surreptitiously selling the house, the avocados are rotting on the trees, one brother is strangling another, little sister is understandably planning to leave, and an idiot called Tilden is lumbering about the front room with the shrunken corpse of the baby his father long ago drowned. The family is less a refuge than a trap which entices, seizes, then maims or kills, and its traditions are also its curse, an inexorable handing over of emptiness and anomie from one generation to the next.

That helps explain the flamboyant and usually empty gestures to which Shepard's people are prone. In an attempt to find personal and social significance, they adopt masks, roles, personalities, sometimes pretending to themselves that they are really faces, identities, selves. Pecos Bill, big-time legend and small-time man, would be an obvious, if minor, example. The best would be the rock star of *The Tooth of Crime*, destroyed not merely by a younger rival but by the impossibility of sustaining the hard, mean style the world seems to respect. "It ain't me," he yells in his extremity, and yet, as he's admitted earlier, he has no longer a "self" to fall back

on when image isn't enough. You might even say he has no
identity at all.

He kills himself, unlike Shepard's other characters, who
bump and stumble on, trying and failing to adjust their internal compasses to a world deprived, so to speak, of its North
Pole. The chances of their ever getting their emotional and
spiritual bearings are, you feel, decidedly slim. After all, the
reason they're lost is that they're simultaneously searching
for things which, if attainable at all, are probably incompat-
ible: selfhood and a persona; excitement and security; the
exhilaration of self-fulfillment and a sense of belonging; freedom and roots. It's surely a quintessential American quest,
and it's chronicled by Shepard in a style whose twists and
leaps and general imaginative restlessness accurately reflect
its substance.

Yet that still doesn't make his work insular. After all, the
feeling of fragmentation, the fear of disintegration, the yearning for wholeness aren't American experiences only, as witness
some of the more striking recent drama in my own country.
There's kinship between Shepard and, for instance, David
Storey and Trevor Griffiths and the late David Mercer, playwrights of working-class origin who see or saw social "better-
ment" as to some extent dispossession, the trading of blood
for water, a birthright for a mess of pottage. He feels diminished by the continuing encroachment of Azusa and its arti-
facts; they, by class mobility, success, comfort, and wealth.
No, Shepard is not "just" American, as some have suggested.
Rather, he is a dramatist of growing international stature who
has brought a vividly American idiom, context, and imagination to universal confusions.

A curious thing happened this afternoon as I was strolling
past that long, heaving bank of word processors and word-
smiths that's called the culture desk at *The Times*. An editor

told me a call had come through that moment from Joe Chaikin, the Uncle Vanya at La Mama, and so I picked up the phone, not without apprehension. My brushes with theater people I have criticized haven't always been happy. When the dramatist John Osborne founded his British Playwrights' Mafia, an organization dedicated to humiliating and injuring critics, he announced that I would be his first victim. Nothing much happened. The Osborne foot shot out and nearly tripped me up as I walked down the aisle of the National Theater one night; I got a children's postcard one day headed "BPM Headquarters" and warning me that it would be safer for my health if I "stayed clear of downtown Chichester," a place I had never proposed visiting in the first place. But it left me aware that the affronted artist could be a vengeful fellow.

Actually I admire Joe Chaikin, as both performer and organizer. Without him the Open Theater, perhaps the most creative force in the U.S. theater in the 1960's, would probably never have existed. If he hadn't again and again brought his mournful voice and woebegone clown face to the work of Samuel Beckett, that playwright would be considerably less well known and regarded than he now is in America. But in my piece this coming Sunday, which he would seem to have seen in advance, I say not merely that he looks rumpled to the point of being slept in but that he reminds me, much more than any Vanya should, of an old bolster with stuffing coming out of the top. Possibly he doesn't feel altogether flattered by this.

As it turned out, he was politeness itself. He wanted me to know that his interpretation, particularly the episode on the professor's lap, wasn't altogether to his liking either. But what can you do, his message seemed to be, when you've subjected yourself to a director's discipline? Well, he's hardly the first actor to fret at that sort of dictatorship. I well recall the outrage still to be heard in Frank Finlay's voice when he spoke years afterward of the crude, redneck Iago it had been de-

creed he should play opposite Laurence Olivier's lordly
Othello. Some might think Chaikin's phone call less than loyal;
to me, it was an understandable reaction to the sort of frustration we'd all feel if we were abused for an interpretation
not really our own. Anyway, I thanked him for the information, mumbled something nice about his work generally,
and rang off.

I daresay he'll have other calls to make. No one much seems
to have liked this Vanya, for all the brouhaha surrounding
its arrival. My colleague on *The Times*, Frank Rich, had some
particularly harsh words for Diane Venora, the actress who
plays the professor's young, bored wife. Yelena, as the character is called, is criticized by both Vanya and Astrov for her
exquisite inertia. Accordingly Miss Venora undulated languidly about the stage with a handkerchief, idleness in excelsis,
huskily luxuriating in the disasters unfolding around her infinite passivity. Very likely she would claim the same alibi for
her performance as Mr. Chaikin would. But whether the interpretation is her own or her director's, it is surely as misconceived as it is exaggerated.

This sounds like a small point. In fact, it takes one right
to the heart of Chekhov, surely an organ as generous in its
sympathies as any that has thumped in theatrical history. In
all his work for the stage there is not a single character—no,
not even the nasty, grasping valet in *The Cherry Orchard*—
whom one can dismiss with derision or contempt. Somehow
he makes you aware that each one has an explanation, a
justification for his or her conduct. At any rate everybody,
"good" or "bad" or anything else, has a point of view worth
trying to understand. The trouble with Miss Venora's performance is that it takes the men's two-dimensional travesty of
Yelena as the full psychological truth. If you listen to the
character as she is, not as she is accused by others of being,
you'll find that she is intelligent and acute, not least about
the way men travesty and misuse women. That's the way I've

twice seen the part played in London in recent years, and it worked very well. That's the way Chekhov would have wished it performed, too. When an amateur actress wrote to him asking if Yelena was a thinking, decent person or an apathetic, idle woman, incapable of thought or love, he replied very emphatically: The first.

Chekhov has often been posthumously hijacked by special-interest groups: socialists; environmentalists; maybe even reformed Shintoists. In fact, he rejected all "tags and labels," all "prejudices" and "isms" as an affront to the complexity of things. He was, he said, "neither liberal, nor conservative, nor gradualist, nor monk, nor indifferentist." Yet it sometimes seems to me that there's one label he would have been happy to wear, and that, curiously enough, is feminist. No other writer of his time saw so clearly how the traditional roles foisted on women robbed them of their individuality. If Yelena has become apathetic and idle, it's because she's intellectually, emotionally, and spiritually frustrated, and if she's frustrated, it's because of a numbing marriage, a paralyzing environment, a deadening society, all adding up to a cage for the mind and the soul. Chekhov would obviously not have liked the narrower, more baleful varieties of feminism, though since he *was* Chekhov, he would have understood how and why that coven mentality came into being. But he would have admired the sort that seeks to release and expand. It would have seemed to him not just feminism but a matter of basic human rights.

We could do with more of that openness of mind and munificence of spirit in these shrill times. If only Serban's production had shown just a little appreciation of such qualities!

To call Raymond FitzSimons's *Kean* the first new play of the Broadway season, as people are doing, seems somewhat pretentious. Can something that began life on the London fringe a few months ago, then moved to the West End, really

be new? Can a long, scattered monologue, interspersed with
bits of the Bard, be dignified as a play? Well, maybe. But in
any case the reason for its appearance at the Brooks Atkinson
has nothing to do with the merits of the text, everything to do
with the identity of the star. America wanted to see Ben Kingsley, who won an Oscar for his screen performance of Gandhi,
and Ben Kingsley wanted to show America that he wasn't just
a small, bald magus serenely twirling a spinning wheel.

   Nor he is. The show admittedly asks the impossible of him.
How to incarnate not only the tormented life but also the
astonishing art of Edmund Kean? Didn't Coleridge say that
to see him act was "to read Shakespeare by flashes of lightning," and didn't Byron admit to shrinking in fear when his
"frown of hatred darkly fell"? Yes, and the official biographer
of Edwin Forrest, who more than once shared a stage with
Kean, raved on about a truth and intensity that "suggested
something portentous, praeternatural, supernal, that blinded
and stunned the beholders, appalled the imagination, and
chilled the blood." Supernal? Blinded and stunned? Poor
Kingsley must sometimes have felt like an electric bulb cast
in the role of that Coleridgean lightning.

   Yet he came nearer to achieving what was required—simultaneously spewing out a shameful life story from a barstool
at 4:00 A.M. and auditioning for the lead at the National Theater—than anyone who knew only his Gandhi could have imagined. He also got me thinking. What makes me suspect, as I
do, that Edmund Kean was the greatest classical actor who
ever uttered in English? Who has matched that tiny, venomous
maestro, and who, if anyone, could match him now, on either
side of the Atlantic? And what is great acting anyway?

   The late Kenneth Tynan once wrote that greatness consisted
of "complete physical relaxation, powerful physical magnetism, commanding eyes that are visible at the back of a gallery,
a commanding voice that is audible *without effort* at the back
of a gallery, superb timing which includes the capacity to make

verse swing, chutzpah—the untranslatable Jewish word that means cool nerve and outrageous effrontery combined—and the ability to communicate a sense of danger." The critic Michael Billington, quoting this list in his *Modern Actor*, rightly wonders why "acute interpretive intelligence, the intuitive reappraisal of a role," is missing from it. But maybe the real trouble is that Tynan was attempting to codify the uncodifiable. James Agate was perhaps wiser, if less informative, when he retreated into metaphor and spoke of "a tiger leaping out on the spectator from the bush of mediocrity and the brake of competence."

You don't analyze tigers, at least not when they're alive and in the same room as you. You watch, tingle, and wonder if you'll get out in one piece. And that seems to have been the very effect Kean had on very many in the early nineteenth century. The elder Dumas actually called him "a wild beast, half man, half tiger." Again, you don't try to put wild beasts on the psychiatric couch, not unless you are very naïve and foolhardy. But one is bound to speculate about the effect on Kean's proud, determined temperament of the calamitous years in which he was doomed to trundle a handcart around the English provinces, reciting Shakespeare to empty houses while his wife starved and one of his children died. By the time he triumphed at Drury Lane, he was a very angry man indeed, and he still had the discipline to sublimate anger into art. He proved that on his debut with a Shylock so powerful it was later described as "a chapter of Genesis" and so cataclysmic at its climaxes that he sent for at least one of his two Tubals in advance of the performance, to warn him not to be frightened.

Yet to take Tynan's "sense of danger" too literally is to fall into romantic heresy. Not all major actors have been bitter, rancorous men, still less raging paranoiacs, like Kean. Anger, though no doubt often present at some level, isn't an essential part of the great performance. There must, you feel, be intensity of emotion inside, and that intensity must, of course, be externalized onstage, but its sources, kinds, and forms will obviously vary. What would appear to have made Edwin Booth great, for instance, is something strange and hard to define, a desolation combined with a sense of horror. His Hamlet, we're told, had "that haunted condition, so expressed as to thrill the imagination with a shuddering sense of spiritual surroundings." What perhaps earns Paul Scofield a place in the pantheon nowadays is something not dissimilar. Behind that gaunt, creased face of his there sometimes seems an almost infinite melancholy, aptly expressed by that dark, mournful voice, rumbling up from his stomach as if from an old crypt.

Actually "anger" only begins to sum up Kean's own range. He seems to have been able to whisper or explode his way to the heart of every strong emotion. Indeed, we have the word of no less an authority than William Hazlitt that his special forte was pain in all its varieties. The last time the critic G. H. Lewes saw him, he was tipsy, hoarse, and sick and (of course) as short, squat, and round-shouldered as ever. Yet when his Othello scuttled in a gouty hobble toward William Macready's Iago, who was much taller than himself, and grabbed his throat with a rasp of "villain, be sure you prove my love a whore," Kean "seemed to swell into a stature that made Macready appear small." Such was the pathos of the performance that "old men leaned their heads upon their arms and fairly sobbed."

As this emphasizes, obvious attractiveness has nothing to do with greatness. On the contrary, the history of acting is a history of physical disadvantage, populated by men who would have difficulty obtaining anything but "character" roles in your average soap opera. David Garrick, like Kean, was tiny. Macready was once described as "the plainest and most awkwardly made man that ever trod the stage" and was something of a stutterer, too. Henry Irving walked clumsily and, like many of the great actors, was vocally less than musical. Kean's voice was "thick and hoarse, somewhat between apoplexy and a cold," like "a hackney-coachman's at one o'clock in the morning": this in 1815, before dissipation and exceedingly large auditoriums had combined to pull his larynx apart.

Indeed, some would say there's only one physical asset a great actor must possess: not hands and not feet—Kean at his most incapable performed while slumped on a sofa—but his own equivalent of Garrick's "far-darting eye." Irving's eyes were small and dark yet could "at a moment become immense and hang like a bowl of dark liquid with light shining through." Olivier has said his eyes are more important to him as an actor than arms or legs. Kean had unusually short lids, so that white was visible above as well as below the pupils, which themselves were "black, large, brilliant and penetrating." Those eyes, said Hazlitt, were "never silent" and allowed him to choke on syllables or even drop words with gain rather than loss of eloquence. John Keats's summing-up of Kean's famous death scenes is suggestive in its emphasis: "the very eyelid dies."

The great actor is truthful and much more than truthful. Somehow he achieves a blend of honesty and audacity that resolves the old quarrels between the realistic and the stylized, nature and art. Garrick had that simultaneous freshness and charisma. When his Hamlet first saw his father's ghost, men cried out and women fainted, so authentic and awesome was his terror. Kean had it, too, and to an extent that seemed barely credible to a generation brought up on the cumbersome gentility of John Kemble, who played the sweet prince "like a man in armour." Macready's skulking yet momentous Macbeth had it, and so perhaps did his great rival Forrest when he played the same part as "the ferocious chief of a barbarous tribe."

Forrest's "biceps aesthetic" wasn't to everyone's taste. Some said that he tended to rant; some, that he hammered out his syllables too unvaryingly. One critic even dubbed him a "bo-

vine bellower." Yet the usually jealous Kean, to whose Othello
he played what seems to have been a notably lively and original
Iago, thought him possessed of a "decided genius," and few
actors have striven so hard and conscientiously for honesty
of effect. So much research did he into aging and senile madness, visiting asylums and old men's homes, that he was able
eventually to claim that his own knowledge of the subject
outstripped that of most doctors. And so thoroughly did he
enter into the part that once he fainted dead away, and another time he hurled off his wig in his fury at Goneril and
Regan. Nor did anyone snigger at the incongruity of a raging
patriarch with short black hair.

The other great Edwin, Booth, probably beats him to the
American bays by virtue of more unpredictability, variety,
subtlety, and depth. He aimed to "reveal the soul of master-
pieces" and seems sometimes to have done precisely that, most
notably with that strange and haunted Hamlet. Yet Forrest
clearly had a physical power and sometimes achieved an intensity beyond either Booth or the next major American con-
tender, John Barrymore. One impressed English visitor found
himself comparing his Macbeth to an angry sea or the Niagara
Falls, "a whirlpool, a tornado, a cataract or illimitable rage."

But who in our time can be compared with oceans, ty-
phoons, geysers, hailstorms, and other such natural yet hy-
pernatural phenomena? Indeed, is the "great" performance,
in the still somewhat romantic sense in which I seem to be
defining it, possible at all nowadays, in Britain or America?
So much seems to be against it, from our ideas about acting
to our feelings about life itself. It's a bit early for me to start
pontificating about what I'm in America to discover, but since
I've started, I may as well crash relentlessly on. Conditions
here strike me in some important respects as less favorable
to the ambitious actor than in Britain. Ian McKellen, who
may one day achieve greatness, once compared what he regarded as his good fortune with the fate of his American broth-

ers. He grew up seeing, ingesting, absorbing Shakespeare as an integral part of the English air. When still pretty young, he had the chance to play Henry V, Hamlet, Richard II, and Christopher Marlowe's Edward II. While still not very old, he was a leading actor at the Royal Shakespeare Company and later at the National Theater. Even when he took time from the stage to appear on TV, the parts he played were never despicable, sometimes positively broadening. "Telly helps," he once told me gravely.

Well, telly in America usually doesn't help. More often both it and the movies are the equivalent of a great black hole, sucking potentially fine talent away from the stage and converting it to antimatter. Nor are the opportunities offered by the nation's theatrical capital, New York, as ample and invigorating as they might be. Actors with a yearning to tackle cliff faces are more likely to find themselves hauling their way with ax and rope up some grassy bank or small suburban knoll. Naturalism rules. The chances to play classical roles, or roles of any great scope or stature, seem to be sadly few, and when they come, they'll almost certainly be with an ad hoc cast, not a permanent or even semipermanent company, the sort that challenges, stretches, enlarges a talent.

Let me not fall into inconsistency here. What Kean considered a company wouldn't have been what we consider a company today. For him, it was a group of underlings, a human landscape for his exotic portraiture. For us, it's a more egalitarian institution, one that expects aspiring stars to subordinate themselves to the demands of the artistic whole. It could be argued, then, that it's inimicable to the big performance, and there are times when that is indeed so. I've seen more than one *Hamlet* played, so to speak, without the prince. Yet no one who saw McKellen's Macbeth or John Wood's Brutus or Alan Howard's Henry V or John Gielgud's Prospero or Albert Finney's Tamburlaine, or any of a score of other performances for the RSC or National, could believe that actors are in practice being deprived of the power to dazzle and astonish.

Perhaps this is also the answer to another doubt that dogs me from time to time. How to project large, bold emotions in an age that hardly seems to believe in large, bold emotions anymore? The shrugging, antiheroic climate of the time wouldn't seem friendly to great performance. Moreover, psychology, psychiatry, sociology, and the other "behavioral sciences" have deprived us of our old innocence about motive and feeling. Evil becomes maladjustment, passion becomes sickness, and everything the dramatists and actors of the past thought relatively straightforward, or at least manageably intricate, disappears in a confusion of subtleties, qualifications, and scrupulous excuses. Hence the socially alienated Iago, the homosexual Iago, the clinically senile Lear, the schizophrenic Leontes, and other such conscientious diminutions of starker, more elemental, and more theatrically powerful truths. And yet there are still some, just a few, who have managed to combine the old force and authority with a contemporary complexity. There was that McKellen Macbeth, for instance: stealthy, hungry, and dangerous; a study of the sexuality of ambition as intense as it was intricate.

An exceptional talent can somehow weather it all: Sigmund Freud, B. F. Skinner; companies, lack of companies; naturalism, the Method; even Hollywood. Orson Welles's lordly, if overblown, Othello is still remembered with nostalgia by those over whom it massively rolled three decades ago. George C. Scott's Antony was by his own confession a failure ("I should have played Cleopatra"); but his Richard III had a spectacular bravado, and his 1962 Shylock was clearly a multidimensional being, capable of "monumental rages and grievances ferociously imaginative." The Canadian Christopher Plummer survived *The Sound of Music*, believe it or not, to offer an Iago whose icy blend of despair and malice left Walter Kerr suspecting it "the best single Shakespeare performance to have originated on this continent in our time."

Yet just because an actor *can* survive Hollywood doesn't mean he *does* survive Hollywood. Scott and Plummer are seen too rarely on the the classical stage, and others never. Think of what might have come from Richard Burton, a smoldering Coriolanus and a blazing Hamlet in his salad days, had he not elected to put down his tents in Babylon. Think of what a rigorous Shakespeare director might have made of Marlon Brando, Paul Newman, and many another. In Britain Fredric March would have died a theatrical knight, and Sir Jason Robards, Jr., would now be in perpetual transit between the National Theater and the Royal Shakespeare Company. In this last case, of course, the American Bard has gained where the English Bard has lost. But it's a pity that an actor so extraordinarily good at baring souls, which is what Eugene O'Neill demands, has so rarely had time, inclination, or opportunity to show those souls' apotheosis, which is what Shakespeare permits. One can imagine the dark fire of his Lear. Maybe he'll give it to us one day. And maybe then the American theater will have an indisputably great classical actor, the first since Barrymore left New York for Hollywood sixty years ago.

But enough of potential and promise, categories not hard to furnish when there are actors like Ian McKellen, Dustin Hoffman, Christopher Walken, Anthony Hopkins, John Wood, Kevin Kline, and Ben Kingsley in the English-speaking world. Who *are* the great classical actors these days? Well, I've already mentioned Scofield and Gielgud in passing and should, no doubt, have invoked Ralph Richardson, too. Yet when one compares their effect on their audiences with that of Kean, one is bound to wonder if something isn't missing. Scofield hasn't that electrifying variety of emotion and expression. Gielgud, a human cello that plays itself with superb discrim-

ination, hasn't any of that animal power. And Richardson—
well, he's a wonderful quirky, inventive actor, but he never
attempted Hamlet or Lear, he flopped as Macbeth and Othello,
and he scored his greatest Shakespearean success in a comic
part, Falstaff. He's as different from Kean as ale from acid.

No, there's only one living candidate for the great Edmund's
mantle and throne, and that's the obvious one: Laurence Olivier. He, too, has been both praised and attacked for the di-
rectness of his realism and for the size of his passion. His
Othello was a black African, so clearly so that one geographically minded critic declared his birthplace to be the west coast
of Africa south of Senegal, and a man in agony, with a "wild
beast sewn up in him and clawing to get out." His Shylock
was a prosperous Rothschild, complete with frock coat and
somewhat awkward urbanity, and a man destroyed. Kean,
with his love of eloquent "hits" or "points," would surely
have envied the terrible howl that reverberated from the wings
after he had stumbled offstage, having brokenly proclaimed
himself "content" to become a Christian. Olivier can scry a
message on a cherry stone or carve a giant face on Mount
Rushmore and, you feel, somehow defy the laws of possibility
by doing both at once.

That's great acting all right, and yet, heresy though it may
be to say it, something seems missing. That Othello was majestic, electric, wonderfully daring, and precise in both intona-
tion and movement—but where were the old men sobbing at
the pity of it all? Or is it just I who feels that while Olivier
may astound my eyes, churn my blood, and do improbable
things to the nape of my neck, he can never touch the lump
I keep poised for action in my throat? Is it just I who finds
him a bit too calculating to be moving?

God knows, Kean was calculating, too, to the extent of
literally measuring the steps to his next flamboyant gesture.
Moreover, he committed sin after sin that our generation would
find outrageous. He appeared with poor casts, upstaged every-

one, omitted or gabbled lines he thought unimportant, sacrificed too much to the bravura moment, and made a mannerism
of his famous switches from dark to light, relaxation to intensity. And in spite of all that, plus booze and sickness and
boorishness, the evidence is that he could command his audience's collective heart as well as its outer organs. He was
terrific even when terrible, awesome even when perfectly awful.
And that is why I suspect he was the greatest actor who ever
lived.

When Americans decide to have fun in earnest, by God they
do so. No, it wasn't Citizen Kane or the Great Gatsby who
sent me weaving back to my apartment in the early hours of
today, filled with champagne and caviar and good cheer. It
was Michael Bennett, director, choreographer, and principal
begetter of *A Chorus Line.* He had spent some $500,000 show-
ing his understandable satisfaction at that musical's 3,389th
performance, which had made it the longest-running show in
the history of Broadway.

They all came, bigwigs and celebrities, Helen Hayes and
Meryl Streep and Joseph Papp, who had first presented *Chorus Line* at his Public Theater back in 1975. They ate, they
drank, they swapped memories of *Chorus Line*, and then they
trooped into the Shubert Theater to see it again. But what
they saw, let's agree, was just a little different. The show has
a cast of 33, generous enough by today's skimpy standards.
Last night no fewer than 332 made their way onto the stage,
at one barely credible moment, all of them simultaneously.

It took weeks to arrange. The organizers apparently tried
to contact 457 performers who had played in the show at
various times and on various continents; they found them at
home and abroad, up the road in *Cats* and resting in Oregon
or Florida; and almost all they invited agreed to come to the
big bash on Forty-fourth Street. Donna McKechnie, who created the part of Cassie and won a Tony for it, was there. So

were Ilona and Judith Papp, twins who alternated the roles
of Connie and Tricia in Berlin. So was Chikae Ishikawa, Connie in Japan. The biographical snippets in the Shubert program demonstrated what the show itself concerned and concerns:
the fluctuating fortunes of a dancer's life. Some had prospered
on the stage; others were "working in advertising and public
relations," "studying for an electrical engineer's degree,"
"teaching computer programming," "compiling a 'gipsy cook-
book,'" "relaxing," "looking for work," and "on the mend
following knee surgery."

A Chorus Line I first saw, and extravagantly admired, on
the other side of the Atlantic seven years ago. It didn't run
so long in London as in New York, for reasons by no means
clear to me. Perhaps Americans found more resonance in its
tale of thirty hoofers desperately auditioning for a dozen roles
under the hard eye of an all-powerful deity invisibly ensconced
in the gallery. If one wanted to be earnest about it, one could
say the show's subject was competition, the dread and pain
of failure, the exhilaration of winning through. In it, those
with talent and skill and personal strength and resilience and
the willingness to endure temporary humiliation get their reward, and the reward takes an almost mythic form. It's a
chance to flash those teeth and tap those feet in the celebratory
center of the great American dream factory, Broadway itself.

But probably that's to overcomplicate the show's appeal,
which more obviously has to do with character, tension, momentum, heart and energy, and, of course, beguiling music.
Back in London I remember thinking it one of those rare
artistic events that had been discovered rather than merely
invented, so logical and right that it was hard to see why no
one had done it before. It was, so to speak, a marvelous bloom
awaiting a naturalist enterprising enough to find it, or long-
buried treasure in search of the right archaeologist, or a pla-
tonic idea that had at last materialized in the land of the
living, thanks to the assorted magic of Bennett and his col-

laborators. The narrative seamlessly became song, and the song effortlessly became dance; and very good that song and dance turned out to be.

So it was again at the Shubert, and in an astoundingly spectacular way. Off into the darkness went the present cast, to fetch their publicity photos, and when they returned, carrying them aloft, they'd been magically transformed into the cast of 1975. As the evening proceeded, there were more such substitutions: the National Company; the Bus and Truck Company; the International Company. One scene was played in a medley of languages, Japanese to German to heaven knows what. At the same time those performing the lead roles dizzyingly multiplied, so that the stage looked as if it were half full of clones of clones or mirrors reflecting mirrors reflecting mirrors. Miss McKechnie, playing the solo performer trying to battle her way back into the chorus, started to dance, and was suddenly joined by eight other Cassies. Paul, the Puerto Rican homosexual, turned out to be no fewer than ten Pauls, simultaneously stammering and shrugging out their secrets.

Then it happened. The appearance of the whole company in its spangled coats and top hats makes a sensational enough ending to the show proper. Imagine what it was like when they trooped by their tens, by their scores, by their hundreds onto the stage and all danced and sang at once. It became a celebration not only of *A Chorus Line*, or just of Broadway, or only of the musical theater, but of the human capacity to enjoy and to share, which is, after all, what the stage exists to express.

Nor was the evening over. You wouldn't think there was more room on the stage or more strength in it, reinforced though it had been for the occasion. But on stepped a willowy, wispy figure in tails, Michael Bennett himself, and in the most unaffected way he proceeded to invite up backstage helper after backstage helper and publicly to thank them for their contribution to *A Chorus Line*. Choreographers, designers, writers, wardrobe mistresses—they all seemed to be there, most of them looking a bit mottled and dewy-eyed. And why not? The performers cried. The audience cried. The ushers cried. *I* cried. We all knew we'd never see anything like it again.

October

Sad, sad news. Ralph Richardson has died in a hospital in London. One can't seriously say it was a terrible surprise, since he was eighty, and yet, of course, it was precisely that. I saw him on the stage of the National only a few months ago, and he looked as immortal as ever. More to the point, the triumvirate of Olivier, Gielgud, and Richardson seemed as solid as, oh, the National Gallery or the Bank of England. Others might be similarly elevated; but they were *the* theatrical knights, inseparable in the public mind, and the passing of one of them is like the collapse of a landmark the presence of which one had long taken for granted.

Not that Sir Ralph shared those big buildings' pretensions. The highfalutin stuff he left to his partners. He was more successful playing Kent to Sir John's Lear or Richard to Lord Olivier's Crookback than Othello, Prospero, or Macbeth. His face was once described, possibly by Richardson himself, as being somewhere between a pineapple and a hot cross bun, and it wasn't really suited to the Shakespearean heroes. Besides, there was always something in him—a mischief edging into prankishness—that undid his best efforts to be portentous. He was a very serious actor indeed; solemn, never.

That made him a little daunting to interview, as I found out when I saw him for *The New York Times* just before his eightieth birthday. I'd been warned that he took sly delight in addling journalists' brains with alcohol. He was also said to dislike answering questions, especially personal ones. "I

don't know myself very well," he once earnestly riposted. "I'll
have to ask myself that one day, and if I tell myself something,
I'll let you know." Many a scribe had been seen weaving from
the Richardson house in Regents Park, doubly disoriented by
the Richardson personality and the Richardson drinks cabi-
net. "Poor chap" was Sir Ralph's epitaph on one such. "Can't
hold his liquor."

My confidence wasn't increased when he appeared at the
front door, a great pink grampus in tweeds, and launched
into an intricate discussion about the relative merits of reaching the second-floor drawing room by elevator or foot. The
question, which was coming to seem as key to our survival as
the right way up the north face of the Eiger, was eventually
resolved in favor of the staircase, so up we trudged, to be
briefly waylaid by Lady Richardson, who somewhat unnervingly told her husband, "Behave yourself." This he proceeded
to do by offering me gin, whiskey, or, "better still, a mixture
of gin and whiskey" and telling a very long, abstruse story
about the drinking habits of the navy.

When was I going to get my interview? Our appointment
was for only half an hour or so, and the time was vanishing.
But suddenly Sir Ralph started talking about his most memorable and satisfying role, which he claimed to have been that
of an arsonist in a movie called *The Ghoul* with Boris Karloff.
"I was a parson, very young with a round face, and the lady
of the house liked and trusted me, but I was getting together
firewood, all the time, to burn the place down. Ha!" cried
Richardson, looking just a little wistfully at the red-hot bar
of the electric heater beside him. "Ha! I've never had a more
enjoyable part."

Greatly cheered by the memory, he began to range from
subject to subject. On acting as a skill: "You dig, dig, dig,
and dig. Find out more about the character. What does he
eat, what trousers does he wear, what does he drink, what's
he afraid of? I get a lot of rags and tags from conversations

I hear and from my dreams. I dream a lot." On acting as a profession: "We're the jockeys of literature. Others supply the horses; we make them run." On acting as a form of beguiling frustration: "You're like a bull in a field, chasing after a cow, trying to get it by the tail, and you never quite catch it. You never quite learn to act." On acting as a career: "Better than being a hangman, at least now the death penalty's been abolished. And it's very cheap. All you want is a stick of makeup. Difficult to think of a career where you need less."

At the time Sir Ralph was filming the part of Tarzan's grandfather in a new screen adaptation of Edgar Rice Burroughs—"I've got this bloody great castle, and no one to leave it to, that's the problem"—and wondering whether to play the lead in Eduardo de Filippo's *Inner Voices* at the National. Retirement did not appear on the agenda. "Can't afford to, not for my inner self. I don't know enough. The older you get, the more you realize how little you know. I'm very anxious to learn more in the short time I've got before I get my ticket. Which might, of course, be very soon."

Well, it was ten months later. I spoke to him briefly on the phone about a publication date ("Nightingale, Benedict? This is Richardson, Ralph") but never face-to-face again. Nor did he introduce me, as I'd hoped he might, to the tiny zoo he was reputed to keep in his house: the white mouse with which he sometimes scared actresses; the ferret he washed in soap suds every Saturday; the parrot he used sometimes to perch on his shoulder when he tooled around town on his motorcycle. Instead, he ended the interview in characteristically offbeat style. First, he told me that, though he didn't expect to survive his death, he could remember having existed before his birth. Then he asked me whom I wanted to kill. "*Everyone* wants to kill *someone*," he declared reproachfully. "*I* do." The intended victim, it appeared, was his biographer, Garry O'Connor, who had implied that Richardson's first, terminally ill wife had committed suicide.

I left the house as unsettled as the journalists who had
preceded me, not at all sure I had an interview but glad to
have experienced Sir Ralph's idiosyncrasies at first hand. Peter
Hall, director of the National Theater, once called him "the
most experimental of the great actors," and he was always
unpredictable, always unexpected, always prepared to try
something quirky and new. For some reason, I have an especially sharp memory of his Fiers in Chekhov's *Cherry Orchard*, a character who gets just one chance to hold the stage
and then only briefly and at the very close. Who but Richardson would have thickly mumbled and vaguely giggled as
he approached his own end? Who else made us feel so strongly
that the sofa on which this hoary dodderer was settling himself
was actually his deathbed? Come to that, how many actors of
his eminence would have taken the part in the first place, let
alone honed so original and exquisite a miniature from it?

Before World War II Richardson's best performance was
generally reckoned to be Johnson in J. B. Priestley's *Johnson
over Jordan*, "an ordinary citizen of the suburbs." Indeed,
his specialty seemed to be the plain, unheroic man on the bus;
his strength, to bring sympathy to the most charmless and
invest the drabbest with humanity. Yet that was never the
whole truth. When Johnson marched into eternity with bowler
hat and briefcase, the bank clerk transfigured in death, everyone agreed that the moment had something else, something
indefinable, something that was to become known as the Richardson magic.

It was a phrase that was meant almost literally. A critic
once said that Sir Ralph, alone of actors, had the knack of
existing in four dimensions simultaneously. Certainly I've never
seen anyone with his gift for making the ordinary strange, the
mundane somehow unsettling. Another unforgettable memory
is the great spectral wail with which he expressed the yearnings
of Henrik Ibsen's doomed John Gabriel Borkman, "love you,
love you, love you," echoing through the National Theater

and into the night beyond. Richardson himself, always a hard-working perfectionist beneath the eccentric exterior, felt he'd got the Borkman, got the John, but somehow missed the Gabriel. He was wrong. There was a remoteness, a purity, a curious otherworldliness in his portrait of the megalomaniac ex-magnate.

Let me not get too monkish and mysterious about this. In many ways Richardson was of the earth, earthy. Another of his specialties was the fleshly, sometimes boozy failure: General St. Pé in Jean Anouilh's *Waltz of the Toreadors*, the lying insurance man in Robert Bolt's *Flowering Cherry*, Hirst in Harold Pinter's *No Man's Land*. Indeed, perhaps his greatest performance was his Falstaff in 1946. I never saw it, being too young, but Kenneth Tynan, then an apprentice critic, has left us a memorable picture of his wild white halo of hair, his majestic eye, his authority and sly, self-mocking humor. That knight was no belching clown, but a serious being, and in the rejection scene, his face red and working in tics to hide his tears, he was clearly a very moving one, too. Tynan found himself weeping when he recalled the "immense pathos" of his reassuring words to Shallow, "I shall be sent for soon at night."

The last time I saw him onstage was indeed in *Inner Voices* at the National. The part he played, an elderly Neapolitan who hallucinates a murder and believes it real, was made for him. He was funny, he was moving, and he had that strange, dreamy look, that Richardson magic. The audience was enchanted, but then it usually was. There was no more loved actor in Britain. There was none who, in the most exact sense of an overworked word, was more extraordinary.

At last, a Broadway musical to review, but unluckily not a new one. On the face of it, it's surprising the impresarios should have decided to disinter *Zorba*, since it's very much a product of the later 1960's and wasn't a great success even then. The hero himself, with his rampaging id, his wanderlust, his boast that "I own nothing, I judge nothing, I am free," was philosophically at one with much of the Haight-Ashbury crowd. The antiwar sentiments he parenthetically mouthed would have gone down well in the Vietnam-obsessed lairs of *Hair* itself. Yet *Hair*, when I saw it in revival not long ago, struck me as not merely dated but puny and feeble. What *had* we seen in that sniveling tribute to self-pitying potheads? What could we hope to see now in the musical it so thoroughly overshadowed back in 1968?

Well, this is ultimately derived from Nikos Kazantzakis's *Zorba the Greek*, which was published way back in 1946, when a flower child was still a young person who liked gardening. That novel gives the show most of its incident, much of its feeling, and perhaps also a certain permanence of spirit. Again, this particular production is directly indebted to a film which, like the book, has proved its power to last. Back in 1968 an objection to the stage musical was that Herschel Bernardi was playing not Zorba but Zorba as he'd been played by Anthony Quinn on the screen. This error, if error it was, has now been cleverly corrected. Quinn himself is once again Zorba, and accompanying him to the Broadway Theater are the man who directed the original movie and the woman who costarred in it with him, Michael Cacoyannis and Lila Kedrova.

Quinn and Kedrova can't conceal what still are, as it turns out, some very serious weaknesses in the show, but they do give class to the evening. Miss Kedrova, her big, ingenuous smiles eloquently offset by her big, woebegone, oyster eyes, brings a wonderful fragility to the part of Zorba's aging, half-cracked mistress. A coo becomes a stricken gurgle, a bat of the eyelids a mothlike flutter of the body as a whole, and the very slant of her nose, jutting from beneath her bedsheet, a

total demonstration of vulnerability. As for Quinn—well, one
has to begin by admitting that his singing isn't what it should
be, nor his dancing what it was.

The one put me in mind of a rusty old cannon, going off
with a tubercular creak and only winging its target. The other
has none of that "savage and desperate" energy Kazantzakis
specified and, at least to some extent, Quinn gave us in the
movie. Instead, an intent frown puckers that long, beetling
face, giving the impression of a great auk straining to lay an
egg, and the egg, I fear, turns out to be his footwork, which
is slow and cumbersome, as if he were stiffly battling with a
cramp. Yet that's only part of the picture. Quinn's lordly,
grizzled charisma is undiminished, and there's a new sensi-
tivity in his interpretation, a tenderness and delicacy, striking
in so burly a man, in his playing of intimate scenes. He is *the*
Zorba, genial and authoritative and more, and (of course) *the*
reason the show is being revived in the 1980's. Quinn in his
archetypal role, Quinn at his most quintessential, is good business and deserves to be.

But we still don't get *the* Zorba the Greek. Musicals, especially those dating from before the reforms of Sondheim,
have their own special magnetic law, which means they gravitate toward the tried, tested, and found wanting. The central
subject of both book and film is Zorba's relationship with his
young master, Niko; the principal conflict involves what those
characters represent, the head and the gut. An intellectual is
given an education in emotion, cured of the chronic bookish-
ness that afflicts him. But that gives us a show without love
interest, or with the wrong kind of love interest for Broadway
1968. So the widow with whom Niko has a tragically cursory
affair in the novel is moved center stage, asked to speak, and,
God help us, required to sing: "Niko, I feel I'm living at last.
Niko, I'll be good for you." A silent, bleak, almost mythic
figure is transformed into a rapturous American housewife,
just back from her encounter group.

Something of the sort has happened to the musical as a
whole, notwithstanding the prowess of Quinn and Kedrova.
Mr. Cacoyannis, who should know better, begins by presenting us with a Piraeus café that's pure Broadway cliché, down
to the balloon seller who inexplicably weaves through the fes-
tive throng. Nor is the island to which the action then moves,
Crete, well evoked by stone steps, a background of what looked
like giant cookies, and a foreground of primitive villagers with
accents that vary from American high school to Greek kebab
house, and clothes scarcely less diversely acquired. Never do
we feel, as we should, that we've been thrust among dangerous
people on a baked earth under a stark sky; the impression,
rather, is of some quaint bohemian community sprung up in
Middle America: Crete, Iowa.

That impression isn't lessened by John Kander's music,
which busies itself with brass and bouzouki but lacks aggression and atmosphere, or by Fred Ebb's lyrics. One number
manages to be vapidly sententious: "Life is what you do till
the moment you die, life is where you wait till you leave."
Another, written especially for this revival, appears to be no
more than a sop to the sisterhood, a ham-fisted attempt to
pretend that Zorba isn't as big a sexist as he actually is: "God
made women to be free, interesting, exciting. . . ." Too often
the great creative goal of the evening seems to be not to give
anyone offense. A climactic murder, the cutting of the widow's
throat by a relative of the boy she supposedly drove to suicide,
is so sedately accomplished that not even one capsule of blood
is spilled.

After *Sweeney Todd*, that and several other things about
the show seem very evasive. After *Cage aux Folles*, its ner-
vousness about Zorba's attraction for Niko may seem equally
so, making Kander and Ebb's effort look doubly dated. But
I wonder. I've been thinking about *La Cage*. Isn't it pretty
evasive, too? Yes, it asks us to expand our moral horizons so
that they embrace the possibility of homosexual "marriage,"

but the marriage it shows is so clubby, so cozy, so unswervingly and reassuringly affectionate, it would surely be exceptional anywhere. One could as convincingly make a general case for heterosexual bonding on the basis of Darby and Joan. Somewhere inside the exoticism of *Zorba* a suburban heart is blandly heaving away. So it is within the gaudy exterior of *Cage*. Have Broadway, and the Broadway musical, really changed as much as all that?

In the intermission of *A Little Madness* by Gerald Zipper, a very crude and confused play about a very crude and confused family, a little old lady came up to a group of us on the sidewalk. "We're from out of town," she said. "Isn't it *great?*" A little old gentleman shuffled and nodded agreement beside her. I said, Oh, well, it was a bit hard to say, wasn't it, sort of. Mel Gussow, who was reviewing the play for the daily *Times*, was more decisive. "I think," he said in his gentle, diffident way, "we should give the second half a chance."

As it turned out, the play continued to seem pretty bad to me, and to Mel as well. Another reviewer, presumably finding all those straw characters just too much for his camel's back, actually began to groan and loudly mutter "My God!" during the performance. But the tiny incident in the street outside got me wondering anew about the very peculiar profession into which circumstances have thrust me. Who am I to set myself up as public taster for people with all sorts of palates, some of them more tolerant than my own? And what's an Englishman doing laying down the law to Americans about their own theater?

They're good questions, doubly, trebly good when the journal that is propagating one's opinions is *The New York Times*. Britain is small enough and the press adaptable enough for a national newspaper also to be a London paper, and that means that the city has four upscale daily critics, three upscale Sunday critics, and a number of other critics whom I, for one, regard as good, serious commentators on the theatrical scene. As my friend Milton Shulman of the *Standard* likes to say, there are about a dozen reviewers of not dissimilar importance. But in New York *The Times* rules, or at any rate rules at the better class of box office. An English director of my acquaintance tells a story of a first-night party that was going very nicely until *The Times'* review arrived. While not devastating, it was unmistakably a downer. Suddenly the waiters began removing the champagne, the revelers melted away, and the party was no more. The play closed a few days later.

Alan Ayckbourn has another story: During a rehearsal of one of his comedies he noticed something curious. Two men were crammed into one aisle seat in an orchestra that was otherwise almost completely empty. Was this an example of this new gay openness he'd heard so much about in England? Or were they, like him, trying to be funny? No, that was the seat that *The New York Times* critic was scheduled to occupy. The two men were jointly ensuring that everything about the production was angled to look exactly right from there.

Of course, it was the daily *Times* they wanted to impress. The Sunday critic, even when he was the great Walter Kerr, is generally held to wield far less influence over the box office. Indeed, it's still unclear to me how much power, if any, I do have. The invitations from the theaters seem more importunate than in England, on occasion becoming vaguely menacing in their efforts to entice me along ("If you don't come, you'll be very sorry"). The dissenting letters seem more aggrieved ("If it cannot talk sense, keep it closed"). The other night in the theater a strange lady with orange and green eyelashes, on realizing I was a *Times* critic, gave my knee a friendly grope and suggested a dinner appointment, which is something that has never happened to me in England, presumably because papers there have less frisson and sex appeal. Oh, yes, and I've had the accolade of being misquoted, or at least misrepresented, in newspaper ads. One such consisted of sentences and bits of sentence wrenched from their context and reassembled, so as to make me sound incoherently enthusiastic about John B. Keane's *Big Maggie,* the play that recently hit the Douglas Fairbanks. A reader would know that it had been "stupendously successful in its native Ireland" because that's in bold type. He wouldn't realize I'd also called it charmless.

If some tiny Tamburlaine has taken up residence at the back of my critical consciousness, that's scarcely likely to slake his thirst for power, but then let's hope none has done so. I would, I think, much rather provoke disagreement, argument, than make or break plays. Indeed, the historical record of criticism, especially on my side of the Atlantic, is so appalling that it would be pretty immoral to crave more power than that. Consider the hostility originally accorded the Ibsen of *A Doll's House* and *Ghosts* ("a wretched, loathsome, deplorable history," the *Daily Telegraph* called the latter). Consider the way in which the first plays of Harold Pinter and Edward Bond, *The Birthday Party* and *Saved,* were dismissed and derided. And over here, consider George Jean Nathan's persistent failure to respond to the talent of Tennessee Williams with remotely the same sympathy he famously accorded that of O'Neill. Sensible readers will treat critics very skeptically indeed, and decent critics will urge them to do so.

Myself, I'm in permanent terror of missing the masterpiece, shrugging aside the master, and have an uneasy feeling I may already have done so. Wasn't I awfully lukewarm about the early work of David Hare, author of *A Map of the World* and *Plenty*? It's a wonder he deigns to speak to me, as he does, just. Am I justified in finding the later plays of John Osborne blimpish and dull? Am I right to think Edward Albee, too, sadly in decline? Posterity may have quite different views, and somehow it isn't quite good enough to argue that changing circumstances mean changing judgments, so that what will seem a masterpiece in the future may not necessarily be a masterpiece now. Think of any major writer. In and out of fashion he or she may go, up and down on the stock market of taste; but wasn't there always a quality there, an irreducible *something*, which the discerning eye should have spotted?

Not that my own purportedly discerning eye has felt greatly stretched in my first weeks here. The problem, as I feared, has been finding anything worth writing about at the length I'm allowed. What my masters at *The Times* seem to want is generalization, whether about a dramatist, a group of dramatists, acting, companies, shifts and trends in the theater, anything. Had I gone to Whitehall to take in the first night of *King Lear* in 1606, I would probably have found myself making a few wise remarks about the play itself ("very, very long"), followed by an assessment of Shakespeare's career to date ("beginning to fulfill his promise") and a word or two about the state of Jacobean dramaturgy ("why this obsession with depressing subjects?"). But his new *Home Again Kathleen* scarcely seemed a strong enough basis for a whole essay on the excellences of Thomas Babe. Nor did Kathleen Tolan's *Weekend near Madison* justify discussion of its subject, the ennui of those who found faith and meaning in the 1960's, even though Lanford Wilson's *Fifth of July* and the new movie *The Big Chill* would suggest that this is becoming an increasingly common American concern.

As this should show, I've been going off- and off-off Broadway in search of stimulation and not finding it to quite the extent I'd hoped, at least in the theater. Life, luckily, is more amusing. I dislike very much being away for long periods from my wife and children—a trip home is coming up, though, followed by their visit to New York—but there are compensations. Consider a day in the life of a critic as enjoyed by me, now I'm settled into a tiny apartment in a co-op building in a neighborhood that I'm told used to be called Hell's Kitchen but is now more sedately known as Clinton. In fact, consider a life in the day of a critic.

Up I stumble at maybe ten, make a cup of coffee, and do

some leisurely but probably constructive reading in bed. Right now, I'm deep into Michael Meyer's biography of Ibsen in readiness for my review of a revival of *The Master Builder* at the Roundabout. Then lunch, which is probably a sandwich. I could, I suppose, make it from one of those cans of tuna hopefully piled in my kitchen, but why risk encouraging the local cockroach population? This is (incidentally) a nuisance new to me, and I've already tried to do something about it, though I've yet to meet the man with the spray gun face-to-face. I simply came home one night to find a vague smell of poison in the air and a black notice, akin to the sort Italians pin to their doors after a death in the family, which read baldly: "Exterminator Was Here." This momentarily chilled me with thoughts of the grave, though not as much as a rather similar happening reportedly did Isaac Bashevis Singer, who lives a mile or two uptown. He opened his door one evening to find on the threshold something that might have doubled as a dybbuk in one of his spookier novels, a caped figure of monstrous size and grim expression. "I am the exterminator," it announced. Singer fainted dead away.

But I'm wandering from the really interesting subject, which is my lunchtime snack. Most likely I bring it in from outside, because that way I can also pick up a copy of *The Times* and see what Frank Rich thought of last night's first night, assuming there was one. If I've the energy, I might walk the block or two to the Carnegie Deli and buy what you'll never convince an Englishman is merely a beef sandwich. Back home, we give the name to two bits of bread inside which, if you look long and hard, you may find a sliver of leather, along with a lettuce leaf. At the Carnegie the bread precariously balances at the top and bottom of an entire ox, deftly sliced. One such sandwich can take two or three meals to finish.

What then? Well, maybe a walk up to the Lincoln Center performing arts library, which has some very useful archive material, or perhaps an amble to *The Times*, dropping into the Drama Bookshop for a browse on the way. The paper itself is beginning to get a bit busy at this time. The deadline for the early edition is nearing. But I can usually find some congenial person—John Corry, Michiko Kakutani, maybe Frank Rich—ready for a clubby chat. If not, well, I'll run through my mail, mull over the latest press releases with Carol Coburn at the theater desk, and decide what to see. Alternatively or additionally, I might do some research in the paper's library or morgue. Right now I'm looking through the interviews David Mamet has given and the reviews of his past work, in readiness for the revival of *American Buffalo* due soon on Broadway.

Shall I hang around for the cart and a dose of the drug to which I'm irreversibly addicted—namely, tea? No, that's one thing I feel I can make better myself. So back to my apartment on Fifty-sixth Street for a pot of tea, followed by a bracing run. Most days I manage to trundle around the circular road at the southern end of Central Park, usually finishing its mile and a half in twelve minutes or so, dreaming as I go of taking part in some future New York Marathon. Now that would be immortality, and immortality of a kind I'm willing to bet neither Frank Rich nor Clive Barnes nor John Simon will ever achieve: to be the first theater critic to make it around that twenty-six-odd-mile course.

But as I drag myself back home, sweaty and bedraggled, I realize the full implausibility of that dream. Aspiring comedians appear from time to time on Columbus Circle, and the other day one used my less than svelte figure for a cheap laugh as I passed by. I block on his precise words, but they were tantamount to a helpful-seeming suggestion that someone should call a doctor, or maybe a mortician. Still, all that presumably adds to the color of this curious, uncategorizable area. Here's Fifty-seventh Street, still ample and imposing, even at its more unfashionable end; here's the rich mix of eateries so characteristic of New York, Japanese and Mexican and Chinese

and French and Italian and Spanish and fast-food American;
here, too, are some surprisingly shabby old brownstones and
tawdry-looking shops, outside which the local down-and-outs
ply their trade. I seem to be on increasingly friendly terms
with a gentleman who wears a skullcap from which tiny American flags protrude and emits coy little calls of "coo-ee" at
you as you pass. Give him a quarter or withhold it, his reply
is the same: "Thank you very much."

But it's getting to be time for dinner and maybe the theater.
I find it depressing to cook for myself and haven't the confidence to cook for anyone else, so I often end up eating out,
either alone or with others. I've in-laws uptown and in the
Village, a cousin with the British mission to the UN, some old
friends, and one or two new ones, so I might inveigle someone
to come with me to sample my favorite sort of food, which is
Indian or (more usually) Pakistani or Bangladeshi. Those
nations' restaurants were scarcely to be found in New York
twenty years ago but now seem to be all over: on East Third
Street, around Twenty-eighth Street at Lexington Avenue, and
vaguely scattered in midtown. If I'm alone, and looking for a
quick, cheap meal, I'm quite likely to go to the India Pavilion,
a short walk east on Fifty-sixth Street.

And so to the theater—perhaps. With so little that's new
on offer, I've been catching up on the already established,
especially the established musicals. *Nine* I thought remarkably
dull: a lot of women standing on silly little boxes, Sergio Fran-
chi equally static as the massive male ego with whom they're
inexplicably infatuated, and nothing else of note. But *Dreamgirls* I liked, and *42nd Street* I shamelessly adored. Fancy
being paid, I thought as I sat there, to go out with a good
friend and see this enchanting fairy story, this showbiz "Cinderella."

That's about it. If I'm alone, I might pause on my way home
for a beer in a bar, though I'm wary of ones with names like
Blarney Stone and Sweet Shannon. The Irish, not without

reason, are less than enamored of the English, and I'm afraid
my accent might end by adding to the existing unruliness in
the Times Square area at night. More likely I'll go straight
home, pour myself a glass of wine, and watch the eleven o'clock
news, though I often find myself exasperated by the emphasis
on local items at the expense of international, the cursoriness
with which important events are treated, and the frequency
of the ads. ABC is presently my favorite network, though not
by much.

Of course, not all days are as tough and demanding as this,
at least not all weekdays. There's sometimes room for a movie,
or a concert, or my favorite recreation, which is simply sniffing
around the city. Or there may be a shindig of some sort. The
other night I went to see the annual award given for services
to the appreciation of O'Neill and found myself seated at
dinner next to Colleen Dewhurst, who had just left the cast
of *You Can't Take It with You* and was, she told me, in a
rather emotional and volatile state as a result. This she proceeded to prove by suddenly and disconcertingly bursting into
tears when she presented the prize to Jason Robards, who
was in Europe and represented only by a videocassette of
himself. It made an odd contrast, her choking back her feelings, him imperviously smiling out of the small screen, while
all around applauded.

Weekends are, funnily enough, the busiest time for me.
That's when I get my column into a shape fit to be phoned in
on Sunday night or Monday morning. I am a slow, laborious
writer, and a neurotically faddy and fussy one, too. For instance, I can compose only in very thin ball-point, never directly onto a typewriter, and if I make the slightest error, I
prefer to begin the paragraph all over again. This means that
what could take a few hours can easily be stretched to fill two
days. Still, I don't seem to get edited much. The problem
seems mainly to be Anglicisms and, I fear, language too louche
for my new employers. "But surely 'fart' is all right," I found

myself arguing to Bob Berkvist the other day. "I mean, Chaucer used it." "There are a lot of things Chaucer said that we can't say in *The Times*," he replied with a grin. How, I wonder, am I to quote from *American Buffalo*, packed as it is with language that ventures below the belt?

But I've wandered a long, long way from the question I began by asking: Who am I to opine grandly about any theater, any drama, let alone American ones? Let me end, I hope not too solemnly, with a moment or two of credo.

I've always felt that my job had to do less with opinion and judgment, more with investigation and analysis, with reporting what's happening in a play, discerning its shape and pattern, and deducing its author's intentions. The reviewer unravels the evidence, so to speak, and then hands it over to his readers, who are the jury. The fault of very much contemporary criticism, so it seems to me, is to leap from the objective to the subjective too hastily and in some cases to make no effort to be objective at all.

Still, it has been wisely said that there can be no such creature as an impersonal critic until there's an impersonal person. In practice, I find it as hard as anyone else to obey principles so astringent, and I'm certainly not as shrinkingly reticent as my critical conscience tells me I should be. After all, the way one describes a play or production, selecting this, emphasizing that, often constitutes a judgment in itself. Evocation and opinion become inextricably mingled. Moreover, one does, of course, find oneself celebrating this, condemning that. I still feel that either enthusiasm or anger is worthless unless it's accompanied by, indeed based on, a long, careful look at the facts of the case. Yet even that is more easily said than done. Which comes first, the feeling or the explanation? It often seems to me that whatever I may earnestly claim to be doing, I am actually engaged in a sort of post hoc rationalization of the amusement, irritation, delight, or boredom I experienced in the theater.

It's a confusing situation at the best of times, and doubly
so if one is writing, as I am, in an alien context. Interpretation
obviously becomes more difficult when one's mind is not, and
perhaps can never be, fully adjusted to the cultural atmosphere and idiom. I can't, for instance, know what's like to
have lived through the Kennedy assassination, the Vietnam
War, Watergate. To me Richard Nixon, while personally less
than salubrious, is the statesman who changed the political
shape of the world by going to China. But I have learned to
be very careful about expressing that view to Americans since
they tend to regard it as maddeningly smug and off the point.
I suppose I might find it hard to remain detached were Elizabeth II and Mrs. Thatcher—and a President, I suppose, is
the equivalent of both at once—were to be found jointly tam-
pering with the electoral process, conspiring against their political enemies, and cursing and swearing like hard hats.

Nor is the problem the large issues only. The small cultural
references, the in jokes of the American family, matter, too.
In England someone has only to say "Bognor Regis," and
everyone in the theater laughs, because of the character and
associations of that rather dull seaside town. Weren't George
V's last words "Bugger Bognor," as someone reassured him
he'd soon be well enough to go on vacation there? Twice since
I arrived here, someone has referred to the "Good Humor
man" on the stage, creating the same automatic hilarity in the
auditorium. I've learned that this lively-sounding personage
is actually an ice-cream salesman, but never having heard his
bell or seen his face as either child or parent, I obviously miss
his precise place in American folklore and, hence, his comic
connotations. I pick up the notes; I don't quite get the tune.

Oh, well, experience will no doubt teach me much. Twenty
years ago I recall going to an American stationery store and
asking for a "rubber," a request greeted with profound mis-
givings by the saleslady, who obviously thought me as mad as
I was beginning to think her. I now know to ask for an eraser.

But until my sense of the nation becomes more complete, it clearly behooves me to be even more cautious in analysis than I try usually to be and therefore even more hesitant when it comes to propagating any judgment I derive from that analysis. Maybe I should also be more ready to follow my practice in England and record the reactions of those around me in the audience, at least when they're blatantly different from my own. If they're self-evidently enjoying what I'm not, then let me say so.

I don't think I and my fellow critics were wrong, and the little old lady right, in the case of *A Little Madness*. But it would clearly be arrogant of us to ignore the testimony of such people altogether and especially arrogant for a foreigner like myself to do so.

Ruby Cohn, the critic and theater historian, recently called David Mamet "virtually bare of ideas." She also cited no less an authority than Edward Albee in support of this severe judgment. His opinion was that Mamet showed plenty of evidence of having a fine ear, rather less of a fine mind. Well, I'm inclined to think that the American theater would be better off if Albee put his own fine mind in the icebox for a while and rediscovered the ear that allowed him to write the blistering dialogue of *Who's Afraid of Virginia Woolf?*, but there's no doubt that his opinion is pretty widely held. I've heard Mamet accused of luxuriating in language for its own sake. I've heard him abused for having perfect pitch, excoriated for writing too accurately, damned for sounding true.

It's not fair. Having just seen Mamet's new *Glengarry Glen Ross* in London and then a revival of his *American Buffalo* at the Booth, I'm convinced it's outrageously unfair. True enough, the ear still seems as sensitive and alert as any cocked in the history of the theater. Whether eavesdropping on the shambling old men of *The Duck Variations*, or the loveless swingers of *Sexual Perversity in Chicago*, or the merchant seamen of *Lakeboat*, or the real estate sharks of *Glengarry*, or the petty hoodlums of *Buffalo*, it has an unerring feel for the cadences of ordinary speech, especially the speech to be heard in and around Mamet's native Illinois. But there's a mind there, too, and one no less formidable for its conscientious refusal to draw attention to the way it is, in fact, shaping its material. Ideas are still ideas whether they're abstracted and explicitly enunciated or whether they're embodied in character and relationship, as Mamet deftly embodies them.

His is a tough, frightening, sometimes merciless world, for all its incidental hilarity, and its inhabitants must struggle to sustain life and limb, let alone the most minimal values. Sometimes they reach out toward one another, like the lovers of *The Woods*, but as that play painfully demonstrates, self-absorption and emotional avarice are difficult habits to conquer. More often Mamet's people seem to be busily rejecting or destroying the possibility of affection, as in *Sexual Perversity*, or trying to dominate one another, as the two actors of *A Life in the Theater* take turns in doing. Mostly they're loners, for whom it's achievement enough precariously to survive the rocks, the currents, and the fellow swimmers in the ontological pond. Think of the title character of *Edmond*, a dull-witted Woyzeck adrift in mean, greedy New York. Think of Teach, the hustler at the center of *American Buffalo* or, for that matter, of the desperate salesmen of *Glengarry Glen Ross*.

Glengarry I hope to anatomize in some detail when it hits New York, as it surely must. But it's harder than ever to dismiss Mamet as a dramatist without ideas when one considers he's written that play, *American Buffalo*, and *The Water Engine*, which is about a machine that costs nothing to run and is suppressed by corrupt moneymen. How much more must he say about the economic system and its effects before we twig his drift? In an interview about *American Buffalo* he went so far as to spell it out for us: "The play is about the American ethic of business. About how we excuse all sorts of great and small betrayals and ethical compromises called business. I felt angry about business when I wrote the play."

Even Arvin Brown's flawed production at the Booth can't conceal that it's about that and more, much more. The three characters—a junk shop owner named Don; his gofer Bob; and their crony, Teach—are planning to burgle a coin collector. This they see as a perfectly normal business transaction and certainly no reason for shame. Indeed, much of what they say suggests not merely that they model themselves on the "respectable" members of the moneymaking community but that they're more scrupulous than many people in that community. At any rate, they manage to convince themselves that the burglary is an act of justice as well as an example of free enterprise. They are simply repossessing the buffalo-imprinted nickel the coin collector bought from Don at too low a price and punishing him for that piece of "stealing." Mamet's implied question is evident. If crooks can so thoroughly identify with businessmen, thinking of theft as trade and trade as theft, what must businessmen be like? In the same interview he answers directly: "There's really no difference between the lumpen proletariat and stockbrokers or corporate lawyers who are the lackeys of business. Part of the American myth is that a difference exists, that at a certain point vicious behavior becomes laudable."

But Mamet isn't just a latter-day Dreiser, itching to trim the capitalist jungle. What really interests him are the shadowy, elusive frontiers between business and friendship, two words that occur again and again in *American Buffalo*, each time defined by their context and the self-interest of the speaker in a slightly different way. Don wants to demonstrate his friendship for Bob, a reformed addict, by allowing him to do the robbery. Teach, who needs money, convinces him that this is bad business and substitutes himself as chief burglar.

Everything then proceeds to go awry, and as it does so, Teach gradually sucks Don into his own embattled, paranoid world view. All relationships are business relationships. Don is being betrayed by Bob and by others he trusts. There's no decency, no friendship: "We all live like the cavemen."

For a time we, like Don, are mentally infected by Teach's poison. When Bob appears clutching a buffalo nickel, we, too, begin to suspect he's stolen it on the sly from the coin collector, thus preempting and vitiating the planned burglary. But then the truth emerges. So far from double-crossing his employer, helper, and friend, Bob has rather pathetically been trying to please him. This is another coin altogether, bought down-town, "for Donny." This seems a small matter, yet somehow Mamet leaves us feeling that it isn't small at all. These people have looked into their lowest depths and found that somewhere down there, there's gratitude, there's honor, there's altruism, there's friendship, there's something that might without great exaggeration be dignified as good. Odd though it may sound, Don's relief is our relief, too. "You did real good," he tells Bob as the play reaches as unpretentiously, unsentimentally touching an ending as I've come across in contemporary drama.

Unluckily the moment didn't have the impact it might at the Booth, thanks to a production overpreoccupied with the surface of things and underpreoccupied with their essence. Sometimes only minor loss results from Arvin Brown's refusal to let his cast isolate, italicize, or artfully point up a telling line. For instance, nothing caused the house more hilarity the last time I saw *American Buffalo* than the news that the ace criminal on whose help Don and Teach are relying has himself been mugged in the street; it perfectly summed up the gap between aspiration and achievement in the play's small, sleazy world. Yet here the line passes as unnoticed as a surreptitious sneeze. What's worse, so do those crucial, climactic two words "for Donny." Substance, you feel, has been sacrificed to style, ends to means—or, rather, to Method.

Though he's the one who drops those particular lines, the worst offender isn't James Hayden's Bob, in himself a marvelously shy, gangling, apologetic presence. Nor is it J. J. Johnston's Don, all pink and paternal, a sort of Santa Claus without a beard. The mumbling, muttering atmosphere is mainly set by Al Pacino's Teach. Black-eyed and mushroom-faced, he paces the junk shop, looping his hands, jabbing with his fingers, nervously flicking at his hair, scratching at his crotch, absently fiddling with the furniture. And he talks with the same fussy restlessness, shrugging and scrambling his way through the text, seemingly happy to be inaudible as long as he is authentically inaudible. And these ostentatious antiheroics have the unsurprising effect of making Teach at once more important and less interesting than he should be.

As a better balanced production would show, he's no more the "lead" than the other two characters, but as a more emotionally searching one might prove, he's a wonderfully well-observed character, a mixture of insecurity, resentment, bravado, and sly, streetwise stupidity, an overage infant dimly aware that he can never claw his way out of the urban trash can. Not least, he's a living demonstration of Mamet's canny command of language, combining (as he entertainingly does) a curt, blunt, violent idiom with solemn rhetoric and sententious apothegm.

"Loyalty," declares Teach, "you know how I am on this, this is great, this is admirable." The next moment he's persuading Don he should forget loyalty and allow him to do the burglary instead of Bob, with a "I wanna go in there and gut the motherfucker." Language is what suits his intentions at the time, part of his street armor, the way his mind sends his frontline feelings into action safely camouflaged. A platitude becomes an attempt to ingratiate, disorient, manipulate, and dominate. A sentiment becomes a way of bolstering his, Teach's, self-esteem and evading what might undermine it. A curse word is a strategy for denying humanity to his victims and thus getting positive moral satisfaction out of fleecing them. Language is many things it may not immediately appear to be, so many that Teach himself often and entertainingly becomes muddled and self-contradictory, simultaneously saying he's calm and upset or declaring that free enterprise justifies uncivilized behavior and proves we're civilized.

But his confusion goes much deeper than that, right down to something aggressive yet defensive, defiant yet fearful at his very center. And so preoccupied with busy detail does Pacino become that he fails to embody that desperation, that feeling of hanging by the fingernails over some infinitely putrid abyss. One sees the fidgety gestures, unstoppably signaling an unstoppable unease. One hears the voice of disillusion and anger. One doesn't quite believe their source is the heart, stomach, and bowels.

Even so, the quality of the play is unmissable. Its quality and, paradoxically, its size. On the face of it nothing remarkable has happened. Three part-time crooks, unconsidered inhabitants of a nondescript subworld, have managed to botch a minor burglary. But actually the junk shop has been the forum for a debate with implications it would hardly be an exaggeration to call cosmic. There, amid the old tires, bicycle wheels, and tennis rackets, David Mamet has posed the most fundamental question any dramatist could ask—do values exist?—and cautiously and convincingly answered in the affirmative. That seems to me quite an achievement. The word "masterpiece" is one that I think critics should take out of their verbal strongboxes only very, very sparingly—but *American Buffalo* is one of the very, very few contemporary plays that deserves it.

Everywhere I go, and I mean everywhere, the theater seems to follow me. The cabby who drove me across town last night had toured Europe in *Bubbling Brown Sugar*. The salesman who gave me my phone was a "resting" actor; the elderly gentleman who tried to let me his apartment, a "retired" one. The genial fellow who was shown another apartment with me turned out to run a theater museum. Even the relatively few people who have no direct connection with the profession seem to want to talk, ask, argue about it. The woman who sold me a paperback insisted, for reasons still unknown to me, on doing an imitation of John Gielgud. That's not coincidence; that's what the pollsters call a significant proportion of a representative sample of the city population.

It could never have happened in London. There we've not too bad a theater, but a citizenry that can, on the whole, take it or leave it. Here we've a theater-mad city and, I'm beginning to think, a less than remarkable theater. The big event on Broadway this October, *American Buffalo*, is actually a revival of a revival, since the play was first produced in New York in 1977 and first performed by Al Pacino some four years later. The big events off-Broadway—well, I've been hither, thither, and yon in search of material that, if not necessarily an excuse for a critical column, will at least keep me usefully abreast of the state and condition of the American theater, and I've yet to feel very richly rewarded. Did I come all this way to review a respectable but unexciting revival of *The Master Builder*? Or *Up from Paradise*, which turns out to be a concert version (all black ties, except when it comes to Lucifer, who sports a raffish little red number between the labels of his tuxedo) of the musical version of Arthur Miller's dramatic version of the Book of Genesis, *The Creation of the World*?

My colleague Frank Rich has stopped saying, "I've never known it so slow," and started intoning, "It can't get any slower." Is he right—or could his be the voice from the *Titanic*, "At last we're pulling away from those icebergs"? More specifically, where *is* the bold new work that off-Broadway and then off-off Broadway came into being to promote? Where's the enterprising choice of program you might expect to find in and around the theatrical heart of a theater-mad city? But it's about time I stopped helplessly whining and moaning and started trying to analyze the situation a bit. And as I rode home from the Manhattan Theater Club after seeing *The Philanthropist* the other night, wondering why so important a playhouse was reviving a decent but not especially vital British comedy at the height of the early season, my program rather spookily fell open at a place that could conceivably help explain its artistic caution. I'm referring to the financial acknowledgments.

These are something quite new to me. In the nonprofit-making sector of the English theater you usually find a single sentence thanking the state-financed Arts Council of Great Britain for funds. Underneath it there's sometimes an equally terse expression of gratitude to the Greater London Council or some other municipal authority. Here even the most important theaters seem to depend on the vagaries of private charity. Whole pages of their programs are crammed with the names of givers, artfully divided into categories designed to advertise their generosity or, perhaps, their meanness.

Who would have thought there were so many names for Maecenas these days? At the City Stage Company there are five; at the Manhattan Theater Club, as many as eight: sustainer, pacesetter, angel, benefactor, sponsor, associate, patron, and supporter. These come with commensurate lures and baits. A pacesetter—that's someone giving between $5,000 and $9,999—gets his or her name engraved on a permanent plaque in the lobby. An angel gets an autographed copy of an original MTC play as part of the reward for donating between $2,500 and $4,999. A patron gets a T-shirt or tote bag for his or her $50 to $149. A supporter, contributing under $50, gets nothing, except perhaps the privilege of not having his or her name published in the program.

Let me not knock this, for heaven's sake. It's testimony to American generosity, evidence of a tradition of philanthropy long since lapsed in my country, thanks to unhelpful tax laws and a thinning of the ranks of the rich. And without it there would clearly be a lot less serious theater in the United States. All the same, as someone who has come to take for granted state subsidy for the arts, I'm worried by the *degree* to which that serious theater, and indeed a good deal of less than serious theater, seem to depend on private philanthropy.

How much does it influence programming? Specifically, to what extent do the tastes of well-to-do subscribers determine the choice of plays? How challenging can a theater be, how many artistic and other risks can it take without imperiling its financial health, maybe its very existence? Again, how competently can its directors and administrators plan ahead, knowing that the hand which generously gives can also whimsically take away? To what extent does the need to woo donors, and sometimes many of them, distract artistic directors from their primary duties and make them less effective? To what extent does it lead to the hiring of fund-raising staff, and with what consequent increase of costs?

Maybe some of these are naïve questions, and as I write, I can see there are prejudices inherent in them: Like almost all Europeans, I expect the government to support the arts. But I've a suspicion they'll loom pretty large in my thinking in the months to come.

November

Take Sam Shepard, add David Mamet, and you've just completed a more or less encyclopedic list of the really interesting American dramatists currently producing work. That's the impression I brought with me to the United States, at any rate, but it's one I hoped would be rapidly revised by experience. Aren't there other young and youngish writers on the stairs, perhaps even up on the landing and banging at the door? Aren't there new voices eager to be heard, new perspectives on America and Americans waiting to be shared?

Well, perhaps there are. Even this sluggish season is beginning at last to demonstrate it. There's Tina Howe and Wendy Wasserstein, both of whom have plays opening soon. There's Marsha Norman, who is still represented on Broadway by *'Night, Mother*, her Pulitzer-winning tale of a daughter readying her disbelieving, appalled, and finally broken mother for the suicide she's long been planning. I caught this the other day and found it grimly entertaining and maybe more. It seemed to involve the bleak underside of the American dream, the cloud in all that silver lining, the sense of powerlessness sometimes to be found in the most powerful nation on earth, the ennui amid the optimism: a life so utterly, so irredeemably drab that the only possible way to change it is, in fact, to end it. Yes—and, while we're on the subject of new voices and views, there are also the two young playwrights who appeared off-Broadway this week, Christopher Durang and David Henry Hwang.

Hwang is a twenty-six-year-old Chinese-American dedicated, so it seems, to interesting the public at large in his people's myths, history, and lives today. In his own words, he wants to "claim our legitimate but often neglected place in the American experience." That has meant writing about a friendship between two young men caught in a strike among the Chinese building the transcontinental railroad in 1867. It's meant contrasting an eager, rather pushy FOB—that is, someone "Fresh off the boat"—from Hong Kong, with a patronizing and somewhat scornful ABC, or "American-born Chinese." It's meant showing the impact of a visitor from mainland China on a Californian clan most of whose members seem mentally enslaved either by superstition and the past or by a gruesome consumerism. If *The Dance and the Railroad*, *FOB*, and *Family Devotions*, as these plays are respectively called, have their awkward and implausible moments, it's at least partly because Hwang is boldly trying to reconcile Western and Eastern forms. Suddenly a long monologue about the devastation wreaked by locusts may intrude into the conversation, or a college student may launch into a story in which he's Gwan Gung, ferocious warrior-god.

Together the three plays suggest that what Chinese-Americans carry on their shoulders these days are less heads than elaborately furnished and richly peopled houses, in which the antique edgily coexists with the contemporary, and Western ways are in perpetual conflict with Eastern. The two shorter pieces now at the Public Theater don't have the same immediacy and urgency, the same feeling of cultural crisis, because they extract the American element, and indeed, the Chinese one, too. They show Hwang expanding his horizons to embrace the island to the east of China. Japan, he implicitly tells us, has a place in his imagination, if not precisely in his heritage. This pan-orientalism of his is no doubt a gain but also, as it turns out, a loss.

His *House of the Sleeping Beauties*, adapted from a short

story by Yasunari Kawabata, fails to bring to dramatic life a subject perhaps better suited to meditative fiction than to the theater: the gradual preparation of an old man for death in a brothel exclusively populated by drugged, immobile, irresponsive beauties. *The Sound of a Voice* I enjoyed more, partly because it has more energy and conflict, partly because one of its two performers is a long, lithe, magnetic actor named John Lone. He plays a Japanese samurai come to the depths of the forest to kill a witch but seduced by her subtle and far from malign enchantments. The piece has the strange simplicity of a fairy tale but, as it turns out, some contemporary point as well. The "witch" ends by hanging herself in desolation at the warrior's departure. Presumably she was a woman with human powers and human feelings, mythologized and misinterpreted, as some of her sisters are today, by suspicion and prejudice and gossipy fear. It's a play in which Hwang moves beyond the Chinese-American community and yet, I feel sure, still manages to touch on some of its concerns: a feminist play in ancient Japanese code.

By comparison with that, indeed by comparison with almost anything, Christopher Durang's latest is a very blunt and direct piece of work. *Baby with the Bath Water*, as it's called, is about spiritual megadeath within the nuclear family. In the cradle "Daisy," who is actually a male forced to wear girl's clothes, is alternately cooed over and terrorized; as a child he's driven into more or less permanent despair by his dipsomaniac father and an erratic mother, who tells him, "I'm giving up my career for you, and any resentment I feel I'll never show"; and as a young and then not-so-young adult he finds himself in perpetual transit between a psychiatrist who can't help him and a college course he just can't finish. Add an almost maniacally unhelpful schoolteacher, and you've what might have been a grim treatise on alienation and anomie but is actually a gleeful, scathing satire on parental infantilism. Imagine one of R. D. Laing's case studies as it might have

been written by a collaboration between Joe Orton and Alfred
Jarry, and you'll have the garish, discordant tone.

What the poet Juvenal called *saeva indignatio* isn't a commodity often found in the theater nowadays, but Durang feels
and communicates it, or something like it. There can't be many
more carefully calculated and concerned acts of dramatic
aggression than *Sister Mary Ignatius Explains It All for You*,
his attack on what he sees as the lunatic contradictions, the
moral beastliness, and the invincible ignorance of hard-line
Catholic theology. This is his principled revenge on a faith in
which he, like David Rabe and Albert Innaurato, was brought
up. There must, incidentally, be an essay or even a thesis to
be written about Catholicism and its influence on several of
America's angrier playwrights.

Actually Durang attacked Rabe, or what he took to be
Rabe's earnestly platitudinous plays about Vietnam, in his
Vietnamization of New Jersey. For Robert Brustein, this was
an important play, satirizing "the cut-rate merchandising of
guilt that permeates so much contemporary American drama—
the heavy-handed symbolism, the piety, the self-satisfied indignation, the clumsy confrontations." It also "declared a
separate peace, and as far as American theater is concerned,
finally managed to bring the Vietnam war to an end." Maybe,
but there are other plays by Durang that seem to me more
slyly venomous, perhaps because the anger in them is more
personal. He endures Mary Ignatius at school, and savages
her and her ilk. He visits a shrink, and lambastes psychiatrists
and psychobabble to marvelous effect in *Beyond Therapy*,
though that play loses its way in the second act and ends
by driveling off nowhere. He lives through a childhood in
which he reports seeing "people being horrible to one another,
over and over and over"—and hence *Baby with the Bath
Water*.

For at least three-quarters of its length this is as black a
comedy as even Durang's satiric tarbrush has managed to

color it. In its carefully considered view, parents are people
who give you asbestos toys to play with, sit blithely by when
you run out and deliberately throw yourself in front of buses,
interpret your suicidal moods as "passive hostility," and (an
instance, this, from the apartment next door) permit the
household dog to eat you. But then the tone changes, not
without a little awkwardness. Durang introduces fresh, unaffected pain into his farce. He allows Keith Reddin to come
forward and explain what it feels like to want to be permanently concealed or dead, and Mr. Reddin does so with a
fragile dignity and, at the end, something more.

"Daisy," after years of psychoanalysis and pathological
promiscuity, has got married and has his own baby. He stands
over it, beginning the same baleful lullaby his father sang him:
"Hush, little baby, don't you cry, Mama's going to give you
a big black eye." But somehow, he manages to substitute
comforting words for the last four ones. The cycle of depri-
vation and abuse, well known to social workers, looks as if it
may at last be broken. The victim appears to have escaped
one of the worst of his probable fates, that of going on to
victimize others in turn. You can't take this optimistic denouement too seriously. After all, the play doesn't exist, and
wasn't meant to exist, on any rich psychological level. But I
found myself surprised, touched, reassured—as who wouldn't
be if he'd spent two hours in the company of a misanthropic
clown and then spotted a tiny, healing smile on the gaunt face
beneath the greasepaint?

Everything feels a bit unreal today, and in a way new to
me. The most recent Sunday *New York Times* contains a
longish review, penned by yours truly in the present tense,
of the first new play to hit Broadway since my arrival. But
Brothers, as it's called, closed after one night only at the Music
Box, just as the issue was being printed. Even the big name
on the billboards, Carroll O'Connor, couldn't save it from a

fell combination of circumstances: poor notices; inadequate advance sales at the box office.

George Sibbald's play asks—sorry, *asked*—whether and when a hale brother should present a sickly one with a kidney from the private spare-parts bank nature has created in his body. A topical enough question, but one that, as it turned out, gave little more than surface frisson to what was actually a rather melodramatic effort, an old-fashioned tale of strife on the family porch. I suspect it would never have been produced on Broadway unless O'Connor had wanted to play the possessive father at its center, and yet, paradoxically, a major reason for its failure was that O'Connor, who also directed, unbalanced the play by making himself too central. What seemed to have been conceived as an ensemble piece persistently brought him mid-stage, where he fruitily chuckled, petulantly growled, and angrily flapped his arms, giving the impression of a large pink teddy bear on the rampage. And the part just wasn't written at the depth to justify that prominence.

But to close after just one night! That seems excessively harsh punishment even for what this came perilously close to being, a vanity production, and for better or worse, I don't think it would have been inflicted on the play in England. There, as I've said before, critics are singly less influential and collectively less powerful. Audiences can anyway afford to take a chance on a play since seat prices are so much less exorbitant than here. Costs are lower, too, and so impresarios are willing to allow shows to run at losses for longer. In any case, the break-even point is usually around 60 percent, lower than in New York. That's why shows close overnight virtually never and seldom after as short a period as a week. Instead, they tend to muddle and blunder on, in hopes of "word of mouth" transforming a critical failure into a popular success.

That can happen, too. How else can one explain *No Sex Please—We're British*? Thirteen long years ago I went to the play's first night and thought it one of the silliest I'd ever seen, as did my saner colleagues. In fact, I didn't even bother to review it at once, so confident was I that it would close within a few days. But a week later it was still running, so I committed myself to the public view that it was undoubtedly doomed. And yet there it still is in the West End of London, a reproach both to my critical acumen and to British taste, the "longest-running comedy ever," with more than 5,000 performances to its credit.

New York does have similar tales. *Grease* wasn't critically well received, yet managed to run up 3,388 performances, more than any Broadway show except the eternal *Chorus Line*. But such unlooked-for success is less common than in London, and prompt and instant failure, much more common. And how can you accuse New York impresarios of being quick on the draw when the sums involved are so large? At the Imperial, or some similar big-musical theater, the difference in takings between a show that fills 80 percent of its seats and thus perhaps breaks even and one that fills only 50 percent is $140,000 a week. A month of waiting and hoping for better times could add $600,000 or more in losses to a production the original cost of which means that it's already deeply in the red. Why lose $3.6 million instead of $3 million? "Twenty-five years ago a play like Shelagh Delaney's *Taste of Honey* could break even at eighteen thousand dollars a week on Broadway," a producer told me the other day, "and so, if you took sixteen thousand dollars or seventeen thousand dollars, you could afford to wait and try to turn the thing around. But now you may have to take ten or twelve times more, so any significant shortfall will soon end up costing you many thousands."

At the 1,000-seat Music Box the difference between 50 percent and a more healthy 80 percent of weekly capacity is $80,000, and those bad notices meant that even with Mr. O'Connor podgily in the lead, *Brothers* would be lucky to achieve 50 percent. The play could have added $200,000 or $300,000 to its debts before "word of mouth" began to transform its fortunes. And who could be sure that "word of mouth" would turn out to be favorable? So the producers acted with American decisiveness, and *Brothers* joined the already daunting list of those cut off at birth in the last year or two.

It wasn't as expensive an overnight failure as the Lerner-Strouse musical *Dance a Little Closer* or the play *Frankenstein*, which came with spectacularly elaborate sets, including the Swiss mountains, a cemetery, Gothic interiors, and a monstrous lab. It wasn't as eccentric an overnight failure as *Moose Murders*, at the climax of which a bandaged quadraplegic, described by someone as "a fetid roll of gauze," reportedly rose from his wheelchair and somehow managed to kick an intruder, inexplicably dressed as a moose, in the groin. But it was still about as absolute as failure can get: a reminder that in this country, as rarely in my own, to be a critic is to be a blend of butcher, gravedigger, and obituarist.

Imagine it. You're walking through the slime and sleaze of Times Square, and suddenly someone taps you on the shoulder and whispers, "Pssst," into your ear. Clearly he's trying to sell you something: drugs, perhaps, or a watch, or his sister. Yet he's very well dressed. In fact, as he tells you, he's a theater owner. He points his finger at the playhouse beside which he and you are standing and then, strangely, at the sky just above it. "Want to buy it?" he asks. "I can give you a knockdown price. Only five million dollars." He's selling you *empty space*.

Actually such sales pitches seem more likely to occur in plush, respectable offices than in the street. But believe it or not, they could soon be happening. To me, it seems a prospect more bizarre and brazen than anything invented by the old medicine men or by the modern Times Square hustler. To a Theatrical Advisory Committee appointed by Mayor Edward

I. Koch, it is a way of saving Broadway from several of the disasters presently threatening it. It's called the sale of unused development rights and is, very literally, a means of spinning money out of thin air.

It's an extension of a practice already current in New York. If an owner of a building doesn't want to tear it down and build one as tall as the zoning laws allow, he may sell the unused space between the height of his present edifice and that putative new skyscraper. The buyer may then translate that space into bricks and mortar, or rather concrete, and put it on top of *his* new building, like a sort of hat, taking it above the limit hitherto imposed by the zoning laws. In other words, one owner agrees to be shorter so that another may be taller. But these weird pacts have so far involved closely neighboring buildings only. The Theatrical Advisory Committee wants the theater owners to be allowed to sell their unused space to developers over a wide area of the West Side.

That way the West Side itself gains, and Broadway is preserved. The key element is that in return for what would be a very substantial windfall, the owners would enter into conventions promising never to demolish their theaters. And why not? The total proceeds could be as much as $160 million, and the owners could expect to get maybe 50 percent of that. In view of the troubles faced by the industry right now, it's no wonder that senior figures among them seem pretty keen on the idea.

Nor is that all. The remaining 50 percent of the proceeds, conceivably as much as $80 million in all, would go into a general fund, to be used for financing new drama. If the first part of the plan would save Broadway physically, that would help save it in a deeper and more vital sense. After all, what's the point of lovingly preserving a theater if you've nothing to put in it?

The mayor's committee was set up after two theaters, the Helen Hayes and the Morosco on Forty-fifth Street, were pulled down to make way for what at present looks like a long, thin cigar but will eventually expand to become the Marriott Marquis Hotel. Most people seem to have expected it to recommend the landmarking of all or most of the forty-four buildings that the city still lists as legitimate Broadway theaters. And several members of the committee wanted to do just that. But representatives of the big chains—the Shuberts, the Nederlanders, the Jujamcyn theaters, owning thirty-two playhouses in all—argued otherwise. Some owners finance shows by borrowing money on the value of their theaters and feel that their value would be diminished if the possibility of development were less. Others think it would prevent them from altering interiors to suit particular shows. How could the Shuberts have ripped apart the Winter Garden for *Cats* if the theater had been landmarked?

Well, it's true that they never could have done that to Drury Lane, the Haymarket, or some equivalent London playhouse. For better or worse or both, West End theaters are far more rigorously protected than Broadway ones. Practically all of them are designated as buildings of historical or architectural importance and are hence almost untouchable; or they are in a "conservation area," such as Covent Garden, where substantial change may not occur; or they are in the London borough of Westminster, whose city plan recently declared that as many theaters as possible should be preserved and that, in the unlikely event of one's being demolished, a replacement should be included in the fabric of the new building. Many are all those things. And just in case one should slip through the thickening net, Parliament recently gave its imprimatur to a theatrical counterpart of the National Trust, which looks after many British stately homes. Neither in nor out of London is it possible to tamper with any playhouse except after consultation with the Theaters Trust, as it's called.

To give the Broadway theaters landmark status, though doubtless discouraging to marauders, would not give them remotely as much protection. The law actually makes it possible for an owner to tear down a landmarked building that proves unable to earn a "reasonable return," or 6 percent, on its value as land. That would probably mean that several theaters, landmarked or not, could be demolished right now. That so many are still standing at a time of rocketing land values suggests, I hope, that the owners mean it when they say they aren't interested in disposing of their playhouses—but their minds might change next week, next month, next year, if times were bad and the right offer came along.

That's why the air rights idea could prove so important. It's more fundamental medicine than landmarking, which might help preserve the shell of Broadway but would do nothing to tackle the slow, creeping illness deep inside. Let me sum up the signs and symptoms of that disease as I, a visitor to the sick ward, am beginning to see them.

Broadway productions played for a grand total of 1,259 weeks in the season that ended this summer, compared with 1,461 in the year 1981–82. Attendance dropped from 10.7 million to 8.1 million. Box-office receipts fell no less alarmingly, from $221 million to $203 million. All this was in spite, or perhaps because, of an increase in seat prices. When I settle into my orchestra seat at a musical these days, glancing at my ticket as I do so, I'm amazed to discover it cost $45. The top for a straight play is around $35, which seems no less exorbitant to me, coming as I do from a country where it's hard to pay more than $17 for a good evening out and easy to pay a lot less.

It's a bit early to make comparisons so early in the season, but present trends suggest that 1983–84 will be no better and conceivably even worse. At the beginning of October as few as sixteen Broadway theaters had plays or musicals in them, compared with twenty-three a year before and thirty in 1980. Some theaters—and I don't mean those of the 44, like the historic Hudson, which have been converted to discos, rock, and other such establishments—appear to be consistently, almost permanently dark. The Eugene O'Neill has been open for only 18 weeks in the last two years. In the past ten years the Belasco has been dark for a barely credible 409 weeks, or nearly eight years, the Lyceum for 294 weeks, and the Golden for 286. This is wasteful. The cost of keeping a theater dark, the Shubert Organization tells me, is between $6,000 and $10,000 a week—and would be more if it, like some owners, had mortgage repayments to make. It emphasizes afresh that the fate of the Helen Hayes and Morosco could be that of others. And it has ominous implications for the future of straight drama, and especially serious straight drama, in New York.

That's because of these theaters' size. The Golden has only 800 seats, and the others, though a little larger, have second balconies, where the seats have to be sold at relatively low prices and are anyway unpopular with American theatergoers. But a straight play costs $500,000 to stage on Broadway these days, and usually more. With running costs no less exorbitant—$150,000 a week in many cases; in some, more—it's hard to see how any of the smaller playhouses can allow an impresario to break even, let alone make money. In other words, the Broadway theaters that are uniquely suited to serious drama are uneconomic and would seem to have little commercial future. And that means that serious drama on Broadway may not have much of a future either.

It's not as if the impresarios can put up seat prices to meet the ever-increasing costs of production and performance. Everyone seems to agree that they're dangerously high already. It is a universal complaint among theatergoers and a universal anxiety among theater owners. To increase prices would only alienate the natural audience for serious drama further than it is alienated now, and that must already be very, very much. How many students, how many teachers, how many young professionals are going to take a chance on

an interesting-sounding piece at the Golden if they have to
pay $35, $40, $45, or whatever would allow the producer
to make a profit at 80 or 90 percent of capacity? Not enough
to keep the theater filled 80 or 90 percent, that's for sure.

It's a vicious circle. Up go costs, so up must go prices, so
down go audiences, so up must go prices again, along with
those unceasing costs. Nor does the fell geometry end there.
Up go costs and prices, and down, with the audiences, goes
courage and derring-do. If theatergoers are less inclined to
take risks with their hard-earned money, so, of course, are
producers. They're going to think very hard about staging
straight plays with large casts and elaborate sets in any theater, whatever its size. They're going to think very hard before
taking risks with unknown actors or obscure playwrights or
touchy, challenging subjects or anything different or difficult.
And who can blame them? Who can blame them when three
of the four most interesting new plays to hit Broadway last
season—Lanford Wilson's *Angels Fall*, Beth Henley's *The Wake
of Jamey Foster*, Christopher Durang's *Beyond Therapy*—
all proved to be failures?

More encouraging news is that the fourth, Marsha Norman's
'Night, Mother, is still running, nearly eight months after its
opening, and it's not in the least bland or "safe." But that
doesn't contradict present trends as much as one might think.
Indeed, in some respects it confirms them. First, it's cheaper
to run than most straight plays, having a single set and a cast
of just two. Moreover, it was flagging at the box office, despite
excellent reviews, until its young author won a Pulitzer Prize,
an honor whose prestige the theatergoing public evidently respects. And now it's faltering again. It is on twofers—that's
to say, vouchers for the show are to be found in Chinese
laundries, Korean delicatessens, and other shops, entitling
the bearer, when he or she presents them at the box office,
to a substantial discount. Again, you can be quite confident
of paying only half the normal price if you stand in line at

the bargain booth in Times Square (which is now responsible, so I'm told, for some 22 percent of all theater tickets sold in New York). Clearly, *'Night, Mother* is not long for this world.

My feeling, along with that of many others, is that straight drama on Broadway will increasingly be represented by the smart and rather bland comedy, the star vehicle, or both. Apart from that, only the occasional big, glamorous musical can expect to flourish. Yet even here, in the area where Broadway has always been strongest and remained so, there are warning signs. *Cats* is doing wonderfully well, but it cost all of $5 million to stage. The "average" large musical, whatever that is, comes with a bill of $3 million, compared with $1.5 million in 1980 and half that in 1976.

Tremendous profits are doubtless still possible. *Annie,* which cost $800,000 to stage, is said to have made $16.5 million. *A Chorus Line* is nearly $25 million in profit. But the risk has become much greater, too. *A Doll's Life,* the big musical adaptation of Ibsen, ran a weekend and lost $4 million. *Chaplin,* with Anthony Newley as the singing tramp, has just collapsed in Los Angeles, losing a similar sum. It received poor notices at first but reportedly was much improved by the play doctors and was all set to come to New York when the producers failed to raise the final $1 million necessary for the move. Risk capital isn't so easy to find these days. Everyone has become more cautious and is likely to get more so.

Hence the relevance of the sale of air rights. Conceivably it would encourage theater owners who are also producers or investors or both to take a few more chances, a few more risks. But its real importance is, of course, what it might do for the drama. The ways things are going, there won't be any at all on Broadway before long. The ways things are going, we'll actually reach the situation half-facetiously prophesied by Peter Brook in his *The Empty Space:* the Great White Way reduced to one show per season, a musical naturally, watched by one man paying $500,000 for the privilege. The only difference is that inflation will have multiplied that sum many times. The theatergoing oil sheikh, or whoever he is, will be lucky if the price on his ticket is as low as $5 million.

Down to the Village to meet Joseph Papp, whom I take to be the most creative, the most influential, and probably the most important figure in the New York and, indeed, in the American, theater. The industry is, as I am discovering, in less than the best of health. But what would it be like if Papp hadn't emerged from nowhere to create the New York Shakespeare Festival, to open the Public Theater, to present production after production, to put forward idea after idea?

The latest of his ideas is for what he calls, with characteristic instinct for the catchy phrase, a National Theater on Broadway. He's a member of the mayor's Theater Advisory Committee and foursquare behind the plan to create a development fund out of the sale of air rights. Indeed, it would appear to have been his suggestion, at least in the form it's now taking. With that and other money it will, he thinks, be possible to finance precisely those plays that the big impresarios aren't financing and to put them in precisely those theaters the impresarios are failing to keep open. That way Broadway is preserved, and reclaimed as a forum for decent drama.

He was born Joseph Papirofsky sixty-two years ago, son of poor Polish Jewish immigrants and reared, so he says, in the streets of slum Brooklyn. As a child he took no interest in drama, but much in dancing and music, and as a sailor in the wartime navy he began to fulfill it, by producing musicals. Though he'd never performed himself, he went on to the Actors Laboratory in California and, instead of going on the stage, became its managing director. Then back to New York, where he started an acting workshop in a church basement; put a stage on a truck and toured it around Central Park; started what's still a free summer festival, mainly of Shakespeare's plays; built the permanent Delacorte Theater beside

Belvedere Lake; acquired the old Astor Library on Lafayette Street and converted it into that marvelous warren of stages and auditoriums known to the world as the Public Theater; moved uptown to Lincoln Center to create what, if he had stayed longer, might have become an American National Theater; tired of the dictatorship of wealthy subscribers, and . . . but the evidence of his drive and restlessness is surely ample enough already.

He sits surrounded by posters of his more successful productions (*That Championship Season, The Pirates of Penzance, Plenty,* and, of course, *A Chorus Line*), a small, neat, dapper, and altogether unpretentious figure. If you saw him on *What's My Line?*, you'd be more inclined to classify him as someone's valet than as a powerful impresario. But energy, incisiveness, and passion are there all right, qualities that have lost as well as made him friends. Recently Sam Shepard stormed out of his life, declaring that he had meddled too much with the production of *True West.* He discovered David Rabe, then had a violent public quarrel with him on the sidewalks of Philadelphia, after he'd walked out of his play *The Orphan.* But now that friendship—a "father and son relationship," according to Rabe—has been reforged. And Michael Bennett, who has had his differences with Papp, surely spoke for many in New York when he brought him onto the stage of the Shubert at the big gala performance of *A Chorus Line.* "I love you, Joe Papp," he said simply, and embraced him.

People say he's a better producer than director, and people say he'd be a better producer still if he did less, spread himself less thin. I've heard him called an opportunist, on the grounds that at Lincoln Center he turned from Public Theater plays to contemporary classics with stars to experimental versions of older classics, in apparent hopes of finding something, *anything*, that would appeal to the uptown, upscale theatergoer. I've heard him called a man without a point of view, and I've heard him called a megalomaniac mainly because he likes to sing commercials for his productions over the radio and tends to appear in prominent positions in ads for the Public Theater.

Well, there are answers to all such accusations. You have to be with him for only a few minutes to see that he's a born communicator, able to articulate an idea clearly and put it across punchily. Singing commercials is just one of many ways in which he's managed to achieve his aims, which is to get people to listen, take notice, and react. As for those accusations of opportunism—well, they take insufficient account of his view of theater, which is that it should be diverse, catholic, rich, appealing to more than one kind of theatergoer and one kind of taste. It should embrace the somber didacticism of David Rabe's *Sticks and Bones*, which Papp brought to Broadway in 1972, and *Hair*, *The Pirates of Penzance*, and, of course, *A Chorus Line*.

Some relevant Pappisms culled from our conversation: "I've always felt that theater exists in its own time, immediately, even today. That's why I'd always do a new play rather than a classic, and classics that have some application to the world around them, preferably with a director with a strong point of view. That's why I started the Public Theater with *Hair*.

"The plays I put on have to fulfill my social outlook in some way. Well, not specifically, because I don't write them. But I have to feel they have some social importance. You can't read the newspapers, see horrors on TV, and do something cutesy, something that's pure entertainment.

"I don't like people who are narrow. I don't like the extreme left, the extreme right, or the extreme middle. I reject them all, because on some days and in some areas I feel to the right, in some to the left, and in some even to the middle. And I don't want any theater filled with plays putting across one point of view, even mine.

"The theater's about talking, about debating. It's dialectic, thrilling and pleasurable and perhaps a bit frightening. If people get too comfortable in one position, I try to put on plays which knock them out of it. I'll put them on even if I strongly disagree with their point of view.

"The American drama is too domestic. I've had to go to England to get plays of a social nature: David Hare's *Plenty*, Caryl Churchill's *Top Girls*. I've had to go to Czechoslovakia, Russia, and Poland for plays this coming season. What a relief some of them are! You feel you're back in the world at last. Here it's so internal."

What's certain is that the kind of play Papp would like to see on the American stage is only very rarely to be found on Broadway. Yet he doesn't, like others I know, go on to conclude that the Great White Way is past redemption, fit only to be ignored. That, for instance, seems to be the opinion of Jose Quintero, who has flounced permanently off to California after seeing Tennessee Williams's last play flop, his plans to stage a revival of O'Neill's *Iceman Cometh* also fail, and the destruction of the Morosco and the Helen Hayes, the respective settings for his productions of *A Moon for the Misbegotten* and *Long Day's Journey into Night*.

Well, Papp, too, fought to save those playhouses from the demolition men, and he, too, feels nostalgic for the days when the great American dramatists could expect to see both premieres and revivals of their work on Broadway. "If David Rabe or Sam Shepard had appeared in the twenties and thirties," he says, "they'd have been Broadway dramatists." Yet he persists, in defiance of much of the evidence, in seeing Broadway as the center of the American theater, the place where writers still hanker to prove themselves and performers still yearn to make it. He's often transferred plays to it in the past, and now he sees a chance to restore it, if not exactly to its old exclusive glory, at least to a place where a healthy mix of serious drama, comedy, and musical can be found. Hence his proposal for a "National Theater on Broadway."

The phrase is rhetoric, and more than rhetoric. It foresees

a chain of Broadway theaters, perhaps as many as ten of the
smaller, more frequently dark, and less economically reliable
ones, given over to production of new drama. Writers would
be lured up there by the promise of at least $25,000, whether
their plays succeeded or failed. Actors of standing would be
attracted there, too, since each production would run for only
eight weeks—"we would," says Papp, in a sentence I find a
bit depressing, "recognize the precedence that TV and movies
take in their lives." Audiences would be attracted back to the
theater by the seat prices, which would vary from $25 down
to, perhaps, $7.

Clearly all this would be very expensive. It would need,
Papp concedes, special agreements with the unions, to keep
down labor and running costs. Above all, it would need the
regular subsidy that a permanent development fund would
permit. Papp obviously hopes that the sale of air rights would
create this, but even if that rather improbable idea never
comes to fruition, he doesn't believe that his plan is necessarily
dead. It could start with as little as $10 million, raised partly
from private donors, partly from the National Endowment
for the Arts, partly from state and city sources. Papp, along
with many others, thinks that New York is doing far too little
to help a troubled industry that, at last count, was directly
or indirectly responsible for an annual expenditure of $1.6
billion. Indeed, a vital part of his plan is that the city becomes
"the purchaser of last resort," itself stepping in and buying
any Broadway theater threatened with demolition.

Coming from another source, that might sound like a pipe
dream. But Papp has achieved so much and continues to
achieve so much. Are black and Hispanic actors underem-
ployed? Well, let's cast them in traditionally white roles or
form them into a repertory company. Are the two Equitys
preventing the English from seeing American actors, and vice
versa? Well, let's do a special deal with the Royal Court in

London, under which productions are regularly swapped.
"Don't tell me anything is impossible," Papp likes to say.
"Let's try it first."

Well, heart transplants were once considered impossible
and now are regular practice. Restoring the old, decadent
heart of the American theater would seem similarly impossible
and should therefore be tried. For Papp it would be the triumphant climax of a triumphant career, and for the rest of us,
an obvious boon. I don't think we've heard the last either of
him or his National Theater on Broadway.

I have only to look out of the window of my apartment on
West Fifty-sixth Street, and I can see two reasons why the
creation of an American National Theater would be difficult.
In fact, I can stay at my desk and hear one of them. The
traffic piles up in the morning and again in the afternoon,
and hoots and hoots and hoots and hoots, unable to contain
its impatience even when it's absolutely apparent there's no
alternative but to wait. And I can peer out at any time of the
day, and the Chinese laundry is still to my left, the Korean
delicatessen to my right, and across the road on Eighth Avenue
a pizza joint and what curiously describes itself as an "Asian-
Spanish" eatery. The faces passing below my window reiterate
and reemphasize that this is not one nation, but many.

Yet the talismanic phrase "National Theater" seems to be
on everyone's lips these days. Actors' Equity has just asked
the government to fund a nationwide network of theaters to
the tune of $1 billion, which could, it says, be raised if the
construction of one Trident submarine were stopped. More
moderately, ANTA has announced plans to start a National
Theater at the Kennedy Center in Washington, financed largely
by the $5 million the organization received from the sale of
what's now the Virginia on Manhattan's West Fifty-second
Street. And finally, of course, there's Joe Papp's National
Theater on Broadway.

I have to say that Equity's appeal strikes me as fatuous and
possibly counterproductive. Do these eager thespians really
believe they can persuade President Reagan, who has been
trying to cut the National Endowment for the Arts's already
inadequate budget, to cash in a slice of the navy and merrily
hand the proceeds to them? The project is so improbable it
makes them look silly and damages what would be, were it
more cannily lobbied for, a good case and cause. The ANTA
plan is clearly more realistic, coming as it does from the organization entrusted by Congress fifty years ago with the task
of creating a National Theater, though unluckily never given
the money that would enable it to do so. Again, the blend of
contemporary and classical work proposed for the Kennedy
Center would fit into most people's idea of what a National
Theater should offer. But the enterprise will need a more
startling director and company than will easily be attracted
to Washington, and more funds than its first five-year plan
envisages, if it's to convince anyone it's much more than a
regional rep with an overblown title.

If a National Theater is to be in only one city, it should,
of course, be in New York, the center of the country's cultural
life and the fount of its theatrical traditions. That's where the
acting and directing talent would most naturally gravitate.
Hence the appeal of Papp's plan. But his motives are to save
theaters, help dramatists, and stop Broadway from becoming
a boneyard jangling with musicals and only musicals. To create a National Theater in any generally accepted sense isn't
his wish. His plan at present is for a season of unconnected
productions, mounted by different impresarios with ad hoc
casts.

It doesn't sound a promising recipe for a National Theater,
if you mean by that, as I do, a permanent company of national
stature and not just a building or series of buildings. Admittedly there's no rulebook, no set procedure in this field. National theaters have emerged for various reasons in various

ways to take various forms. Louis XIV wanted to construct a culture worthy of a sun king, Gustavus III of Sweden enjoyed writing as well as watching plays; and so Paris got a Comédie Française, Stockholm a Royal Dramatic Theater. Konstantin Stanislavsky and Bertolt Brecht needed to put new ideas to the test, and hence the Moscow Arts Theater, the Berliner Ensemble. Peter Hall took charge of summer stock at Stratford-on-Avon, decided he couldn't maintain satisfactory standards with ad hoc casts, and formed the Royal Shakespeare Company. A century of pressure by the theatrical faithful—two centuries, if you remember David Garrick was suggesting an English equivalent of the Comédie Française many decades before the birth of Matthew Arnold, let alone that of Shaw—at last resulted in the creation of the National Theater of Great Britain. And the fundamental purpose of these institutions varied from safeguarding French culture, to staging the Bard accessibly and well, to propagating Marxist thought, to (the British and Swedish idea) presenting the widest possible selection of good plays from all periods and places.

They're different in every respect but one, which is, of course, that they're companies first, bricks and mortar only secondarily. That's a point that seems not always to have been appreciated over here. It was wonderfully generous of the late Vivian Beaumont to give money for a building she hoped would become "a National Theater comparable in distinction and achievement to the Comédie Française," but also a little naïve to think that an American Comédie Française could simply be built. Molière's troupe came to a triumphant halt in Paris only after eight years of honing its skills in the provinces. More recently Britain's National Theater spent a decade in, and sometimes out of, the shabby Old Vic before moving to its permanent home beside the Thames. Indeed, that great cultural Oz might never have been built had not its prospective tenants first appeared to prove their value and its practicability, and their experience in humbler surroundings did much to determine its eventual shape.

Twenty years and no less than four regimes after Mrs. Beaumont Allen made her gift, the building bearing her name would seem less likely than ever to end up as the American National Theater, let alone its Comédie Française. In retrospect, it seems a pity that the Lincoln Center Repertory, as the group that eventually moved to the Vivian Beaumont was called, didn't stay longer in the steel tent in Washington Square where it began its life. As it was, it moved uptown before it had begun to develop a coherent identity or, some would say, even the basic skills necessary for the job. That historic error is one of several reasons why the Vivian Beaumont now stands untenanted and looks perilously like fulfilling the prophecies of Robert Brustein: "A Stonehenge of the future, visited only by scholars engaged in speculation as to what its function could have been."

Companies should precede buildings, not vice versa. Indeed, it's tempting to go further and wonder if companies need permanent buildings at all, let alone the rather grand sort that tend to be associated with "national theaters." In many ways—from the cost of its upkeep to the kind of upscale audience it attracts—the structure will tend to dominate, control, limit, and sometimes spoil the troupe inside. Standards dropped disconcertingly when the British National Theater made the trip from the Old Vic to its present building. It's only in the last few years that it has reestablished itself creatively. It's fortunate the Royal Shakespeare Company had evolved a still stronger character and more distinctive style or it could hardly have survived its recent move to the Barbican Center in the City of London, an edifice which combines the quaint charm of a Hilton Hotel with the intimacy of Heathrow Airport. As it was, there was much unhappiness in the ranks and some uncertainty onstage.

Perhaps a truly national theater should be out traversing the nation, not stuck in the metropolis, like a gem in a brooch. This isn't some odd foreign notion either. Back in 1935 America created the most authentically "national" theater the world has ever seen in the Federal Theater Project. In three-odd years some 10,000 people gave 63,000 performances to 30 million people in forty states. But congressmen hostile to the New Deal and, in one notorious case, suspicious that Christopher Marlowe was a Communist, denied it the money and time to develop into something the country might soon be celebrating as a fifty-year-old National Theater.

Nor have more mandarin initiatives made the progress that might have been hoped. The Theater Guild became indistinguishable from commercial Broadway. Its offshoot, the Group Theater, found it financially impossible to sustain the greater austerity at which it aimed. According to Harold Clurman, one of its founders, "The basic defect in our activity was that, while we tried to maintain a true theater artistically, we proceeded economically on a show-business basis." The Group's failure was its "utterly destructive" dependence on the box office. Europe may not always, or even often, be a helpful model for America. But if there's one generalization that can confidently be made from the European experience, it is that national theaters can't survive on tickets sold over the counter and probably can't thrive, as the Lincoln Theater Rep tried to thrive, on subscription lists and other such philanthropic gestures. From the Mediterranean to the Baltic, from the Urals to the Irish Sea, there's agreement that it's impossible to create a sizable company, plan competently ahead, take artistic risks, maintain standards, keep seat prices sensible, and attract an audience diverse enough itself to be called national without the regular injection of public money.

This is a subject likely to preoccupy me rather a lot in the months ahead, so I'll content myself here with saying that American suspicion of subsidy—I've heard it called socialized

theater in the same dark way people talk of socialized medicine—is one of the reasons why the creation of a local Comédie
Française or RSC will be difficult, if not impossible. There
are others, some practical, some psychological. There's the
lure of Hollywood, always likely to disrupt a good permanent
company with promises of wealth and fame. There's the relative narrowness of acting traditions. How are American performers, whose strength is naturalism, to cope with the slippery
and exotic rhetoric likely to be found in the classics that would
presumably be part of a National Theater's repertory?

More subtly, where's the "coherent idea" without which
Clurman once said, no group "can survive beyond the flush
of its first flight"? Well, perhaps it would be enough to have
a burning faith that theater matters to great and low alike,
an unyielding determination to find what is fresh, what is
stimulating, and (without descending to the chic vulgarity that
would turn Petruchio into Hugh Hefner, Katherine into Kate
Millett, and set *The Taming of the Shrew* aboard an executive
jet) what is *American* in the oldest and most seemingly alien
works. Actually Elia Kazan surely had it more or less right
when he first addressed the Lincoln Rep Company as its director: Since they were American, they'd create an American
theater; though they were in New York, they wouldn't aim at
one section or group only; they'd hope to become "a world
theater, expressing the way we Americans see the world";
they'd try "to speak for all men by expressing what is deepest
and most enduring in the lives of all men."

What a National Theater needs is a leader possessed not
necessarily of some abstract "idea" but of a crusading passion
and the charisma to communicate to others. Kazan hadn't the
passion of a Bertolt Brecht or an André Antoine, or the charisma of a Laurence Olivier, founder of the British National
Theater, but he had enough of both commodities to be the
obvious candidate for such a job back in 1963. For whom
could one claim that today? Robert Brustein, scourge of the

Vivian Beaumont, has made a great success of the American Repertory Theater up in Cambridge, Massachusetts. But his unconcealed contempt for the meretricious has given him a rather elitist image and certainly can't have endeared him to the theater establishment. Joe Papp is the obvious choice. But he actually ran the Vivian Beaumont for a time and found that plush uptown environment and those plush uptown audiences not at all to his taste. Nor does he seem interested at the moment in forming a permanent company in more congenial surroundings, let alone a "national" one. It's a sign of the lack of qualified Americans that the Lincoln Center people have had to look abroad for someone to revivify the Beaumont, trying, but failing, to lure Peter Hall from his present job as director of the National in London.

But here's another problem. Suppose Hall, or someone else, had the money, the talent, everything else needed to start an American National Theater. Would he get other things no less important: the time painstakingly to build a company and the right to fail, fail again, and fail yet again? To flop in America still tends to be what Clurman ruefully called it years ago, "a moral disgrace," and success is expected to be not only complete but quick. But the philosophy of wanting it all, wanting it now, and shame to those who don't deliver, isn't very helpful to someone trying painfully to create an ensemble of national or even international stature.

Those symptomatic horns tooting and blaring outside my window aren't altogether vexatious to me. American restlessness, American impatience for results, are among the native traits that we in Europe, where it sometimes seems that nothing can change, tend to envy. But they are also a main reason why that enterprise to which I keep returning, the Lincoln Center Rep, never fulfilled the hopes invested in it. Kazan and his codirector, Robert Whitehead, said from the beginning that they'd need three years to create any sort of company, and the regime collapsed before the end of two, the victim of what Kazan called the "venom" of critics and others, of dissatisfaction in the boardroom, and perhaps to some extent their own folly in trying too much too quickly. The production of Thomas Middleton's *The Changeling*, at the beginning of the second season, was universally execrated and was clearly far beyond the powers of an embryonic company. Kazan might have condemned impatience, but he showed signs of it himself.

What the enterprise needed was not what the *Village Voice* kindly gave it at the end of its very first year, an award for "outstanding disservice to the American theater." It needed restraint, forbearance, understanding, patience, and a willingness to take the long, long view, and it needed it from everyone involved, from directors to reviewers, audiences to board members. That it didn't get this, then or later, must largely explain the would-be National Theater's history, with its changes of policy, its swerves of direction, its fumblings and bunglings and exasperatingly occasional successes, all culminating in the closure of the Beaumont itself. Imagine if within months, if not weeks, of forming his troupe Molière had been attacked by the cognoscenti for not being highbrow enough, abused by regular theatergoers for not being lowbrow enough, damned by everyone for unevenness of standards, given an award for outstanding disservice to French culture, then sacked. What sort of Comédie Française would Paris now have?

And what sort of Comédie Française would it have if France itself had been a cultural Babel, divided among Chinese-Frenchmen, Hispanic-Frenchmen, Polish-Frenchmen, and Mongolian-Frenchmen? When I first spent that extended period in the United States, twenty years ago, something called the melting pot was much admired. It was supposed to transform any immigrant into a good, standard American within a generation or two, and the implication was that this cooking process was a healthy one, to be welcomed by those being benignly whirled around in the blender. The feeling seemed to be that if blacks, for instance, only tried that little bit harder they, too, could enter the great WASP paradise, with all their differences bleached away. Well, that particular dream appears to have ended, even reversed itself. Now I find an America unapologetically fragmented into different groups, each one proud of its separate cultural identity, be it black or Hispanic or Chinese or gay or militantly female.

This "Balkanization of American culture," as Brustein brilliantly calls it, is not good news for those wanting an American National Theater, which would not have to be absolutely homo- but could obviously not be infinitely heterogeneous. As he says, how can there be a National Theater when there's not a nation, only a series of subnations, each with its own ambitions, language, and symbols? That's a poser all right. Yet Brustein himself acknowledges that at some level there's a common experience, or at least a common imagination, that binds human being to human being and therefore American to American. The same problem exists, admittedly on a far lesser scale, in present-day Britain, a much more culturally and racially diverse nation than it once was, and it's been faced by both the RSC and the National Theater. We're becoming used to Englishmen of West Indian or Asian origin cropping up among the Shakespearean nobility. We've seen an all-black *Measure for Measure* at the National and also an all-black version of Pinter's *Caretaker*. Both productions have found new resonances in old plays.

Is it naïve to say that good plays are good plays are good plays? There is "minority" drama, for instance, LeRoi Jones's *Dutchman*, that has the power to arrest and stimulate the majority, whatever that majority may be. There's "majority" drama, if directed and acted with flair, that can do the same for minorities. A sensible first season for an American National Theater is impossible to select in abstract since it would obviously depend on the strengths of particular members of the company. But it might be the one with which Tyrone Guthrie launched his theater in Minneapolis: *Hamlet*, Molière's *Miser*, Chekhov's *Three Sisters*, Miller's *Death of a Salesman*. It is cautious, the sort of program to get a director accused by the impatient of "playing safe" but also the sort that might enable a company to find its feet. Those plays are all capable of exciting the nod of recognition anywhere, anytime.

To talk more precisely about the kind of American National Theater that might one day emerge can be only to indulge in fantasy, and highly personal fantasy at that. My own crystal ball, for what it's worth, shows a large, ethnically diverse troupe dividing its time between a main theater and a studio theater and between there and the road. In fact, I see at least two companies alternating between New York and points beyond. Am I sounding implausible? Then let's continue.

Time, shared aims, long periods for rehearsal would transform those companies into ensembles, but not ensembles with any rigid style. The American National Theater would not ossify, as some would say the Comédie Française and the Moscow Arts Theater have ossified. It doesn't keep the same production in repertory for decades, putting new actors into the same fixed slots when one leaves or dies. Its offerings aren't books in a college library or exhibitions in a museum. Though permanent, it constantly renews itself, making a virtue of what would doubtless still be necessity. Though the salaries and the prestige it offers are enough to give pause to those tempted by Hollywood, the performers and directors come, go, return, each time committing themselves for as long as it takes to belong.

The theater's programming gradually grows in confidence. It knows that America has produced three dramatists of international stature in O'Neill, Miller, and Williams and many others well worth either safeguarding or encouraging. It also knows that while it hasn't a Molière as a direct ancestor, it can claim more kinship with (say) William Shakespeare, Pedro Calderón de la Barca, and Sean O'Casey than either the Comédie Française or the Scandinavian theaters. It can counter accusations of rootlessness with the argument that America's cultural roots are everywhere. It can even claim that Balkanization is to some extent a gain because it gives the few access to theatrical traditions which they can then perhaps share with the many.

The theater is obsessed with new American work, commissioning plays from all around and in turn being overwhelmed with scripts, many from writers who have numbly concluded that their future was only in TV or the movies. It mounts seasons of experimental or "rough" theater in its studio. It moves the occasional success to Broadway, though only if that doesn't disrupt other productions and hence the repertoire as a whole. It invites companies from abroad and visits other countries, learning something both ways. It . . . but to go on would be to risk sounding as farfetched as Actors' Equity itself.

What one can say, though, is that there isn't likely to be a much more congenial time for a really substantial initiative than now and that it would be a pity if that were preempted by a lesser one, such as an ersatz National Theater in Washington. As far as both the classics and serious new plays are concerned, Broadway's dereliction is as apparent as off-Broadway's insufficiency, and at last everyone seems to be acknowledging the fact. The Papp plan would be a great step forward. That, combined with a repertory company, maybe even an American National Theater Company, would be a greater, if much more improbable, one. At least people are urgently thinking and talking. You might almost say that things are bad enough to be hopeful.

Peter Brook's chamber version of *Carmen*, which I've visited no fewer than three times to date, seems already to be escalating from event to phenomenon to *casus belli*. It has reactivated the row between those who think that the Vivian

Beaumont, where it's staged, is a perfectly adequate theater
and those who think it a perfectly inadequate one. Moreover,
a sort of civil war seems to have developed between the theater
critics, most of whom have tended to admire and applaud
Brook's reworking, and the music critics, some of whom have
been deeply upset by what they see as an awful atrocity per-
petrated on the pristine form of Georges Bizet. Indeed, I'd
only to let slip a hint of my enthusiasm to a leader of the latter
faction, Harold Schonberg, *New York Times* cultural correspondent, and his normally benign face turned not merely to
stone but into a plausible imitation of an ancient bust of Mars
at his most implacable. How (he asked) would *I* like to see a
Hamlet that contained bits and pieces of Holinshed as well as
Shakespeare? How would I like one that was hacked, chopped,
dismembered, then so reassembled as to quarter the cast,
treble the violence, and swap Act 2 with Act 4?

Well, I've seen Shakespeare productions not unlike that,
and I didn't like them at all. I'm conservative enough to have
had my doubts even about Brook's celebrated *Midsummer
Night's Dream*, before whose clowns, jugglers, and trapezists
most theater critics ignominiously abased themselves, impres-
sionably gaping at the three-ring circus of that director's imagination. Where, I wondered, was the unease, the lust, even
the horror that are to be found in the original? Yet Brook's
eighty-minute condensation of *Carmen* exhilarated me each
time I saw it, although his policy of rotating the principals
meant that some performances were stronger than others. Is
this reaction testimony, as I'd like to think, to the opera's
mythic stature and power? Or simply to the gullibility of myself
and my comrades in the theater regiment when confronted
with attention-grabbing travesties in an alien genre?

The question raises interesting questions of principle. For
myself, I feel less protective to Shakespeare's *King John* than
to his *Macbeth* or *Lear*, so I'm relatively unconcerned when,
as once happened at Stratford-on-Avon, a director adds ma-

terial from an earlier play on the same subject. Perhaps a line can be drawn between work that can on occasions be subjected to surgery and work so momentous that it must never be tampered with even by a Dr. Michael De Bakey of the theater. But then many people would place *Carmen* in the second, untouchable category, along with *Giovanni* and *Figaro*. A better defense of what Brook has done to the opera is that he doesn't pretend that the result is *the Carmen*.

It's *La Tragédie de Carmen*, a new work adapted by Jean-Claude Carrière and others from Prosper Mérimée's original novella, as well as from Henri Meilhac and Ludovic Halévy's libretto and Bizet's score. The choruses of cigarette girls, bandits, and the like have gone. Instead, only four singing parts remain, and those principals aren't greatly outnumbered by the orchestra, a tiny gaggle perched in the wings. Well-known songs turn up in unexpected places, and one or two not at all. In this version Don José kills his commanding officer and also Carmen's husband, a sinister intruder from Mérimée's original. And so far from triumphing in the bullring, the toreador Escamillo is mortally gored offstage, increasing still further a death count higher than any Bizet himself contemplated.

It sounds sensational. On the contrary, it's dour, spare, and, literally as well as metaphorically, earthbound. Earth, plus a little gravel, is what covers the small circular stage thrusting out into the Beaumont's auditorium. Earth is what Carmen is lying on at the very beginning, a sprawling heap covered by a tarpaulin, and earth is what she's absently fingering just before her murder. Everything about the production emphasizes that we're down here, in the grime, blood, dirt, and sweat, where men and women feel and unspectacularly suffer. We're not up there, in the high operatic air, where larger-than-life figures strike romantic attitudes. At times Brook's dark, stark fable put me in mind of Goya, at times of Beckett, at times of Büchner. As he sees him, Don

José is very like Woyzeck, a simple, inarticulate soldier, lost
and bewildered, who ends by helplessly murdering his woman.

Of course, the two men's circumstances and motives are
different. Social pressures are driving Woyzeck to ruin, and
social pressures are trying to save Don José from it. But in
Brook's production, we're little aware of the bourgeois mother
offstage, the respectable sweetheart from home, and other
such manifestations of the nice, safe world from which Carmen
is trying to seduce her would-be lover. We're aware neither
of "good" society nor of "bad" society, the smugglers and
bandits of the original. We're somewhere beyond the reach
of the sociologists and the topographers, in a hot, dusty forum
where feeling nakedly clashes with feeling, and even Micaela,
the childhood sweetheart, comes to us stripped to the raw.
Wherever one looks, one sees bleak yet vibrant testimony to
the destructive power of sex.

Does this make Brook's *Carmen* sound dauntingly astringent and abstract? Actually there's room in it for plenty of
human detail. Patricia Schuman, the most sensual of the Carmens I've seen, does all sorts of intimate, suggestive things
with her eyes, her tongue, her toes, a cigar, smoke rings,
grapes, an orange. Laurence Dale is an especially fine José,
a pale, desolate boy, deceptively still outside, stricken within.
Escamillo becomes, most memorably in Carl Johan Falkman's
performance, a lordly, sauntering roué, confident enough in
Lillas Pastia's tavern, but even there half-aware that his time
as master of the bullring is nearing its end. He injects a sudden, quiet foreboding into the great toreador song and shows
the tension before what does in fact turn out to be his last
public appearance: puffing at a cigarette, making rather groggy
practice sweeps with his cloak, kissing his rosary, then sitting
side by side with Carmen and singing a grave little duet with
her. Somehow Brook manages to reconcile the elemental with
the very ordinary. This is myth, with human rumples.

The adaptation has its occasional awkwardness. It's a bit

odd to hear Carmen rhapsodizing about the gaiety to be found at Pastia's inn when it's been reduced to a rug, a few cushions, and a vaguely comic proprietor in a battered hat, and odder as she sings about sun-kissed gypsies dancing intertwined when we don't actually see a single one so much as entwined around himself. But the rough simplicity of the story is always arresting, often haunting. At the end, for instance, José and Carmen kneel quietly and mournfully side by side on the earth. Then he whips out his knife and plunges it into her back, a sudden, silent murder that made the audience gasp each of the three times I saw it. She knows death is coming and accepts it with melancholy resignation, as the unavoidable end of his obsession and her fortune.

As I say, I haven't seen all five of Mr. Brook's Carmens or all five Josés or all four Escamillos. But each time his production has seemed to combine immediacy and vitality with a strange, troubling depth. It's as vivid as a nightmarish dream and as hard to pin down the next morning. Clearly it needs no apology as a piece of theater in its own right, and even the puritans must concede that it's possible to defend it as a version of *Carmen* itself. We forget how much upset the opera caused when it was first produced in the Paris of 1875. A director of the Opéra Comique resigned at the mere prospect of those "thieves, gypsies, and cigarette sellers" on his genteel stage; audiences, critics, and even Bizet's librettists were appalled by what would seem to have been a notably realistic production. Celestine Galli-Marié, who created Carmen, was accused of "taking pleasure in accentuating the unlovely aspects of this dangerous role."

It wasn't until later the same year, when the Viennese inflated the spectacle, interpolated ballet, made cuts in the story, and replaced dialogue with recitative, that the opera became the blander success most of us know today. Only by stripping him of the accretions and adulterations of tradition can the essential Bizet be heard. Perhaps only by returning to the original, and then toughening it up, can a director make a less squeamish generation feel what those first spectators felt. Madame Galli-Marié, said the librettists Meilhac and Halévy, played "the Carmen of Mérimée." So did Miss Schuman and her sisters.

But this is a line of reasoning that would, admittedly, make me very anxious if it were applied to Shakespeare. One can imagine all kinds of cheeky perversions justified by specious appeals to the groundlings in the Globe. However, I see no need to hedge or shilly-shally or make nervous qualifications in the other argument reactivated by *Carmen*, the one I mentioned at the beginning. Before the production opened, Brook was quoted as describing the Beaumont Theater, which has been dark for most of the last six years, as a "highly workable instrument." And he's proceeded to prove it precisely that.

As I argued a few pages ago, the reasons for the theater's inactivity are probably more fundamental, to do with a historic failure to coordinate its erection with the creation of a company. But the obvious and immediate one is this. The Vivian Beaumont board believes that up to $5 million should be spent improving sight lines and acoustics, transforming the thrust stage into a proscenium, increasing a seating capacity totaling only 1,100 and making other supposed improvements; the Lincoln Center board, which leases it the theater, believes that this expense is unnecessary. The Vivian Beaumont board has kept the building closed in readiness for change, even though it has yet to raise the necessary finance; the Lincoln Center board thinks the theater should be open and busy. In short, the Lincoln Center board hates the Vivian Beaumont board and vice versa. It's stopped its adversary from using the name Lincoln Center Theater Company, ceased to support it financially, and heaven knows what else.

People say you should never take sides in a family fracas unless blood is actually flowing, but the Beaumont is important enough to involve even temporary participants in the theatrical scene, such as myself. Brook fiddled about a bit, building a huge wooden back wall flanked by equally tall slats on the sides, pushing the action out into the orchestra, and raising the level of some seats, and, lo, performers and audiences found themselves intimately interlinked. It's true that Brook is Brook, not the least gifted and experienced of directors. But in the past others have often followed where he has led, and can't all be incapable of doing so here. The Beaumont isn't infinitely adaptable—how many theaters are?—but it looks to me like a very workable instrument, which should and could be playing all year round.

Something festering in me for a month or so came sharply to a head last night. I was leaving Václav Havel's *A Private View* at the Public Theater when a solemn-looking young man just ahead of me turned to the solemn-looking young woman at his side. "My God," he said, "we're missing something. My God, are we missing something!" Now, it might be that he and she had chosen that moment to agonize over their emotional lives, like parody characters in a Woody Allen movie. Or perhaps it simply was that they had bad colds and were imploring the unhearing gods for Kleenex. I prefer to think they were talking about the New York theater. In fact, that stricken but eloquent cry will make a good opening to my next piece. It's about time I started bemoaning the narrow horizons of most American playwrights—and how better than to compare them with those of the Czechoslovakian dissident and sometime political prisoner Havel?

This is hardly a new complaint. Americans often make it themselves, though more in conversation than in print, and then usually with a resigned shrug as something regrettable but incurable, like herpes. But the relentless domesticity of the American theater seems more surprising and less inevitable to someone like myself, who comes from a country and a continent where drama tends to be more social and often more political in its emphasis. Kenneth Tynan had the same reaction when he came from England for a stint as theater critic of *The New Yorker* back in 1958.

He began bright-eyed and bushy-tailed, remembering the American theater that had bowled him over a few years before. It had the best young actors and actresses, the most exciting directors, and in Miller and Williams the greatest English-speaking playwrights. But for one reason or other—principally, he thought, commercial pressures—that feeling of excitement and danger had disappeared by 1958. Tynan found an ingrowing, unchallenging theater, "an island of shuttered anxieties, unrelated (except cursorily) to the society that created it." He found "a one-eyed drama with a squint induced by staring too long down domestic microscopes and never looking out of the window." Confidently expecting a fertile orchard, he found a fetid hothouse and returned in 1960 to England, John Osborne, Arnold Wesker, John Arden, and other such talents.

The other day I came across a piece of mine, written in 1969, in which I declared that America seemed to be producing "more exciting drama than anywhere else in the world." Kopit's *Indians*, Albee's *American Dream*, Van Itallie's *America Hurrah*, Michael McClure's *The Beard*, and others "used striking, provocative imagery to make points which, though often disconcertingly sweeping, could nevertheless be isolated, defined, and related to recognizable social problems, be they urban violence or middle-class emasculation." But the turbulence of the sixties is long over, and the American drama seems once again to have renounced the public for the private, the large for the small, the world outside for the hothouse.

Consider my professional visiting list in recent days: Tina Howe's *Painting Churches*, which is about a young artist's attempt to understand her parents and have them understand her; Michael Cristofer's *The Lady and the Clarinet*, about a woman's repeated failure to find and keep a satisfactory man;

and Michael Brady's *To Gillian on her 37th Birthday*, about
a grieving widower hesitantly disinterring his sexual feelings.
Add *A Weekend near Madison*, *Baby with the Bath Water*,
Brothers, and one or two others I've already seen, and you
begin to get the feeling that all that matters to American playwrights is self-discovery, self-fulfillment, and the raveled relationships of husband and wife, lover and lover, father and
son, mother and daughter, mother and son, brother and
brother, sister and. . . .

Obviously such subjects have a place in the drama. It's not
the existence of the hothouse that is disturbing; rather, it is
its pervasiveness, the way it dominates the theatrical landscape to the exclusion of so much else. Again, such subjects
can be well or badly treated. There can, so to speak, be elegant
lilies as well as anonymous lichen, dangerous and bizarre
flytraps as well as weeds. *Painting Churches*, in particular,
would always merit a showing, whether or not the American
theater recovered its old interest in social and political problems. It's humorous and graceful and touching, and if the
production at the Lambs lacks the idiosyncratic energy of its
author's earlier work, it's more because of the director and
the acting, less because Miss Howe had nodded at the typewriter.

In her *Art of Dining* she showed us a scattering of gourmets
gorging themselves on a fancy restaurant's crepes, rather as
their ancestors must have done on speared boar, and in *Museum*, she set art lovers rather similarly amok, touching, then
moving, then ripping apart avant-garde sculpture. Under the
civilized surfaces of her characters you could spot atavistic
hobgoblins, trolls nostalgic for anarchy, and you can see just
a little of that, too, in the Boston Brahmins of her *Painting
Churches*. At one point Father, a poet teetering on the edge
of senility, and Mother, an unabashed eccentric given to crazy
hats and fey squawks in public, jointly retreat into gleeful
infantilism, scattering some of his unpublished manuscripts

and making paper darts from their pages. If George Martin weren't so muted in one part and Marian Seldes so exaggeratedly febrile in the other, the moment would be unsettling and sad and maybe more. But they are and it isn't.

Elizabeth McGovern, as their daughter, seems strangely uneven, too. She has her moments of truth, yet gapes and boggles at manifestations of her mother's outré malice and barmy callousness, like a caricature patient faced by a monster dentist with a road drill.

The play's quality is as apparent as its limitations. Indeed, its quality *is* its limitations. It successfully brings onstage that blend of love, dread, rage, embarrassment, boredom, and incomprehension many children feel for many parents into middle age and beyond. What gives these maddening people influence and power over us? Why can't we place them, or shake them off, or both? Why do we crave their approval long after their biological purpose is achieved? These are the questions that emerge from Miss Howe's three-person fracas, and she asks them with delicate inconclusiveness.

To Gillian has been widely praised, but I have to say it seemed to me thin, very thin, where *Churches* was acceptably slim. One should always be wary of plays containing lines like "The one rule we have here is that you can't sound like a made-for-TV movie." They mean the author has the uneasy suspicion that the smell rising from his typewriter is that of soap, and he may be right. Again, one should mistrust such forms of address as "I love you, you overeducated, self-indulgent shit." There is a bantering avoidance of sentimentality, very common in the American theater right now, that manages to be more sentimental than straightforward sentimentality itself. Unsurprisingly the sudden conversion of the widower at the play's center from a bristling curmudgeon into an aspiring lover and devotee of life isn't especially credible. The play just doesn't introduce anything fresh and original into the emotional hothouse.

Nor does *The Lady and the Clarinet*. Six years ago its author, Michael Cristofer, won a Pulitzer with his study of cancer cases facing the void, *The Shadow Box*. I don't know whether candidates were light on the ground at the time or whether the prize committee was light in the head, but the play strikes me as earnest, pedestrian, and by no means as interesting as the subject should make it. His latest effort is sprier, more theatrically accomplished, more enjoyable, and also, I fear, harder still to take seriously. It's scarcely more than three rueful and amusing anecdotes, narrated by the admirable Stockard Channing to a sort of Harpo Marx of the clarinet, a benignly smirking musician whose function is to say nothing at all, toot out squeals and squiggles in response to her questions, and add atmosphere to the evening with longer bouts of woodwind.

In the first act Miss Channing forces herself on a clownish young Lothario, who falls goofily in love with her. Then she's competing with wife and children for the time and attention of an adman who feverishly spirals in and out of identity crises. Then she's married to a male housewife so jealous of her attempts to cook and clean that he slams out with a screech of "I want this place looking like a pigsty when I come back." And we leave her hopelessly yet hopefully welcoming a new gentleman caller, one whose foibles Cristofer would doubtless depict with the same brittle humor had he time. Indeed, the play seems infinitely extendable, right up to the inevitable episode in which Miss Channing, now creased and bent, has a sweetly sad fling with the crusty yet lovable mortician she's chosen to bury her. Perhaps it should be a TV sitcom. Perhaps that's the plan.

The overriding point, though, is that all these plays take place in a social vacuum. There are references to a world outside—an art exhibition, a university, an office—but that world does not intrude, still less define. It doesn't seem to have shaped the characters and their relationships any more than, say, the surrounding furniture could be said to shape the goldfish in a bowl on the sideboard. Everything important has happened and will happen in that glass bubble, and there only. Yet one doesn't have to be a bug-eyed Marxist or behavioral psychologist to know that people are what they are and do what they do for reasons that go beyond the influence of parents, siblings, lovers, and others close to us. Insofar as the American theater suggests otherwise, and it often seems to do so, it's distorting the truth.

Not all American dramatists have retreated into emotional isolationism, of course. David Mamet's *Glengarry Glen Ross* offers, as I've said, a scathing picture of dog-eat-dog in the business jungle. Sam Shepard, though concentrating more and more on family relationships these days, still manages to say something about a wider American rootlessness, a more general sense of loss and bafflement. An exceptional dramatist can, of course, write about the small and seemingly private and leave you feeling you've seen something large and public, too. *American Buffalo* would be a good example of that, as would *True West*. But I can't think of many other instances.

Still more rarely do American dramatists seem to be tackling social and political issues directly these days. Where's the Kopit of *Indians*? When last heard from, he was worming around the crannies of a dying woman's memory bank in *Wings*. Where's the David Rabe of the Vietnam plays? Robbed, so it seems, of a profitable subject. Where's the Jules Feiffer of *Little Murders* and *God Bless*? Silent. Where's the Miller of *Salesman*? Old.

Even when dramatists appear to be about to confront a social or political subject, they commonly wrench around the steering wheel at the last moment and avoid it. A good example was Lanford Wilson's recent *Angels Fall*, which looked as if it might have something to say about the danger of nuclear power but turned out to be using an explosion and contamination simply as an excuse for keeping a cross section of characters in one place, where they could proceed to work out their personal problems. The play might as well have happened on a desert island after one of those convenient plane crashes so popular one time among film directors.

Why this retreat from the big, bad world into that of personal relationships? Have all those domestic sitcoms on TV terminally imprinted a generation of dramatists without their realizing it? At this stage of my visit to America it would be pretty presumptuous to assay any explanation, let alone one as insulting as that. In any case, there's plenty of mind-numbing nonsense on TV in Britain, and there the dramatists seem to feel a positive need to utter on matters of social and political moment. So why isn't that the case here? Why the difference between the two countries?

Well, it's getting on to thirty years since 1956, when John Osborne's *Look Back in Anger* came to sear the British with its eloquent contempt for the old values, the old ways, the old establishment. But it changed the direction, the tenor, the concerns of our island theater so strongly and sharply that we feel its influence and aftereffects still. We are, if you like, in the late *Anger* period. In any case, the feelings of national anxiety and purposelessness that lay behind the play are with us still, rather different in nature but perhaps in some ways more intense. The economy stumbles; unemployment rises; the schisms of class seem as great and unbridgeable as ever. Americans who visit Britain, and see London, Stratford, and the odd cathedral city, are bound to return home with a false faith in the nation's serenity and security. In politics the boundaries of the conceivable are much wider than in America, the distance between left and right far greater—and who knows in whose hands we'll end?

So the drama reflects a national uncertainty that in America exists on no such scale. True, relations with Russia have rarely been worse, Central America is a perpetual worry, and the Middle East is as dangerous as ever, as the massacre of 241

marines in Lebanon has grimly proved. Yet there's no sense
of crisis, no urgent feeling of threat, as there was in the days
of the Depression and the Vietnam War—the last two occasions, I suppose, when the American theater took a markedly
social and political turn. One might even argue that the lac-
erations suffered by the nation during the Vietnam era, and
then during Watergate, are as responsible for the domesticity
of the drama now as they were for its greater public consciousness then. If *that* is politics, who wouldn't prefer mentally to retreat into the relative serenity of hearth and home?

Not that everyone's hearth and home in America can feel
stunningly secure. Think of the poverty and crime to be found
in New York itself. But such things can hardly appear particularly pressing or menacing to most playsmiths. The prosperity of the country is more evident than its problems, and
those problems seem strangely amorphous, hard to diagnose
and define, when they don't seem remote. After all, how many
writers are made to feel even subliminally uneasy by the gross-
ness of the budget deficit? How many feel that the troubles of
unemployed steelworkers impinge on them? Besides, there's
always the belief in this country, largely missing in Britain,
that change and renewal can actually occur. There's always
a feeling of space and fresh possibility. If you don't succeed
here, well, why not try there? And that, too, is inimical to the
kind of earnest tussling with social issues you get in so much
British drama these days—or, for that matter, in the work
of Václav Havel.

On the face of it, then, it would be naïve in the extreme to
use that much misused Czech as a sort of human bludgeon
with which to belabor American dramatists and bring them
to a greater sense of social awareness. As far as I know, none
of them has been tortured, imprisoned, banned, and humiliated for mildly asking President Reagan to fulfill his own
promises on human rights. None of them has been forced
either to lug beer barrels for a living or to risk being accused

of social parasitism, which is what happened to Havel himself and what happens to his autobiographical character, Vanek, in the first of the three short plays that constitute *A Private View*. They aren't trapped physically, intellectually, spiritually in an oppressive and seemingly inescapable social system, and therefore, they've neither the experience nor the motive to be burningly political in their work.

And yet one still feels what the solemn-looking young man said: My God, we're missing something, and my God, we shouldn't be missing so much. In fact, Havel wrote his most biting social satire, *The Memorandum*, before the Russians destroyed Alexander Dubček and his reforms. Does its subject, a dehumanizing bureaucracy, not exist in this country? My own experiences are so far limited to being shifted from endless bank line to endless bank line to endless bank line and, another time, being politely informed I couldn't be told my own phone number "because you see, sir, it's unlisted, and we can't give unlisted numbers out." But I've a suspicion that the iceberg runs many hundreds of fathoms deeper than that and would seem a perfectly proper subject for any playwright.

But maybe the crucial point is that *A Private View* is not the sort of play one would expect from a dissident who has suffered what Havel continues to suffer and not one that seems remote from American experience and American concerns. Vanek is never seen with secret policemen or jailors or censors or self-serving politicians or any of the other scullions of the state. His fellow characters are less sensational, more agreeable: his boss at the brewery, so befuddled with the task of informing on Vanek that he asks him to compose the necessary reports himself; his "best friends," a married couple who have prospered in the new Czechoslovakia and crave his approval for the signs and symbols of their success; and finally, a broadcaster, who wants to inspire but not sign a petition to the government for the release of his daughter's politically em-

barrassing boyfriend. They're not bad people, any of them.
If they browbeat, insult, and seek to manipulate Vanek, it's
because his very presence, mild and unjudging as it is, seems
to them a moral reproach. They've consciences that, especially
in the last case, they're edgily aware of having tailored to the
year's fashion.

Havel's accusation against contemporary Czechoslovakia is
not that it encourages the bad but that it maims the decent
and disfigures the good. Indeed, it's directed less against the
Czechoslovakian regime per se, more at those who allow themselves so to be maimed and disfigured. His finger is quietly
and not unsympathetically pointed at his audience, any audience, you and me. How many, persistently cajoled with
sticks and carrots by Big Brother, would stick unyieldingly
to their principles? After all, how many refuse to compromise
when they're subjected to lesser pressures from the somewhat
smaller brothers set over them?

A Private View is about people squirming to survive in any
organization, under any system. True, it has the authority of
Havel's particular calamities. But is there any overpowering
reason why the same fundamental perceptions shouldn't have
come from an American eye and an American pen? Lives in
this country are not free enough from social pressures, nor
the country itself empty enough of problems, for anyone to
be content with a drama as slender in its concerns as seems
currently to be thriving here.

December

"I put all the nice things I had to say about people into *The Glass Menagerie*," the young Tennessee Williams said of his first successful play. "What I write hereafter will be harsher." It was harsher, too, much harsher, and consequently more to the taste of earnest curmudgeons like myself, whose view is (I guess) that drama should properly be prodding and whipping me to yet higher levels of awareness. I'm the sort of person who responds with little cries of puritan glee to the madness of Blanche DuBois in *A Streetcar Named Desire*, or the sexual atrocities of *Sweet Bird of Youth*, or the despair of the defrocked priest of *The Night of the Iguana*, or the exotic cruelties of *The Red Devil Battery Sign*. *The Glass Menagerie*, on the several occasions I've seen it in England, has left my more masochistic side feeling sadly neglected.

All the same, I wouldn't like to think I went to the O'Neill last night in a wholly negative frame of mind, having just dropped by a Broadway bar where, I've discovered, Williams himself used sometimes to drink in his later years. This is a very ordinary place, farther north than most theaters and without a theatrical photo on its walls. Mainly it seems to be frequented by rather grumpy old men talking about sports. "He used to sit over there," the bartender told me, pointing to a battered-looking booth. "Nice enough fella, he didn't seem anyone special. Never said much." That memory wouldn't seem to add vastly to Williams scholarship, but the thought of the great man in that dowdy corner, his round, ravaged face mournfully poised over a lonely bourbon, put me rather more in the mood for the evening to come. Maybe American performers would find more juice, more gumption in *Menagerie* than their English cousins. And yet there I was an hour or so later, fully persuaded I was seeing not just the wrong play but the wrong play staged by the wrong director on the wrong set and performed by the wrong starring actress and the wrong juvenile lead.

The trouble, of course, was that I was the wrong critic. That would certainly have been the view of Brooks Atkinson, who thought *The Glass Menagerie* Williams's most perceptive creation, filled with a "pity, coolness of perception, poetic grace and forbearance" lacking in his later work, and it might also have been that of my esteemed predecessor, Walter Kerr, who announced in *The Times* last week that the very prospect of seeing Jessica Tandy as Amanda Wingfield sent tingles of delight rippling up his backbone. Still, I can call some equally impressive witnesses in my support. These would include Joseph Wood Krutch, who thought *Menagerie* was enveloped in "a fuzzy haze of pretentious, sentimental, pseudo-poetic verbiage," and George Jean Nathan, who decided it was "rather less a play than a palette of sub-Chekhovian pastels brushed up into a charming semblance of one." Finally, let me summon to the box Tennessee Williams himself, who scrawled "a rather dull little play" on its typescript and from the first regarded it as too soft to be characteristic of the drama he felt he could and should write.

One can imagine how Williams's shade, that disheveled spirit that recently abandoned its old, earthly haunts to take up residence in the Latin Quarter of the Elysian Fields, would react to the news that *Menagerie* was the first of his work to be importantly revived after his death. He'd get drunk on ambrosia cocktails in the Paradise Saloon. "I gave them a *Measure for Measure* and a *Troilus and Cressida* and a *King Lear*," one hears him grumbling to Shakespeare as he orders yet another round from the angel behind the bar, "and they persist, not only in putting on my *Twelfth Night* but in thinking it the best thing I ever did." And the Bard would nod sympathetically, perhaps interjecting the polite little caveat that, well, *Twelfth Night* wasn't *that* bad a play, was it?

Nor it was. Let me not get carried away by my enthusiasm for some of Williams's later, more underrated plays. There's a place for tender, melancholy chamber music as well as for brash, unruly orchestral efforts, and *The Glass Menagerie*, like *Twelfth Night*, is no doubt very good of its kind. In fact, let's go further and admit that there's to be found in it an authenticity of feeling not altogether undermined by the flatness of Miss Tandy's performance, or by further evidence of John Dexter's discomfort as a director with anything much smaller than epic, or by a set that defies Williams's precise and pointed instructions by transforming his St. Louis tenement into a sort of transparent pavilion, inexplicably floating in a blue-white sky.

The parallels with Williams and his backgrounds are well known: the aspiring writer, like him called Tom, like him fretting away his life in a shoe factory; the shy, repressed, ailing sister, cloistered away with her collection of glass animals; and, of course, the domineering mother, with her everlasting nostalgia for a lost Eden in the South. When Miss Edwina, as her son wryly called her, first saw *The Glass Menagerie*, she jumped "like a horse eating briars" to see a version of herself so unnervingly similar in mannerism and pet phrase. Then, as if to rub the point fully in, Williams introduced her to the actress responsible, Laurette Taylor, who could be relied on to be tactless. "The woman was a silly fool," she told Miss Edwina; "that's why I wear bangs."

Poor lady. She'd spent the evening enduring not only what her son later admitted to be an "exact portrait" of her but his attempt to punish her for her treatment of himself and, especially, his sister. To the end he blamed her "monolithic puritanism," her dislike of Rose Williams's sometimes unruly sexual feelings, for the girl's nervous troubles and finally for the prefrontal lobotomy that turned her into a permanent invalid. *Menagerie* is part revenge, part an act of atonement for having himself, as he thought, neglected a sibling he adored. It's an elegy to the (very literally) burned-out hopes of Rose, alias Laura, and a deeply personal play.

Miss Tandy is, of course, a considerable actress—wasn't she arguably the finest Blanche DuBois of all?—and a case can certainly be made out for her dogged, unpretentious Amanda. She seeks to play the person, not the prejudice. That's to say, she presents Amanda from Amanda's own point of view, as a concerned mother bravely battling against impossible odds to save the daughter she loves from becoming an emotional anchorite, and she forgets Williams's dyspeptic memories of that "little Prussian officer in drag," Miss Edwina. This makes the play morally subtler than it sometimes seems, since it means that Amanda's more domineering and destructive aspects come beguilingly camouflaged in more or less sympathetic guise, and yet something is clearly missing. Where's the character's resentment, her rage at the present's persistent refusal to transform itself into that sentimentally imagined past of hers? Where's the volatility of mood, and where, for that matter, the fear, the desperation, the feeling that Amanda is clinging by the fingertips to the splintering sill of her family's collective security? But then Dexter's production never ventures very far into such fissures of feeling as lie beneath the play's surface. Bruce Davison's Tom, affably slouched and smiling behind a cigarette, seems to be on a nostalgic ramble down memory lane, not revisiting events that traumatized his author and obsessed him the rest of his life.

But then, to be fair to him, the play itself doesn't altogether help. It doesn't obviously bleed or exactly suppurate with unresolved miseries. Indeed, that's perhaps what's most unusual about it. Most writers begin by serving up their personal agonies pretty directly and only afterward distance them, put them in perspective. Williams reversed that process. *Glass Menagerie* is remarkable for the coolness with which it crystallizes firsthand pain. It's the later work that confronts that pain in all its grisly chaos.

Yet it's for the courage to do precisely this that we value Williams and will, I think, continue to value him. No recent dramatist has looked harder at his own moral ugliness and at the darkness inside his fellow beings, and none done more to earn understanding and sympathy for what he called "my little company of the faded and frightened and difficult and odd and lonely." Such was the intensity of his vision that he was sometimes able to raise the personal into the general, the domestic into the metaphysical, the conflicts between and inside people into the everlasting tangles of mind and body, spirit and clay, what tends to pull us up and what conspires to drag us down. And those are the reasons why I'll always prefer a *Suddenly Last Summer* to a *Glass Menagerie*.

That's no casual comparison because *Summer* may be seen as a *Menagerie* that has shed its inhibitions. There, again, is the powerful older woman and the ailing, troubled girl, but now the one is blatantly scheming to cut, scrape, and sear the "filth" out of the other's mind, leaving her as clean and harmless as Williams suspected his sanctimonious mother wanted to leave the sometimes loose-talking Rose. And once again there's the aspiring writer, a young poet who also ends by escaping the maternal fold; but now he sees the same stark and terrible things that haunted Williams's imagination, he's as corrupt as Williams felt himself to be, and he's as horribly punished as Williams thought he should be. Not to beat about the bush, he's torn apart and eaten by the hungry urchins with whom he's been sexually toying.

It's scarcely surprising, of course, that the impresarios should prefer to revive *The Glass Menagerie*, which demands a modest set, four performers, and an interest in that apparently

unsinkable subject, the pathology of the American family.
Again, *Summer* is in many ways a less theatrically effective
play. It consists largely of reportage, its most interesting character doesn't appear, and it has a weak ending. Yet even so,
it rises to the emotional occasion with a savage and gaudy
majesty that makes *Menagerie* seem sub-Chekhovian, a bit
sentimental, and one or two other things the ruder reviewers
called it forty years ago. When will Broadway pay its posthumous respects to the Tennessee Williams who could write
like *that?*

Was that strange, shambling figure with the big, bushy off-
white beard really Rex Harrison? Indeed, it was, and looking
as much like a cross between Tolstoy and an old-fashioned
shaving brush as he did when he played the same role, Captain
Shotover, in the same play, George Bernard Shaw's *Heartbreak House*, in London last March. With *Kean* and Michael
Frayn's *Noises Off* already arrived on Broadway and Tom
Stoppard's *Real Thing* among the British work still to follow,
I'm beginning to think I may be spending much of my tour of
duty in America reliving events I've already experienced back
home.

Still, everyone except Harrison is different, down to the
director, who is Anthony Page and no longer John Dexter.
Even Rosemary Harris, the shriller and more arrogant of
Shotover's two daughters in London, has switched to the role
of her sensual, musky sister, who was played there by Diana
Rigg. Not that it matters a lot. The production at Circle in
the Square is what the one in the West End was, too, perfectly
adequate without being especially remarkable, let alone definitive.

Definitive did I say? Let's not forget that the only work that
can be "definitively" revived is work hardly worth reviving
in the first place. Anything with richness, resonance, or even
ambiguity can be performed in different ways, with different

emphases, different lights and shadows, peaks and deeps. You can't imagine a definitive production of O'Neill's *Mourning Becomes Electra* or Miller's *Death of a Salesman* or, whatever its limitations, Williams's *Glass Menagerie*. Actually history makes this last point rather well because it's evident that Jessica Tandy's interpretation of Amanda Wingfield is very different from that of Laurette Taylor, who radiated the "glow of lost, aching illusions," or Helen Hayes, a superannuated and somewhat self-parodying coquette, or Maureen Stapleton, whose dominant mood would seem to have been despair. Maybe *Menagerie* is a bigger play, or at least Amanda a bigger part, than I've been suggesting.

Only the meager and monochrome can be "definitively" produced because only that leaves the director and actors no room for intellectual or emotional maneuver. There's work by Shaw that admittedly could be placed in that category: *Misalliance* or *Getting Married* or *Too True to Be Good*, plays in which the characters scarcely seem much more than attitudes or opinions in abstract conflict with each other. But though *Heartbreak House* often sounds as if it, too, were occurring in a debating chamber, the debaters themselves give a plausible imitation of flesh, blood, and other such animal alloys. It lives, or sort of lives, and sort of lives again at Circle in the Square. My doubts and worries are, I find, rather different. Should the play be at this address at all? Why expensively bring to America a piece that's all about the impending collapse of Britain? And a lesser question: Why sell it to the New York public as Shaw's "most uninhibited comedy?"

That's what Harrison has been doing on local radio in recent weeks, creating the impression that the play Shaw thought his greatest, and actually described as his *King Lear*, is actually a bit like *Cage aux Folles* without the music, rather naughty but very, very funny. It's a kind of salesmanship which, if you think about it, opens up all sorts of beguiling possibilities.

"Master clown Eugene O'Neill's wacky *Strange Interlude* will have you rolling in the aisles." "You'll never see funkier Furies than those in Aeschylus' laugh riot *The Oresteia*." With quotes like that embellishing its frontages, Broadway might once again find audiences for serious, challenging drama.

Yet there's more substance in Harrison's view of the play, and less in his author's, than one might at first suppose. Shaw once said that his dramatic talent was "to take the utmost trouble to find the right thing to say, and then say it with the utmost levity." He was in earnest yet joked, or joked yet was in earnest—a contradiction often felt in *Heartbreak House*. It begins as a serious-seeming comedy about a lovelorn girl shedding her romantic illusions and deciding to marry for money; it evolves into a lively argument about several of Shaw's pet themes, principally the inadequacies of English democracy and the tendency of Englishwomen mentally and morally to castrate the more energetic sort of Englishman; and it ends on a strange, sardonic, and rather obviously symbolic note, with the characters awoken from Shavian reverie by the flash and bang of bombs and most of them enjoying the experience and wanting to repeat it. By now the pretty somber joke is the apparent death wish of what Shaw defines as Heartbreak House.

Heartbreak House is both the rickety mansion in which the characters are gathered and, evidently enough, Britain itself: a land irresponsibly ceded by the more cultured of its citizens to the Philistines and moneymen and go-getters; a ship of state, in Shaw's insistent metaphor, in danger of drifting to disaster on the rocks. "The Captain is in his bunk, drinking bottled ditchwater, and the crew is gambling in the fo'c's'le," cries Shotover, who is guru, eccentric, and Shaw's own half-satiric portrait of himself. "She'll strike and sink and split. Do you think the laws of God will be suspended in favor of England because you were born into it?" It's a speech that remains as ringing an assault on our island smugness as it was in the

Great War, when Shaw wrote it, the sound of zeppelins bombing British citizens in his ears. Never mind the plot, which barely exists; feel the passion, which indisputably does and still has power to grip and surprise, at least in Britain.

But what of America? I can think of several reasons why the play is worth showing here. First, it offers an unusually complete tour around one of the century's more interesting minds, giving us a good, hard look at Shaw's prejudices, fears, and something hinted at by that violent ending, hopes of revolutionary change. Secondly—well, are Americans so free from emotional self-absorption and political sloth that Shaw believed to be imperiling his Heartbreak House? Is the play hopelessly anachronistic when it warns of the heavens "falling in thunder and destroying us" and ends by showing them doing precisely that? And thirdly, there's the opportunity, not common nowadays, to see Rex Harrison on the stage rather than on the screen and to discover if he can act without a cameraman and a film editor between him and the audience.

He can. In fact, he's a fine Captain Shotover, a shaggy old tar who shambles about the stage, blinking and mumbling and gurgling and querulously bleating and disguising none of the character's octogenarian impotence. Yet his internal compass can quite suddenly veer from sou'-sou'west to true north, from near senility to absolute sanity and sense. The confused burble becomes a downright growl, and there, in all its grizzled eloquence, is the voice of Shaw himself, incredulous at the waste, drift, and general foolishness around him. *Heartbreak House* isn't the sort of play one would wish to see too often, long and lacking in action as it is, but I was glad I saw Harrison himself twice.

Harold Clurman, into whose criticism I find myself often and profitably dipping, says that the musical is the "one theatrical form in which America excels," and he seems to me wrong only in the undue emphasis he gives that "one." After all, O'Neill excelled in domestic hyperdrama, or psychological tragedy, or whatever the peculiar form may be to which his *Long Day's Journey* belongs. No one wrote Eugene O'Neill plays quite like Eugene O'Neill, just as no one wrote Tennessee Williams plays like Tennessee Williams, and no one writes Sam Shepard plays like Sam Shepard. That's to say, each carved out a category for himself and was or is inimitable within it.

But the musical is, I guess, the broadest form in which Americans excel. It's partly a matter of the individual talent involved. True, Andrew Lloyd Webber has been a very gainful export for Britain in the past few years—but how successful would *Evita* have been without Hal Prince's wonderfully inventive staging, or *Cats* without John Napier's creative dismemberment of the Winter Garden Theater? Beside Stephen Sondheim, Webber seems lacking in adventure and musical sophistication, though fairness obliges me to add that so does every other theatrical composer now living. But even his reputation for melody seems a bit thinly based, considering that "Memory" and "Don't Cry for Me, Argentina" are pretty well the only numbers sustaining it. Think of Richard Rodgers, Irving Berlin, Frederick Loewe, and even Jerry Herman now, and then think of two-tune Webber.

But America's supremacy extends to performance. Confronted back in Britain with musicals either native or imported, I regularly find myself nostalgically thinking of the drill sergeant who tried and failed to make something authentically military of me and the fellow members of my school cadet force. "That's it, lads," he'd yell, "but that's not bloody it." Our footwork was, so to speak, more grandfather clock than electric metronome. The beef we managed to muster was fatty hamburger rather than prime porterhouse. It would, of course, be unjust to compare the cream of London choruses with some semidemimotivated boy soldiers, but I often feel, without quite being able to say why, that their energy is not as precise as that of their American counterparts, nor their precision as energetic. That's it, and that's not bloody it.

Why the difference? Clurman says the reason is social and historical. "The story of America," he writes, "has by and large been one of energy, adaptability, youthfulness, buoyancy, optimism, physical well-being and prosperity. No matter what troubles beset us, we try to remain sanguine." His inference is that all these virtues are reflected in the snap of the shoe on the boards and in all the other zippy and zesty qualities that go to make up musicals over here. That's why so many of their stories involve resilient people bouncing their way to what Clurman perceives as their most characteristic subject and concern: a success which may sometimes be mildly deplored for its materialism but is rarely deplored the least convincingly. Of course, he was writing before Sondheim brought his sometimes misanthropic wit to the Broadway musical; yet couldn't it be argued that there's something almost positive in the apparent negativity of a *Company*, a sort of enjoyment and even glee in its cynicism, a relish in its evocation of the woes of contemporary marriage in contemporary New York City?

In any case, Sondheim is scarcely very representative, as for better or worse I've been discovering in the past few weeks. The glummer times America has lived through since Clurman made his analysis, back in 1962, don't seem to have resulted in a glummer American musical theater. Every other show on Broadway would appear to be about the struggle for success, and in virtually every case the struggle is crowned *with* success. There's the eternal *Chorus Line*, still celebrating the success of the unnoticed and unsung. There's *Dreamgirls*, which shows the success not just of a group of singers but of the group member their manager elects to drop. There's *42nd Street*, about the success of a hoofer given the chance to shine on Broadway. And now there's something called *The Tap Dance Kid*, which is about two varieties of success and their

claims on the young scion of an upwardly thrusting black
family: Should he be a successful lawyer, as his father is and
wants him to be, or should he be a successful dancer, like his
uncle and like his maternal grandfather, an aged trouper given
to turning up in dream sequences and tapping across the living
room in a spangled topper?

It's an old conflict—son yearning to escape from the superglue of his dad's expectations—and not one that produces
an especially interesting book or particularly beguiling songs.
Yet the show has that captivating buoyancy of which Clurman
spoke, and not only because all the expected resolutions are
reached at the end. It's there from the very moment the company rattles en masse onstage, its feet banging away like perfectly coordinated castanets, just as it's there at the opening
of *42nd Street*, when the curtain rises a few feet to reveal a
lot of chirruping toes and chattering heels. Come to think of
it, is there any more upbeat and invigorating human activity
than tap dancing? To me, long an aficionado, it seems the
ideal antidote to all negative emotions, to European habits of
fatalism and resignation, perhaps even to greed, hatred and
despair. If Genghis Khan had had the right shoes, he'd have
stayed in Ulan Bator, and Asia and eastern Europe would
have been saved from massacre; if Othello had been similarly
blessed, he could have hopped and clicked Desdemona out of
his system, and both he and she would have survived. There
should be a pair at either end of the hot line today. Tap
dancing seems to me not merely to encapsulate what's most
appealing about the American musical and its preoccupation
with success but to symbolize the optimism and resilience of
the American character itself.

Of course, not everything about the musical, still less its
preoccupation with success, could be described as appealing.
In his *Acting Out America* the critic John Lahr argues that
what it generally encapsulates is the American dream at its
most mercenary: "The proof that opulence, capitalism, con-

flict and peace can co-exist . . . creates a moral universe compatible with the worst instincts of middle-class life . . . the symbol of America's conspicuous waste." Well, perhaps, sometimes—yet isn't that a bit of a heavyweight attack on opponents who never claimed to amount to anything very awe-inspiring in the moral or aesthetic scales? One could, I suppose, say that *42nd Street* and *A Chorus Line* celebrate the bubble reputation and a transitory prosperity, but even in my most puritan moods, I couldn't regard either as terribly corrupting. As I've said before, the former is only a variation on the "Cinderella" myth, and the latter has some of the enchantment of a fairy story, too.

My complaint is more that there's a certain sameness in the subject matter of musicals these days, and something about their treatment of it I don't altogether like. Others have drawn attention to a lack of diversity in former times. Clurman writes of a period when the fashion was for "appeasing our jarred souls with sweet, smiling images of the past or of remote places": *Oklahoma!*, *Carousel*, *Brigadoon*, and so on. Lahr, writing in the early seventies, rather similarly categorizes them as "entertainments nostalgic for a earlier time": *Gypsy*, *Hello, Dolly!*, *Funny Girl*, and so on. Perhaps this is only to say that the genre has traditionally been sympathetic to an audience's desire for what critics nowadays tend to deride as "escapism" and has found different ways of demonstrating that sympathy and allowing that escape. Perhaps one of those ways is what I see all around me at the moment, a preoccupation with the fantasy business and imagination industry in all its forms and varieties.

Broadway has, let's face it, always been a pretty self-absorbed place, profoundly fond of shows about show people and most especially show people who are also Broadway people, but right now it must be breaking its own records for rapturous narcissism. Look at the opportunities for vicarious dreaming it's offering the stage-struck and starry-eyed. He or

she can identify not just with the dancing or singing protagonists of *A Chorus Line*, *42nd Street*, *Dreamgirls*, and *The
Tap Dance Kid* but with a jazz-fixated ballerina in *On Your
Toes*, an eminent movie drector in *Nine*, the transvestite nightclub performers of *Cage aux Folles*, and, if one wishes to push
the point perhaps a little too far, Grizabella, the glamor cat,
the fading Marlene Dietrich of Andrew Lloyd Webber's salute
to the feline classes. Not so long ago the list would have included Peggy Lee in her one-woman act of homage to herself,
Peg, and a musical called *Marilyn* about guess who.

You can't talk of these shows as if they were uniform, either
in nature or in merit. Some of them should feel more satisfied
than others when, so to speak, they contemplate their coun-
tenances in Narcissus' pool. Several I loved and have already
lauded; others I didn't and can't. Indeed *Marilyn* was so bad
as to be interesting, an instructively awful case study of what
musicals should no longer be and do in the 1980's. They should
reject numbers involving cheery high school kids and happy
frankfurter salesmen or featuring plumbers in pink, frolicking
around a bubble bath. They should shun dances of passersby
on New York sidewalks, especially ones backed by glitzy gold
skyscrapers. They should think hard about employing a trio
collectively called Destiny, particularly if it has little more to
do than sprinkle fairy dust on the heroine and most particularly if it's dressed in mauve nightgowns and baseball caps.
They should introduce neither Joe DiMaggio if he's going to
say things like "It isn't me you love, it's those damn cameras—
well, I hope they'll warm you at night, because I'll not share
you, I'm not built that way," nor Arthur Miller if he's going
to talk like the sort of play he'd rather die than write: "That
fragile beauty turns to me, and I feel like a giant of a man,
the only man in the world."

Well, well. *Marilyn* scarcely seemed very characteristic of
the Broadway musical these days—except, of course, in its
subject matter. It invited the dreamers in the audience to

identify with the late Miss Monroe, a sensitive soul whose innocent wish was simply to be very, very famous indeed. It was the sort of thing that made you long for musicals about plain people and ordinary happenings. Certainly it left me more than usually receptive to the new arrival at the Barrymore. *Baby*, as it's called, involves a matter as common in life as it's rare on the musical stage, getting and being pregnant, and it's the work of collaborators who seem personally familiar with the subject. Richard Maltby, Jr., and David Shire, lyricist and composer respectively, don't only know how to fit lively tunes to adroitly turned lines, but know about ovaries, stretch marks, the tendency of some older women to get jealous when confronted with young and vulnerable mothers-to-be, and much else.

To me, it's of interest for another reason, too. It's the first show I've reviewed in New York that has emerged from what appears to be an increasingly important source. Gone are the days when an aspiring Broadway success would have spent time shedding the fat in its book, toning up its melodic muscle, and otherwise improving itself in Boston, Philadelphia, and other such remote places. Even the system that replaced the out-of-town tryout, a harried pruning during previews in New York, is regarded as dangerously extravagant and extravagantly dangerous. Now it seems more sensible to bring composer, lyricist, librettist, choreographer, and performers to a "workshop," like one of those humming away at any given time in the big building at 890 Broadway owned by Michael Bennett. There they can experiment, fiddle, rewrite, recast, and inexpensively discover if they've a show worth taking uptown at all.

Workshops mean that otherwise unaffordable risks have been taken. Without them we'd have had no *Nine*, though I personally wouldn't think that a terrible loss since I regard it as a pioneering innovatory show that is actually pioneering and innovating a profounder type of boredom. More seriously,

we might not have had Bennett's own *Dreamgirls*, which was
the fruit of workshops costing some $150,000, a sum infinitely
more easily raised than the $3.5 million that was the eventual
bill for producing it on Broadway. And we might not have
Baby now.

Nevertheless, people are beginning to worry about workshops. They are, it's said, becoming more institutionalized,
less experimental. Less and less they're what they were originally meant to be and actually were when *A Chorus Line*
emerged from a whole year's testing and tinkering: a way of
liberating an embryonic show from commercial pressures and
allowing it to evolve over a long period. More and more they
seem to be a cheap means of staging more or less finished
musicals and thus attracting the extra investment necessary
for a move to Broadway. "They're turning into backers' auditions," an experienced producer told me.

Could this process explain the limitations as well as the
merits of *Baby*? When it was slowly cooking in its workshop,
all sorts of ingredients were apparently tried. There was, I'm
told, a possibility that one of its three couples should be homosexual, another decide on an abortion. As it turned out, nothing so outré materialized: For the youngest and most unorthodox
of the couples, marriage follows pregnancy; for the oldest and
most doubting, conception leads to birth; and the one in the
middle is barren, not because both partners are the same sex
but because the husband is "shooting blanks," as a less than
sensitive fertility clinic put it. If their stories were plots or
subplots in a straight play, we'd find them certainly flimsy,
perhaps cozy, possibly a bit of a cop-out, given the issues they
raise.

Yet its creators could, of course, have spent a decade in a
workshop and still have ended up with a show that steered
clear of the disturbingly downbeat. That would probably be
because they'd be nervous that such stuff wouldn't appeal to
the people on whom they'd eventually have to depend: inves-

tors prepared to risk a lot of capital; a public ready to pay $45 a seat. The real brake on originality and derring-do seems to be the same as with straight plays, the economics of Broadway.

Clurman says that musical plays or musical comedies are potentially nearer to "true theater" than any other form or genre because they can use every means, from dramatic action to speech to ballet to song, to tell their stories—and may contain or embody ideas as well. That's idealism speaking, of course. That sort of intellectual, emotional, and physical wholeness has always proved elusive, however prosperous times were for the musical. But for all the merits of the shows on Broadway—*Baby* not least—can there have been a period when that "true theater" was less likely to come comprehensively to imaginative fruition than now?

Every nation has its clichés, in the drama as in other areas. I daresay little murmurs of dismay would ripple around that fifth-century Athenian hillside as yet another dramatist attempted to win the tragic contest with yet another treatment of the Oedipus myth: "Not all that resignation stuff, not all that count no one happy till he dies again! Surely old Sophocles milked that one dry. . . ."

Well, justifiably or not, I'm getting surer and surer in my mind what the cliché American play is these days. About its English counterpart I'm not so confident since our drama, for all its insularity and lack of passion and other failings, is more diverse in its subject matter. As I've said before, American horizons are almost unrelievedly domestic these days. The British usually admit that society exists, too. In fact, they write a lot about society, and their own society in particular, and they don't always do so very freshly or interestingly. If an ersatz Freud rules the American theater, a bastardized Marx is responsible for a good deal of the British and, for that matter, the European one.

A play I seem to have seen three, four, ten, twelve times is set in a municipally owned apartment block of awesome seediness and involves an eighteen-year-old boy who has passed the day being aggressively unemployed. On the way home from a soccer match, where he and his broken bottle ran amok among fans of the opposing team, he mugged a few cripples. On the way up to the urine-filled fourteenth floor where he lives, he pushed an old lady down the elevator shaft. Now all this makes him an object of deep sympathy to his author because it means he is alienated, and the rest of the play is an attempt, conducted in quasi-documentary flashback, to discover how he got that way. The result is a searing indictment of teachers, social workers, policemen, callous housing authorities, and an economic system knowingly described as "capitalism." Finally, a quivering finger is pointed at you and me; what, after all, are we doing sitting in a bourgeois theater watching a bourgeois play instead of working for the revolution out there?

All right, I exaggerate, but not much. What can be exhilarating about the British theater—its willingness to analyze and attack the undoubted inequities and injustices of society at large—can also be and has often become what's predictable, repetitive, clockwork, and dull. Still, at least the track it rather monotonously follows has a broader gauge than that of the American theater. How would one sum up the cliché play here?

It occurs in or beside the back porch of a well-to-do household in a comfy suburb. The main characters are Dad, a tyrant with a warm heart, and Mom, an emotional vulture but no less lovable once you get to know her, and a child of indeterminate age—maybe twenty, thirty, forty. Let's call this last character him, although strictly speaking, his gender is irrelevant, because he's presexual, having not really been allowed to grow by his parents.

Well, as middle age begins to encroach, the infant turns

rebellious. He wants his latchkey, goddammit! He wants to stay out after dark without being nagged. He would like a friend or two of the opposite sex, or maybe of the same one. And so the three main characters gather on the porch for two and a half hours of in-depth recrimination. The past is not just examined for wear and tear, as so often in American drama, but turned inside out, scrubbed and scoured, until every tiny last secret is out in the open. So to the triumphant climax, in which the overage baby brings himself to turn on his mother and cry, with every appearance of meaning it, "Mom, from here on out it will no longer be appropriate for you to change my diapers."

Again, I exaggerate, but not all that much. I've just seen Wendy Wasserstein's *Isn't It Romantic* at Playwrights Horizons, and its climax is, in fact, strikingly similar. Janie Blumberg, aged around thirty, is trying desperately to find a belated independence in Manhattan, but her doting father and voracious mother still sometimes turn up in the early hours with food and importunate advice. This she tolerates for a time, then begins to wonder if it's altogether conducive to her emotional growth. So when her mother again knocks on the door at 7:00 A.M. or thereabouts, Janie refuses to let her in unless she first acknowledges her maturity. She must stand outside and repeat, "My daughter is a grown woman." And she does so: which to some might seem an absurdly overdue achievement, but to Miss Wasserstein it is a victory, accomplished not without courage.

Nor does this denouement seem particularly exceptional. Indeed, I'm beginning to realize that I was too vague when, a week or two ago, I mildly deplored American dramatists' seeming inability to look out the windows of the emotional hothouse within whose clammy confines they and their work had become terminally trapped. The theater here does indeed seem more preoccupied than ever with personal relationships, but not all that many could be dignified as truly adult ones. For quite a few dramatists, some very talented, the great contemporary question seems to be whether, when, why, and how to grow up at all.

The first essential ingredient is at least one parent capable of obsessing and preferably mesmerizing his or her progeny. This may be done by bullying and brainwashing, as in Christopher Durang's *Baby with the Bath Water*, or by love and brainwashing, as in *Isn't It Romantic*, or by love, bullying, and brainwashing, as in George Sibbald's short-lived *Brothers*. It may be done by a sort of disorienting eccentricity, as in Tina Howe's *Painting Churches*. It may even be done by divine diktat, as by the heavy father, God, to His apologetically squirming son, Adam, in Arthur Miller's recent *Up from Paradise*. Anyway, it *is* done, bringing us to the second essential ingredient. This is a long, nervous, nail-biting struggle by the child in question either to stand up to his parents or to reach a new understanding with them, or both.

Thus the middle-aged lawyer in *Brothers*, having cravenly submitted to his father's plans for his kidney, manages to break it to the old tyrant that he'd prefer not to donate it to his sickly brother, thanks very much. The bruised and baffled hero of *Baby with the Bath Water* emerges from a zillion sessions with his psychiatrist to tell his parents, on what must be his thirtieth birthday, "I must be going now—I'll call you in a few years if I feel less hostile." Less contentiously the young artist of *Painting Churches* diffidently shows her mother and father the portrait she's painstakingly done of them, listens first to their carpings and complaints and then to their growing approval, and is finally seen bouncing about in undisguised exultation: "They like it, they really like it!" At long last they have ratified her adult identity, as Janie Blumberg's mother does here in *Isn't It Romantic*. And like Miss Wasserstein, Miss Howe clearly regards this belated renunciation of the diapers as a major accomplishment, maybe even a triumph.

In fact, it occurs to me that a good general phrase for this sort of play would be "diaper drama." I'm not altogether easy in my mind about it because it has a glib adman's ring to it and simplifies an admittedly complex phenomenon, embracing material that varies a lot in character and quality. But slogans have some use if they make people more sharply aware of something they are, and shouldn't be, missing—or, in this case, of something they are and shouldn't be getting, at least in such quantities. The slightly derisory sound of the phrase, though perhaps unfair to the better plays on the subject, is, of course, intentionally provocative, an attempt to stir, irritate, and make dissatisfied. Anyway, "diaper drama" is the phrase I'll throw at my readers this week, just to see what, if anything, they make of it.

Mark you, I had better put plenty of qualifications into my column. For one thing, *Isn't It Romantic* isn't a play that deserves to be treated derisively. Though I think I prefer Miss Wasserstein's *Uncommon Women and Others*, in which she entertainingly smuggles us into the ghetto of female higher education, this is written with warmth and verve and a sometimes captivating wit. "I want badly to be someone else without going through the effort of actually changing myself into someone else," characteristically declares Janie, herself an aspiring artist so rumpled she wanly describes herself as "an extra from *Potemkin.*" If the jokes and repartee sometimes become a bit self-conscious, it's because the people in the play are pretty self-conscious people, nervously and sometimes feverishly using language to keep their more unmanageable feelings at bay. Miss Wasserstein can't be accused of succumbing to that not uncommon American habit: flinging about smart one-liners which momentarily tickle the audience's mental armpits but tell it nothing about situation or character.

Again, it would be absurdly complacent to say that diaper

dramas aren't to be found in life itself. Many psychiatrists, their couches overflowing with the paternally maimed and maternally mutilated, would tell you otherwise. Nor is literature exactly lacking in instances of people who have found it hard to sever what Sidney Howard, in his brilliantly observant study of a manipulative mother and a half-castrated son, called the silver cord. I suppose *The Oresteia*, containing as it does the seeds of almost everything written for the theater since, could fancifully be called a diaper drama. So in a pinch could *Hamlet*, along with Ibsen's *Ghosts* and John Millington Synge's *Playboy of the Western World* and T. S. Eliot's *Family Reunion* and O'Neill's *Moon for the Misbegotten* and heaven knows what else. So, of course, could *The Glass Menagerie*, *Death of a Salesman* and Marsha Norman's *'Night, Mother*, which could be one explanation of their presence, actual or promised, on the Broadway of today.

The trouble with most contemporary contributions to the genre seems to me twofold. First, they're narrow in scope. That's not to attack poor Miss Wasserstein for not having written *Hedda Gabler* or condemn Durang for not having created an identity crisis as complete as Hamlet's. It's rather to point out that when O'Neill or Odets or Williams wrote about parents and children, they didn't write about that and that only. Arthur Miller could be said to be preoccupied to the point of obsession with the relationship of fathers to sons and sons to fathers, yet in *All My Sons* he insists on the insufficiency of that relationship even at its warmest, and in *Death of a Salesman* he makes it clear that his protagonist's inadequacies as a father are directly and indirectly caused by the consumer society to which he belongs. Both plays are firmly rooted in a context that, for most American drama nowadays, seems to exist only in the vaguest, haziest outline, like the shimmer you can see around the moon.

The second trouble is that there are just too many diaper dramas. The proliferation is such this season that the theater is beginning to look like a kindergarten and feel like an incubator for overblown infants, though that's something which, as I write, I realize I'd better not say quite so bluntly in my column this week. I'm still very much aware of my alien status over here, as I'm sure some of my readers must be. What might sound robust and stimulating coming from an American could well seem presumptuous and patronizing and self-important, and worse, coming from a foreigner. I don't want to be the sort of guest who, kindly invited to dinner in a strange house, spends the evening complaining about the cooking and attributing its supposed monotony to deep-seated lacks and flaws in his hosts' personalities. Such a visitor shouldn't be surprised if he ends up on the doorstep, with the dessert dribbling down from the top of his head.

Nor is it just a matter of protocol. Perhaps this is another instance of my hearing the American music and not quite getting the American tune. Perhaps I'm the victim of my own misdirected expectations. I came to this country looking for new young writers, or even new old writers, who would tell me something about this country. Indeed, I had hopes of discovering one or two who would tell me something not merely about this country, but about the world as a whole, as Sam Shepard seems to me to have managed to do. Have I any right to complain when I find a Durang, a Howe, a Wasserstein, and he or she elects to write a little more modestly? After all, the New York public is currently thronging to their plays and may, for all I know, find them more resonant than they seem to an intruder. Where I see nothing but parents and children redundantly at odds with one another, they may sense some larger American preoccupation: the search for roots, perhaps, or at least the fear of rootlessness.

And yet, and yet. There's no point my being here unless I say what I feel, and what I feel is that there must be more exhilarating subjects than how to look Papa in the eyes or stop Mama from pouring chicken soup down your thirty-year-

old throat. There must be more inspiring rallying cries than
the one which comes at a climax of *Isn't It Romantic:* "It's
just too painful not to grow up." There must be more exciting
things for a hero or heroine to do than what should, surely,
be an everyday occurrence, an unremarkable feat: become
an adult.

January

Tom Stoppard once told me that if he weren't himself, he'd probably be me or someone not totally unlike me. Had not he been infected by the playwriting bug that swept Britain in the 1960's, he'd probably still be what he originally was, a journalist, and maybe composing bright notices of other people's plays. I took this as a compliment and, almost every time I see his work, feel like returning it as far as fantasy will permit. If I wrote plays, I wouldn't at all mind writing plays like his. *Jumpers* is, as it happens, a personal favorite of mine—how many dramatists these days are capable of writing about metaphysics at all, let alone mounting a scathing critique of modern materialist philosophy, let alone making that investigation and that attack consistently hilarious? But then many, most of his plays are similarly blessed. They're detached, clever, sophisticated, scintillating, fun.

Mark you, some people would say that's what's wrong as well as what's right with them. Stoppard has been accused of lacking both emotional power and the social and political clout English reviewers seem to expect of English dramatists these days. To write about the class system, the education system, even the sewage system is considered responsible and relevant. To ask whether there's such a thing as an absolute good, or such a being as an absolute God, gets considered irrelevent and hence not very responsible. And to present this moral quest in comic terms, as Stoppard does in *Jumpers*, is to risk

136

being dismissed as pathologically flippant, terminally clown-ish, or worse.

Well, he answered this particular accusation in a rather abstract way in *Artist Descending a Staircase* and *Travesties*, two erudite and enjoyable attempts to define the purpose and power of the writer, and more concretely in *Every Good Boy Deserves Favor* and *Professional Foul*, which involve political dissidents in (respectively) Russia and Czechoslovakia. Stop-pard was born in the second of these countries in 1937, didn't come to England until after the war, even now speaks with a just discernible foreign accent, and, as both plays show, clearly cares very much about the abuse of human rights in Eastern Europe. But neither they nor his recent *Night and Day*, which was in part a grim warning about the threat to freedom al-legedly posed by union restrictions in the British newspaper industry, have altogether satisfied his severer critics. Why, they've asked, doesn't he write more often and radically about his adopted country, England?

The other accusation has been less frequently made but possibly has more justice to it. Stoppard's characters have lacked strong personal feelings. A sort of rueful *tristesse* has, on the whole, been their dark night of the soul. Wasn't he the dramatist who sent the protagonists of *Rosencrantz and Guil-denstern Are Dead* to their violent deaths with no more than a shrug, a smile, and a wry quip on their lips? Yes—and in the sixteen years since that dazzling debut he hasn't created a single character one could imagine in any sort of ecstasy, whether of pleasure or pain. His people don't exult or howl or even hurt very much.

Not until now. Not, that is, until *The Real Thing*, which has just reached Broadway from London, in Mike Nichols's production a deeper, finer play here than it was on the other side of the Atlantic. In it, Stoppard rounds on both sets of accusers: the political puritans and, more unusually and interestingly, those who have presumed to find his work cold and loveless. Indeed, he brings both accusations together in a single theme or at least under a single heading, which could, I suppose, be called commitment.

To what should we, can we, commit ourselves, privately and publicly? What has substance and value? What, if anything, is the "real thing" in love, in politics, in writing? The play confronts these questions with style and panache and often something more. Thanks to the performances of Jeremy Irons and Glenn Close at the Plymouth, we've a remarkably complete and satisfying play: sharp, amusing, and everything we knew that Stoppard was; moving, painful, and several things we never dreamed he could be.

It begins with deceptive virtuosity, as if nothing has changed. A husband urbanely quizzes his wife about her professed trip abroad. "Franc doing well?" "Frank who?" "The *Swiss* franc." Then he reveals that she left her passport at home, and the curtain falls on her cool dismay, his polished delight at this proof of her adultery. It is, one begins to realize, an amusing piece of self-parody on Stoppard's part, and it is promptly rejected with something akin to self-disgust. What we've been watching is, in fact, a scene by a dramatist noted, like Stoppard, for his educated ability to be detached, clever, sophisticated, scintillating, and fun. His life, into which we're plunged for the rest of the evening, turns out to be considerably less bland and brittle than his art.

Henry, as he's called, begins an affair with an actress, Annie. She tells her husband she's leaving him, and his reaction is embarrassingly, abjectly tearful: "Don't, please don't." Then Annie, now married to Henry, sleeps with an actor, and it's the dramatist's turn to wail and sob like a stricken child: "Please, please, please *don't.*" They're words that have surprising impact, first and most obviously because Stoppard wrote them. Here's Tom, the intellectual dandy, juggler with words, upscale acrobat and clown, admitting that love hurts, hurts hideously.

The second reason for the impact of that "Please, please, please *don't*" is that Jeremy Irons speaks them. Roger Rees, who created the part of Henry in London, was the Royal Shakespeare Company's Nicholas Nickleby and is a bravura performer, refreshingly unafraid of bold, volatile, un-English emotions, yet there was, is, something external about his acting. He shaped and pointed Stoppard's many witty lines more adroitly than Irons, who lets several escape, but Irons does something more important—that is, open himself to the possibility of pain and, without ado or pretension, show this pain when it strikes. Early on, one senses a vulnerability, a yearning behind the banter; later, something melancholy, even somber; and by the end that long, willowy figure has drooped, blanched, and vocally crumpled into what, were a chain attached to its legs, one might almost suppose to be Marley's Ghost. Much more than Rees, he shows us that the play is centrally about Henry's emotional education, his evolution from a man who could write that opening scene to one who knows how thin and cold it is, and in this endeavor he's greatly helped by Glenn Close, a more vibrant, magnetic, and sexually formidable Annie than Felicity Kendal in London. The two of them—she the elemental force, he the heart she brightly smites—seem to me pretty terrific.

It would be a bit extravagant, though, to acclaim Stoppard for having written with feeling about adultery. Others have done as much. Though the subject fell into theatrical disfavor some years ago—those eternal triangles came to seem interminable, too—it has had something of a resurgence of late in Britain. Didn't Harold Pinter spend *Betrayal* charting the dark and furtive politics of infidelity, and Peter Nichols use *Passion* to show the mental and emotional destruction inflicted by sexual disloyalty? Yes, but those examples suggest that the old subject is being treated rather differently these days. To a dramatist of a hundred, fifty, even thirty years ago, adultery would usually have been wrong just because it was wrong, and it would, of course, have been especially wrong for the woman in the case. Now it's wrong, if wrong at all, because it turns people into cheats and liars and causes pain and damage. And that, as it happens, is the emphasis of Tom Stoppard, too.

Yet one wouldn't wish to suggest that he has renounced his old strengths. He has not left his mind in the cloakroom and brought only a bruised and indignant heart into the theater. On the contrary, the play is as much an argument about Eros as a demonstration of its power, with literary references—to August Strindberg's tormented *Miss Julie* and John Ford's tragedy of incest *Tis Pity She's a Whore*, in both of which Annie is performing—bolstering the abundant and often contradictory evidence supplied by the characters' own deeds and words. Is love an unimportant biological drive or "colonization," as Henry's daughter seems to believe? Or "mess, tears, self-abasement, loss of self-respect, nakedness," as Henry himself finally decides? What is this thing that alternately gives joy and (a recurrent image) impels respectable married people to rummage through each other's closets and drawers in search of incriminating sexual evidence?

And what of that other variety of commitment of which I spoke? Like Stoppard himself, Henry is an artistic perfectionist who stands accused of being more interested in the dance of language and ideas than in the plod and grind of everyday life, and his professional dilemma is whether or not he should help revise an earnest, didactic TV play which has been written by one of Annie's protégés, a soldier imprisoned for violently protesting against nuclear weapons. He thinks the piece naïve, stupid, "half as long as 'Das Kapital' and only twice as funny," and yet he compliantly transforms it into something actable. Why? Not because he's undergone a political evolution similar to his emotional one but simply because he wants to please Annie. Personal motives explain what seems to be a principled, "committed" action, as they do throughout the play. The protest that landed soldier Brodie in prison was a casual act of vandalism, done only to impress Annie. Annie is helping Brodie and promoting his play because she feels guilty. Stoppard would seem to agree with Henry's epigrammatic sneer: "Public postures have the configuration of private derangement."

Now, there's plenty of room for objection here. Henry's mandarin views, about both art and political commitment, seem more beguiling than they should justly be, not only because they are expressed with such superb finesse but because they are contrasted with those of Brodie, who is a travesty of the contemporary British left-wing playwright, stupidly stuck in an inflexible ideology, professionally blundering and inept, and personally loutish to boot. In fact, there are dramatists— Trevor Griffiths, Edward Bond, Howard Barker, others— who hold opinions rather similar to Brodie's and can express them articulately on the stage. Since they'd suggest that art and a zealotry alien to both Stoppard and Henry can occasionally be reconciled, it might have been fairer somehow to have introduced voices like theirs into the debate. As it is, Stoppardian literary sophistication seems to be claiming victory without ever having really done battle.

Moreover, the suggestion that public postures are the indirect expression of personal quirks and manias is, if you think about it at all, pretty outrageous. Tell that to William Wilberforce, or Abraham Lincoln, or Andrei Sakharov today. Are those who wonder if it's morally acceptable to aim H-bombs at Moscow or Washington or London, which is what Brodie claims to wonder, really to be numbered among the deranged? Is Stoppard simply sublimating feelings of childhood nostalgia or rejection when he himself writes with indignation of events in Czechoslovakia? Is all political conviction only intensely felt whim? It's surprising that a writer who queries so much should not have found a way to introduce questions as basic as these. It's astounding that after flaying both his protagonist and (by implication) himself with so many sharp-edged doubts, he should come close to enshrining a cynical simplification.

Yet I say "comes so close," not "ends by definitively stating." The world of *The Real Thing* is a deceptive one, of dramatists, of actors, and of plays and plays within plays. Moreover, it's a world invented by Stoppard himself, a master illusionist, and a pretty wily, elusive one at that. Just when you think you've got him firmly pinned down, he's off on the wing, slyly teasing you with some new inconsistency or paradox. He once said that he wrote plays because "dialogue is the most respectable way of contradicting myself." Their algebra, he added, was "firstly A and secondly minus A," with rebuttal following thesis and counterrebuttal following rebuttal, and no point of rest at all. I've an uneasy feeling it may be I, not he, who is the simplifier and simpleton. For instance, isn't Annie's actor-lover Billy allowed to say that Brodie "sounds like rubbish, but you know he's right," while Henry's views "sound all right, but you know they're rubbish"? Can Stoppard himself really be intellectually identified with Henry, and even if he can, is he entirely lacking in self-doubt?

Well, there'll be time and opportunity enough to decide his moral position because *The Real Thing* looks destined to captivate New York as it captivated London, to do well in the regional theaters of both nations, and then, no doubt, to establish itself as a fit object of study in the world's academies. But I don't think Stoppard has written with more wit, intricacy, and humor, not in *Rosencrantz* or in *Travesties* or even in *Jumpers* itself. His search for some "real thing" propels him in all sorts of directions. His attempt to see if we're collectively doomed to endless relativity—perhaps the play's fundamental subject, perhaps the fundamental subject of most of his work to date—takes him from the very serious to the pretty slight, from love and politics and art right down to pop music, to the Big Bopper, the Crystals, the Supremes, and the other groups his Henry incongruously adores.

So I could go on, but it's clear enough that Stoppard, who once declared that his hope was to "dislocate an audience's assumptions," has this time succeeded in wrenching our mental bones from their sockets. Not only that, he has given our collective heart a rare and salutory shaking. The intellectual osteopath has, in short, expanded his range and his credibility. After *The Real Thing* we can surely say that his future is in the theatrical equivalent of holistic medicine.

Something strange happened at the Living Theater's press performance last night, as I discovered when I left the Joyce, to find little eddies of critics on the sidewalk, gasping and expostulating. What on earth was wrong? "Frank Rich has been assaulted," they told me. "My God," I replied. "Is he hurt?" "Not like *that*," they said, "like well, like something else."

Gradually the truth emerged. At one point in the evening the Living people had gone on their customary prowl through the audience, whispering, "Are you afraid if I touch you like this?" to those unlucky enough to be on the aisle, and occasionally stroking or even bussing them. Julian Beck, the skinny, bleating guru whom one would call their leader if they admitted having leaders, had apparently picked Frank as his personal victim. After a fellow member of the tribe had given him a retchy kiss on the ear, he shot his hand between his legs, pausing for a quick, intimate fumble.

I was relieved to hear that my colleague and friend hadn't had his neck ritually broken by the crazed anarchs and showed it. At this the doughty Douglas Watt of the *Daily News* looked disapproving. To him, the incident seemed to warrant a complaint to the police and, I daresay, the mass deportation of the Living Theater to France, whence Beck had brought them. Hypocrite that I am, I promptly started frowning and concurring, only to discover that Frank himself wasn't exactly traumatized by Beck's attempt to liberate him from his inhibitions. "It was the *intellectual* assault I really minded," he told me, grinning all the way from the contaminated ear to the uncontaminated one. I, too, would have put up with much to be able to make a remark like that.

Beck and his wife, Judith Malina, founded the Living Theater in the early fifties, though it wasn't until their production of *The Connection* that word of their originality began to trickle across the Atlantic. I saw this in its film version and had to agree that naturalism could go little further. Jack Gelber's vague, rambling, seemingly improvised dialogue left me convinced that yes, these really were heroin addicts waiting in their shabby loft for the arrival of the genie with the needle. But, as I've said before, I didn't see the company onstage until 1963 and *The Brig*, which was superficially an evocation of the hyperdisciplined savageries inflicted on erring marines and more fundamentally a somewhat sensational metaphor for American society itself. That piece was very different from *The Connection*, yet it, too, had documentary authenticity and authority and, though perhaps less for that reason than that it wasn't paying its taxes, got the company into serious trouble. Both Becks ended up in prison, to emerge more fiercely hostile to the big, bad world of rules, laws, police, judges, and money.

That hostility they chose, however, to express in what turned out to be a continuing exile in Europe. By the time I caught their *Frankenstein* and *Paradise Now* in London in 1969, they'd become preachers for freedom, missionaries for their own brand of anarchism, rejecting their earlier naturalism for sweeping verbal and visual rhetoric. They used the theater sometimes as a sort of private joss house, complete with incense, chant, and vaguely Eastern rites, and sometimes as a forum for a revivalist meeting, with supposedly challenging slogans and purportedly salutory insults hurled at us in the audience. Though I seem to remember Frankenstein's monster (alias purified, regenerate man) being spectacularly arrested by the eternal fuzz and equally exotically released from prison, there wasn't a lot that could be described as performance.

It had its funny side, especially when the company, naked to G-strings, started moving around the audience, laying on hands and blessing bits of our bodies. The elderly gent beside me had been puzzled enough by their decision to open the proceedings with half an hour's cross-legged meditation on-stage. "Haven't they got a prompter?" he kept repeating, not realizing they were willing one of their number to levitate, an accomplishment that would have brought about the cancellation of that or any other performance at which it occurred. But now worse was happening. "Holy nose, holy mustache," a performer whispered to me as he went about his priestly duties, then turned on my neighbor with a certain sadistic relish: "Holy cheek, holy teeth, holy gums." The conversion of what he'd assumed to be actors into a pack of inquisitive, prowling dentists was too much for him to bear, and he left.

Who could blame him? Was anything being communicated except a sort of sterile astonishment? What the company described as a "meaningful dialogue" turned out to be the modern equivalent of a hellfire sermon, with us variously denounced as capitalists, exploiters, living corpses, motherfuckers, and "bourgeois intellectuals getting your bourgeois thrills out of tickling your brains." If we answered back or reacted to the cast's shrill yowls of "I'm not allowed to smoke hashish" and "I'm not allowed to travel without a passport," we were curtly and rudely silenced. Our function was humbly to join in communion at the Living Theater's altar—that is, shout, "Feed all men," when Julian Beck, squatting before us, intoned, "Free the blacks," or reply, "Down with money," to his chant of "Abolish the police." The initiated were then invited to make their way to Holloway Prison and start the revolution by freeing the women inside. I tagged along to see how the police state would react to this challenge to its authority and found a forlorn little group of Becks, Beck affiliates, and Beck supporters huddled on the sidewalk in the rain, ignored by everyone. The Bastille still stood, as I fear it does to this day.

What had happened to the most striking and important of American avant-garde groups? What has happened to it now? If one can judge by *The Archaeology of Sleep*, the show staged last night, sadly little since 1969. The tribe, though not without its younger members, simply seems older, more bedraggled, and, as is often the case with quasi-religious cults, a bit more cranky.

"Have you seen a group of cats, all of whom are in delta sleep?" cries Beck, and there they are, in the hospital beds that litter the stage, electrodes on their heads. Rather later one of these felines, disoriented by the disruption of its brain patterns, mimes "something unprecedented in the animal world": an act of necrophilia with a furry corpse. The establishment, it seems, is once again abusing, tormenting, thwarting, distorting the personality, instead of taking the opportunity to liberate and expand it. This particular establishment happens to be scientific, and its victims are animals, not people; but the point is as obvious as the tenor of the evening as a whole.

The Living Theater, having spent the last decade or so proselytizing for paradise in the outer and visible world, has decided it's time to explore the hidden utopias supposedly lurking within. That's why its members spend so much time reenacting their dreams and perhaps why we all were eventually invited onstage to sway together "in solemn flow," in imitation of what my incredulously scribbled notes tell me was a "molecule of sea." But what did we actually learn about sleep, about dreams, about the human imagination, about untapped capacities waiting to be revealed, like precious jew-

els in a deep mine? Not a lot. What we'd seen was more like
a long, slovenly piece of group therapy, plus a little groping
and fondling of critics during the rest periods. Still, let me
not rush too speedily to judgment. The Living Theater is in
town for a while yet. I'll return to see what else it's brought
from Europe to unsettle the land of its birth.

The British actor Ian McKellen is in town, rubbing his
refined salt into what I am increasingly finding a wound. One
of the pleasures of being a critic at home is that one is re-
currently exposed to the great dramatists of the past, especially to the greatest of them all. I must review productions
of Shakespeare, by the RSC, the National and others, twenty
or more times a year. Not all are particularly good, of course,
but at least they occur. As McKellen's one-man *Acting Shakespeare* reminded me, I've seen remarkably little classic work
of any kind during my time in New York and just two plays
by the Bard, neither of them at imposing addresses. Had I
not been preparing a general piece on Shakespeare production
for *The Times*, I probably wouldn't have gone to either. *King
John* at Cocteau Rep had a forceful Bastard in Craig Smith
but otherwise struck me as a pretty amateurish affair, notable
mainly for the odd eccentricity, such as the rifles protruding
from the jungle camouflage affected by its medieval armies.
Hamlet was more ably acted at City Stage by a company
nominally headed by Noble Shropshire, a pale, grave, fastidious prince in a leather jacket. I say "nominally" partly because the performance lacked size and charisma—it was, so
to speak, Noble Shropshire rather than Princely Denmark—
and partly because the play was so altered that one wasn't
quite sure whether Hamlet was the main character anyway.
    In fact, it began with Ophelia's funeral, ended with the
gravediggers exchanging glum riddles about their trade, and
in between appeared to have been torn up, shuffled, and then
speculatively glued back together by someone who saw nar-

rative flow in terms of loops, twists, and sudden, dizzying backward somersaults. Why? Presumably to take us inside the prince's mind, show us his stream of consciousness at work, and focus our attention on what the theater's publicity called "the emotional fulcrum of the play, the death and burial of Ophelia." And that, of course, was the first trouble with Christopher Martin's production. The death and burial of Ophelia are not the play's fulcrum. Moreover, *Hamlet* proper is about rotten Denmark as well as its hero's perception of it.

As I said when I was talking about *Carmen*, I've seen some remarkable things done to the classics, especially to Shakespeare, during my reviewing career, and had I been based in America, I would have had oddities enough to record. New York was, after all, the home of Joe Papp's famous *Hamlet*, with Claudius a South American dictator, Ophelia a rock singer in a miniskirt, the prince killed by a member of the audience with a gun, and textual liberties galore: "What is't thou read'st, my lord?" "It is *The New York Times*." And didn't Peter Sellars recently set Handel's pastoral *Orlando* in the Kennedy Space Center, Richard Foreman transfer Molière's *Don Juan* to a madhouse full of keening corpses, and Lee Breuer turn the villains of *The Tempest* into mafiosi, Caliban into a punk, and Trinculo into a parody Mae West?

Myself, I tend to take a conservative and possibly reactionary line about such changes, while making several admissions possibly damaging to my own case. First, mutilation of the classics has plenty of historical precedents. To have seen *King Lear* between 1681 and 1823 would have meant enduring the cosmetic surgery of Nahum Tate, who married Cordelia to Edgar and sent the king to live serenely ever after in the English outback. A production of *Pericles* in the eighteenth century would have contained more bawdy language than Shakespeare actually wrote and in the nineteenth century would very likely have telescoped the play's two brothel scenes into one, leaving it (as a critic of the day said) "without a syllable at which true delicacy could conceive offence." Every age has imposed its biases on classic plays, so why should we complain when a contemporary director does the same—especially if, as seems so often the case, the aim is to make the piece more accessible, more topical and novel, more relevant to our concerns and those of the society around us?

Second, Shakespeare production has in many ways improved. Staging has become sparer, less cluttered; and acting, less selfish and ostentatious. No longer can a classic production simply be a showcase in which a great performer strikes bravura attitudes. Nowadays we tend to see plays as organic wholes, in which the least may have something vital to contribute. Nor could a critic nowadays complain, as Tynan did back in 1952, that you need only "give an actress a round resonant voice and a long Shakespearean part, and she'll have to enter smoking a pipe to avoid being acclaimed." We've come to expect meaning, not music—meaning unearthed by intellectual and emotional hard work on the part of both performers and director, who these days is expected to be something of a textual scholar and a social historian as well.

Third, let me admit that a thoroughly unconventional production may take us closer to the heart of a great work than a more obviously respectful one. Many felt that was the case with Brook's sci-fi *Midsummer Night's Dream* fifteen years ago, and many feel that to be so with his *Carmen* now. The nineteenth-century setting Trevor Nunn gave *All's Well* recently made that difficult play more fun and more comprehensible, with matters of class and honor made clearer by being removed from the Elizabethan twilight to the world of our great-grandfathers. No one wants safe, soft classics, mumbling their moribund truisms to bored or uncomprehending audiences. It goes without saying there's a place for risk, theatricality, astonishment, and, above all, the determination that a play should speak to us here and now. The trouble is that surprise often becomes a sterile end in itself, and "rel-

evance" a buzz word for superficiality and a kind of narrowness.

If a director transports a play to a different period, for
instance, he's in danger of emphasizing only those aspects of
the play which that period is peculiarly fitted to illustrate and
so neglecting or omitting others of importance. If he brings
out one particular idea, italicizes one special meaning, he's
all too likely to sacrifice other ideas, other possible meanings.
The real objection to the swinging sixties *Measure for Measure*
I once saw or to the ecological *As You Like It* I expect to see
any day, the one with Jaques turned into Ralph Nader, is not
what they do but what they don't do, not what they put in
but what they leave out. I well remember a director filling
Coriolanus with swastikas and jackboots and other such re-
galia and managing only to shrink that complex play to the
bald statement that its hero was a fascist and that fascists
were bad. What seemed daring was safe to the point of truism.
How much more daring, how much less safe to have given us
the contradictory evidence actually provided by Shakespeare
himself.

Is a director necessary in classical production at all? That
has sometimes seemed a good question. Well, a guiding hand
is helpful, if only to achieve a minimal consistency and ensure
that Antony and Cleopatra aren't performing in two quite
different plays. The trouble nowadays is that many directors
go on to make inessential choices and decisions, forgetting
their primary task, which is to give the author as complete
and vivid a showing as a sympathetic reading of his intentions
will permit. That does *not* mean substituting a single "interpretive line" for complexity, "messages" for ambiguity,
topicality for relevance, transitory social truths for lasting
human ones. It does *not* mean selecting bits and pieces of a
play, packaging them into beguiling shapes, and manipulating
an audience into believing the result meaningful. It means

stating the thing in all its variety and abundance and letting the audience conclude what it will.

If the classics were more freely available in New York, City Stage's *Hamlet* could perhaps be rated an interesting experiment, justified because another production would soon arrive to give us something closer to Shakespeare himself. But that argument rings pretty hollow in a town where even the best-known of his works are performed far too infrequently and the lesser-known ones scarcely ever. Americans deserve the opportunity to see the Bard, not someone's mereticious gloss on him. As McKellen says in his one-man show, "The most reliable director of his plays is Shakespeare himself."

That show, I should add, struck me as highly enjoyable, and I don't think that's just because I admire McKellen, an actor who sometimes seems to rely too much on melodic throb yet is far more courageous than most British actors when it comes to reaching inside himself and finding and exploring the darker parts within. True, he doesn't get much opportunity to demonstrate such strengths in the set speeches he intermittently delivers here. How can the definitive utterances of Jaques, Henry V, and others mean much unless their characters have been established first? But the show isn't just an anthology of Shakespeare's greatest hits; rather, it's an attempt to share an educated bardolatry.

The enthusiasm is evident throughout, and the education, too. At one point McKellen anatomizes Macbeth's melancholy ruminations on endless tomorrows with a care and thoughtfulness difficult to imagine from an actor only twenty, thirty, forty years ago, and when he comes actually to perform the speech as a whole, we can both hear the nuances of thought and feeling he's injected into it and appreciate the deftness with which they're integrated into its flow. And the spirit of sharing is no less unmissable. Amiably, unaffectedly, he chats, confides, asks the odd question. Can anyone name a single

happy marriage in Shakespeare? *The Taming of the Shrew,*
someone suggests. "I try to do the jokes in this show," he
ripostes with a grin. Then down from the stage he comes and
walks through the auditorium reciting that "tomorrow" speech
from *Macbeth* as Richard Burbage might have spoken it, in
an accent that weirdly combines Somerset, Lancashire, and
parts of contemporary America. The contrast with the Living
Theater came inevitably to my mind. There one had felt hec-
tored and menaced, in the name of a specious enlightenment;
here one was actually enlightened but also drawn gently and
considerately into a collective celebration, a party whose genial host was McKellen and whose guest of honor was Shakespeare himself.

My only reservation was this. Why wasn't it an American
actor up there, sharing the delight of discovery? Is Shakespeare an exclusively British possession? In the fields of scholarship and criticism that is laughably little the case, yet when
we come to the place that really matters, the theater, there is
this strange loss of nerve on the part of Americans. The system
is, of course, less than congenial to the production of the
classics, Shakespeare not excluded. One can't imagine *King
Lear* being presented at all on Broadway or even being very
satisfactorily staged off it. And that would be first and fore-
most for reasons of finance. Neither the most enlightened of
the commercial producers nor the most ambitious of the nonprofit-making theaters would be likely to risk their hard-won
funds on a difficult and painful tragedy with no fewer than
twenty-five characters.

But the conventional wisdom seems to be that the problem
is as much finding competent actors as finding sufficient money.
Indeed, I've heard it baldly stated that Americans "just can't
do Shakespeare." Somehow they're disqualified, not merely
by training that still tends to neglect the classics, not simply
by a theatrical tradition that is overwhelmingly naturalistic,
but almost by birth. They come into the world with mouths

so built, or tongues so shaped, that they can't cope with Shake-spearean rhythms. This is nonsense, pernicious nonsense, as McKellen himself manages indirectly to show. The first per-formers of Shakespeare probably spoke more like a modern New York actor than a modern London one.

It's beyond me to comprehend how the lie can persist when American theatrical history includes Forrest, Booth, Barry-more, Welles, and now George C. Scott, all of whom attracted acclaim from the snootier side of the Atlantic. Yet how can their successors disprove it when they're given so few chances to do so? How, when the only significant opportunity offered by New York itself is a single production of Shakespeare in Central Park? In effect, the American acting profession stands accused of failing to deliver what is scarcely ever asked of it. It doesn't make sense.

What would make sense would, of course, be more govern-ment money for the American theater and the creation of at least one large, permanent repertory company. By its very existence, that would probably influence and alter the training of actors generally, and it could in any case compensate for any inadequacies in the training of the particular ones it en-rolled in its ranks, much as the RSC and the National now do with those it recruits from drama schools in Britain. But I'm back to what's becoming a bit of an *idée fixe* of mine, one I've mentioned before and will no doubt rehearse more fully later.

Has Broadway a death wish? The news from the Plymouth Theater makes me wonder anew. Those responsible for Tom Stoppard's *Real Thing* have decided to celebrate its enormous critical and public success by putting up the price of their better seats from $35 to $37.50. Agreed, it's not much of a jump in itself, hardly more than the cost of eating your bread unbuttered for a week or so. But won't the investors and impresarios be using the same argument when, in the not so distant future, they ask us for $100 instead of $95 for the privilege of spending a couple of hours in orchestra seats? As they must realize, each step upward helps alienate the young, the not-so-rich, the not-so-grand, and all those the theater should be actively courting today if it expects to exist at all tomorrow.

To admonish backers of plays for lack of patience is, admittedly, a bit like rebuking a paraplegic war veteran for lack of enthusiasm for the fray. Considering the mauling so many of them have received in recent times, it's remarkable that any exist at all. Yet a little forbearance, a little longsightedness, a little concern for the future of the American theater would surely have meant broader audiences in the long run for *The Real Thing*—and only a short delay in the arrival of those inevitable profits. Is it so essential that the play should make back its $800,000 investment by June, as now seems possible, rather than by July or August?

Tennessee Williams once publicly lamented that the greatest of the arts should have fallen into the receivership of businessmen and gamblers. Were he alive now, to see the terrible artistic dereliction of Broadway, he would doubtless express his criticism more strongly—and range it more widely. About the same time as the producers announced that it would be more expensive to see just about the only halfway serious play on the Great White Way, my colleague on *The Times*, Samuel G. Freedman, published a cool but devastating comparison of the cost of putting on plays in London and New York. This showed that the tongues lapping the Broadway trough belong not only to capital but to labor as well.

Sam's conscientious research concentrated on Ben Kingsley's one-man show *Kean* and found it had been roughly five times dearer to stage in New York than in London. Virtually everyone connected with the production received rewards that were far higher when not only considered in themselves but adjusted to take account of the relative weakness of the pound,

the greater expensiveness of America, and the higher wages
usual here; and some of those people did little or nothing to
earn them. A curtain man made $549 a week, even though he
had to lower and raise the curtain itself only once during the
show. A wig man got $500 a week for perhaps one hour's work
a day. An understudy was hired at $800 and was told he
needn't even bother to learn the lines since the performance
would have been canceled had Kingsley been absent. What
annoyed me was that the secretary of Actors' Equity, so far
from being embarrassed by so outrageous an instance of featherbedding, defended it on the ground that his union was "allowing an alien actor to come into our country and take a job
away from an American." Really? Who is this all-American
Kean that the predatory Brit was being allowed to cheat? The
truth, as this smug dignitary should have known, is that the
Brooks Atkinson would have been dark for six more weeks
without Kingsley—and thirty-six Americans would have been
out of work.

The problem is complex and not new, but in its present
form it could be dated from the mid-seventies, when Broadway
began to recover from a slump that looked to be even worse
than the present one and the union won excessively generous
contracts from excessively complacent producers. That was
always dangerous in so labor-intensive an industry, with anything between 62 and 80 percent of the cost of a new show
going in salaries and royalties. And though all appeared well
for a time—no fewer than 10.8 million people coming to
Broadway in 1980–81 to see shows that ran for a total of 1,545
weeks—the circle of rising costs and rising prices soon began
to display its viciousness. In the 1982–83 season the number
of theatergoers fell to 8.4 million, the number of playing weeks
to 1,259, and 1983–84 promises to be worse, perhaps a lot
worse.

As a member of a union myself, indeed one of those re-
putedly avaricious and balky British ones, I feel a little uneasy

to find myself wondering if some work rules in the American theater aren't a little absurd and some wages not altogether justified. Anything that increases employment in so barren an area is surely to be welcomed. But that is the short-term view, one damaging to the health of Broadway, hence to the future of the American theater, hence to the prospects of labor itself. If costs were more sensible, more theaters would become commercially viable, more risks could be taken, more work and especially more "straight" work could be staged, and more people would be employed, though perhaps at rather lower wage scales and under more flexible conditions. Some would get less in order that more might get something—in my opinion, a perfectly responsible union position.

Stars on Broadway can get huge sums in fees and percentages. Indeed, Ben Kingsley grossed a weekly $12,500 from *Kean*, by no means a record. Lesser luminaries often earn what, were the show to run a year, would be six-figure annual salaries. So it seems outrageous to pick on the actor or actress who is paid the present Equity minimum of $610 a week as a rogue or spoiler. Others should no doubt be more self-denying. And yet, when even a walk-on must be paid at a rate approximately four times that of his counterpart in London, one can see why Broadway producers are so chary of straight plays, let alone ones with casts of any size whatsoever. As for musicians—well, is the rule that four must be put on the regular payroll if more than four minutes of recorded music are needed in a play, or six if that figure rises over twenty-five minutes, really good for the future of straight drama in America? Is the rule that in certain theaters no fewer than twenty-six performers must be paid, no matter how few actually play, really good for the future of the musical and for the long-term employment of musicians?

No wonder we're in the era of the $5 million musical and the $45 ticket, or the $750,000 to $1 million straight play and the $37.50 ticket. Back in 1960 Albee's *Who's Afraid of Vir-*

ginia Woolf? cost a then daunting $40,000 to stage. Now that
bill would be fifteen, twenty times higher, far more than inflation alone can explain, and the play would probably not
be risked on the Great White Way at all. What's the solution?
Is there a solution? Can there be any hope for the poor goose
Broadway when everyone is busily pulling at its feathers, trussing
its feet, and otherwise mistreating it in hopes of garnering a
little extra golden egg for himself?

Management talks privately of getting tough with labor over
featherbedding, but as far as I can see, only Joe Papp is
addressing the problem in any large-minded way. Part of his
solution is a new deal with the unions, putting some of the
smaller theaters into a special category when they house straight
dramas. And part, of course, is to take the financing of serious
plays away from the sort of people who promptly put up seat
prices when they smell a killing. But there's been no movement
at all on the ideas he floated three months ago. We're clearly
at an early stage of a long chapter in a very long saga, one
that may well end tragically.

The Living Theater has cut short its promised season at the
Joyce, leaving us with a New York where the purportedly
avant-garde, the professedly experimental, seems as insufficiently represented as everything else, the big musical always
expected. Where's the Mabou Mines, that company of which
I've heard so much? What's happened to Richard Foreman's
Ontological-Hysteric Theater? What's Andre Gregory been
doing since he had dinner with Wallace Shawn in that long,
garrulous movie by Louis Malle?

Their absence at the present time seems symptomatic, at
least to me. When the Living Theater and its offshoot the
Open Theater visited London in the 1960's, there was great
excitement among the British faithful. We may have had reservations about some of their offerings, but at least they provoked argument, controversy, and imitation. But since then

we've lost the habit of looking to this side of the Atlantic for theatrical astonishment, notwithstanding the odd astonishing visitor from America. Andrei Serban brought us his exotic versions of Greek tragedy, as I've already observed, and Andre Gregory came to plunge us into the surreal menace of his *Alice in Wonderland*. The Bread and Puppet Theater made the crossing twice, first with its *Cry of the People for Meat*, in which a huge Byzantine Christ was crucified on a shark-nosed airplane, and later with a less spectacular offering, packed with images of dereliction and decay but also of resilience and permanence. The main characters, I recall, were members of the International Union of Washerwomen, stolid figures wearing heavy, phlegmatic masks, who spent the evening cleaning, sewing, trudging about with tatty shopping bags, and generally representing a spirit of dogged endurance beyond the power of our temporal rulers to destroy.

Oh, yes, and then there was Robert Wilson, who came to London from New York via Paris, where he was very, very big. So big, in fact, that one of his productions, his *Life and Times of Joseph Stalin*, ran for twelve hours, from sundown to sunrise, though that was brevity itself beside his *Ka Mountain*, which lasted just a little longer than it took God to create the world, seven days and nights. But we English were permitted to see only the more modest *I Was Sitting on My Patio This Guy Appeared I Thought I Was Hallucinating*, which consisted of three-quarters of an hour of free association, followed by another three-quarters of an hour in which the same, seemingly random monologue was repeated.

As even this somewhat slim list demonstrates, it's pretty meaningless to talk of the "avant-garde" or "experimental" theater as if it were a single phenomenon. By definition, it must be many. There are, after all, countless places in which the barriers of the orthodox may be breached and more than a few ways of doing so. One may go across by foot or air balloon or even rocket—or, to translate the metaphor, by

script or mime or dance or energetic improvisation or heaven
knows what. Bread and Puppet uses masks and marionettes
to represent human archetypes and put across simple hu-
manist ideas. Wilson is a former artist and is interested in
creating visual and verbal paintings arresting in themselves
but without obvious moral or social purpose. Those with a
reputation for experiment in my own country—the Pip Sim-
mons Theater Group, for instance, or the Cartoon Archetypal
Slogan Theater, or Red Ladder—tend to be more political in
their interests and aims than their transatlantic cousins. Some
overtly and angrily espouse a radicalism that these days seems
as alien to the American avant-garde as to every other area
of the nation's theatrical life.

Obviously we need an avant-garde to snipe and challenge,
to make us dissatisfied and force us to revise our notions of
what's possible and permissible. But equally obviously yesterday's pioneering event becomes today's conventional one.
The land the other side of any artistic Cumberland Gap is
eventually likely to be absorbed into mainstream America.
This doesn't always happen or at least happen so straightfor-
wardly. There's a superficial astonishment that dates very
quickly, but there is, of course, also a profounder originality.
It wouldn't surprise me if the year 2000 thought Robert Wilson's work a series of quaint period pieces, but it would surprise me very much if it shrugged off Sam Shepard, say, quite
so easily. Or Beckett or Pinter. Let genuinely disturbing content somehow find its own distinctive style, and you've something that will always escape the lengthening tentacles of
theatrical respectability.

Some may feel the Living Theater's work still falls into such
a category, some but not very many, as the Becks would seem
to have unintentionally demonstrated by their hasty exit from
New York, the victims not merely of a killer notice in *The
Times* but of sheer lack of interest among the cognoscenti.
Their kind of radicalism has come to seem as old-fashioned

as their stylistic invention. The company's time was the 1960's, and though it seems often not quite to realize it, the 1960's are long gone. Loud liberal rhetoric, generalized denunciations of state oppression just don't seem enough these days, whether or not they're accompanied by ostentatious attempts to engage the eye. We want passion, to be sure, but we want a passion able to explain and justify itself. We want concrete observation, analysis, argument, *evidence*, at any rate from those who, like the Living Theater, aim to convert us into crusaders against all aspects of the status quo.

I got to all three productions the theater staged after its somewhat soporific *Archaeology of Sleep* and found, I fear, little but dull thinking, inept performances, and desultory visual effects. There was, I suppose, always likely to be something secondhand about their offerings since they were all adaptations of other men's plays: Ernst Toller's *The One and the Many*; Brecht's *Antigone of Sophocles*; Shaw's *Back to Methuselah*. But I hadn't expected quite so much fustian, quite so little imagination.

Part of the problem is that Judith Malina plays the lead in the first two of those plays, and she increasingly sees the stage as a pulpit, in which she can make righteous noises and strike righteous attitudes. Of *The One and the Many*, in which she's a principled pacifist caught in a violent strike the objectives of which she supports, I can bring myself to say nothing, so incredible did I find her rotund denunciations of erring comrades and malign social enemies alike. Nor has *Antigone*, which first entered the Living Theater's repertory as long ago as 1967, remained the relatively invigorating experience I recall when I first saw it. She's melodramatic in the main part, and so for that matter is Beck's Creon, a scrofulous pixie much given to scowling, growling, twisting the necks of his subjects, and holding his own testicles, a gesture presumably meant to indicate that power is macho aggression. If only tyrants proclaimed their moral characters so guilelessly in the real world!

How much easier it would be to inhabit the world that the Living Theater prefers self-indulgently to postulate!

They rechristened the Shaw *The Yellow Methuselah* in tribute to what the program called another "experimenter bent on answering the needs of a dawning century," the painter Wassily Kandinsky. His contribution to the evening, however, seemed little more than some multihued squiggles on the backcloth and a few thoughts on creativity and science. Mostly we got *Back to Methuselah*, heavily cut but recognizable enough. It still started in 400 B.C., allowing the performers to squawk, wail, and disguise themselves as red sausages, and it still ended in A.D. 31,987, allowing Julian Beck to disguise himself as a bald seer and stalk wisely about the stage. In between, supposedly representative politicians were parodied, more laboriously than I remember being the case in the original. Also, some human butterflies jumped about, chorusing "Chains," which I don't remember in *Back to Methuselah*, and Beck walked around the audience with a microphone, this time camouflaged in an orange suit and orange whiskers, in obvious imitation of Shaw himself.

He didn't sound like Shaw, though, notwithstanding the slight brogue he was affecting at the time. "Are you protesting against the militarization of the entire planet?" he asked one mumbling respondent, and then turned to another equally surprised and inarticulate face, asking it, "Are you against capital punishment, and what are you doing about it?" In fact, Shaw thought weapons of war rather a good thing. Out of them would come violent revolution and, in the long run, a better society. Capital punishment he thought a better thing still. He recommended it for both the mentally and morally unfit, for the seriously defective and the incorrigibly criminal and even the socially or politically troublesome. The Shaw who praised Stalin, and spoke up for the Cheka, isn't the one the admirers of his better-known plays care to remember, but he existed all right, eloquently and unapologetically.

He wasn't a pacifist. He believed in a degree of social discipline that would be anathema to Beck and his fellow anarchists. He had little but contempt for the "greasy commonplaces," flesh and blood, regarding the body, the emotions, love itself as mere distractions from the important business of life, which was the enthusiastic exercise of the intellect. He'd have found the Living Theater people muddled, sentimental, and worse, with their cries of "Abolish the police" and their whispers of "Are you afraid if I touch you like this?" In fact, he'd have despised them, and they'd have feared and hated him. It's a sign, surely, of the extent to which the Living Theater has lost its bearings and its way that it should end its stay in New York by enshrining this improbable, alien figure in its personal pantheon.

February

Nearly five (yes, *five*) months into my time as a critic here, a second (yes, a *second*) new play has come to try its luck in what Americans still touchingly consider the center of their theater, and as it happens, it's neither altogether new nor likely to be a lot luckier than the only authentically new play to have hit Broadway this season. *Brothers*, I recall, ran just one performance back in November. What hope for Shirley Lauro's *Open Admissions*, a brave, tough, and surely uncommercial piece padded out to six to seven times its natural length in what would appear to be a vain attempt to become commercial? What hope for American playwrights when one of the most promising feels impelled to adopt such an expedient in order to achieve recognition and success?

In its original version *Open Admissions* lasted for just twenty minutes and came at the audience like a broken bottle thrust into its collective gut. Calvin Jefferson, a black student thrust into a city college without the wherewithal to cope academically, sobbed and raged at Ginny Carlsen, the teacher of speech communications who was teaching him nothing; then the two of them launched cautiously into an ad hoc lesson that at long last recognized that the young man's level of literacy was roughly fifth-grade; and that, more or less, was that. But now we learn about other people, too, notably Ginny's slovenly husband and worried daughter and Calvin's harassed sister and troubled niece, and the effect is to muffle and mute the play's attack on an open admissions policy that promises much

163

and delivers little. The finger that was pointed at the educational system starts to waver. The public insidiously becomes private. A type of play scarcely ever seen on Broadway transforms itself into yet another thin study of domestic crisis.

Still, I've spent enough ink berating American dramatists for not quite managing to be capsule reincarnations of Shakespeare and Büchner, Ibsen and Brecht. Maybe it's time to acknowledge the difficulties they face at a time when the traditional center of their theater is so inhospitable to even their less serious efforts, let alone their more challenging ones. Nearly fifteen years ago William Goldman complained in his book about Broadway, *The Season:* "We have not had a first-rate playwriting debut in almost a quarter of a century, and the wait is getting painful." Since he wrote that, the prospect of such a debut has become so slight, so slim that any sane person would give up the wait as hopeless. Indeed, the best may not be seen on Broadway at all. Mamet's *American Buffalo* may have slipped past the sentries, but Sam Shepard, whom many would regard as the first among the first-rate, has yet to have a play produced there.

Even those writers who make it to Broadway don't necessarily find the trip rewarding. The risk of producers' cutting their losses and instantly taking off a play is greater than ever. Many must wonder what no less a dramatist than Lillian Hellman asked a few years ago: "Why should I spend three years writing something that might close in three nights?" And those whose work is to all appearances more successful may in effect be subsidizing it out of their own pockets. Marsha Norman long forwent half her royalties on *'Night, Mother* in order to cut its costs and keep it running. Lanford Wilson, David Hare, Harvey Fierstein all have waived or deferred their earnings at one time or another. The most important producers on Broadway, the Shuberts, never now put on a show unless its author first says he's willing to do this. The result can be that a play in difficulties survives and the playwright once again earns full royalties: the case, one understands, of Fierstein's *Torch Song Trilogy*. It can also mean that a writer gets little or nothing: the case of poor Martin Sherman, who wrote that well-received play about the plight of homosexuals under the Nazis, *Bent*.

It seems hideously unfair that virtually all other labor costs should be regarded as fixed and those of the creator of the play which keeps that labor employed should be disposable. It leaves one feeling that the proper human reaction to the inhospitality of Broadway should simply be for the infrequently invited and ill-treated guest to say to hell with the place. But the trouble is that it's still the only area of the American theater where a playwright can occasionally make good money. To adapt Robert Anderson's well-known saw, he may not be able to make a living there, but he can just conceivably make a killing—$10,000 a week or even more. His play might have to run several months at some less prestigious address for him to earn so much in all. A dramatist who relies on off-Broadway, the regional theater, and the publication of his scripts is certainly going to have a hard time making ends meet.

That's why the continuing collapse of Broadway as a forum for new work is so very bad for the future of drama in America. As long as there was some faint possibility of eventual success there, there was at least some financial incentive to write for the stage. But why should someone with a family to support, a mortgage to pay, or even just himself to feed gamble on a possibility that has become less faint than invisible? No wonder one hears story after story of gifted playwrights abandoning the stage temporarily or even permanently for more financially reliable work, Jason Miller, for instance, or Paul Zindel, or Murray Schisgal, now mainly the author of novels and screenplays. And who can say how many potentially considerable talents have been deterred from writing for the theater in the first place?

It's tempting to start making comparisons with Britain, where, rightly or wrongly, it seems to me that never have so many dramatists been writing so many plays at any time in our history. Back in 1954 Ken Tynan wrote a celebrated piece in which he described a French student airily assuring him, "Oh, Paris is in decline. Apart from Sartre, Anouilh, Camus, Cocteau, Ayme, Claudel, Beckett and Salacrou, we have almost nobody." From the England of the 1980's a similar plaint might go up about our dramatists. Apart from Pinter, Stoppard, Gray, Ayckbourn, Nichols, Churchill, Hare, Brenton, Wesker, Bond, Storey, the Shaffers, Bolt, Mortimer, Rudkin, Poliakoff, Gems, Bennett, Hampton, and Frayn, we, too, have almost nobody. Why such abundance there and not here in America?

Well, one or two reasons must be apparent already. Though the West End shares many of Broadway's problems, they aren't so severe, and impresarios are more ready to produce contemporary dramatists. And though the regional theater is becoming ever more important in America, and off- and off-off-Broadway continues to produce new work, it still seems easier for a playwright to find a slot in their British counterparts, especially now their number includes a National Theater with three auditoriums. The Arts Council funds more than a hundred theatrical companies in England alone, and they know that they risk losing their subsidies if they don't produce at least some new plays. And can America match the eighty-odd bursaries, residencies, and other awards given by the council to our dramatists last year? Of course, many of those would look pretty small if translated from weak pounds into strong dollars; but then it's cheaper to live in Britain, and in any case, British writers seem to expect more modest salaries.

Financial conditions are more favorable then. So, of course, are geographic ones. A London-based playwright who takes up a residency in, say, the highly regarded rep in Leicester or Nottingham is hardly more than an hour by road or rail

from the center of things, something that can't be said of a
New Yorker offered a temporary home in Minnesota or Ken-
tucky. He can stay in close touch with the metropolis, and he
can expect the metropolis to stay in close touch with him. The
leading British critics seem increasingly willing to range the
regions, and in any case, word travels fast within a theatrical
community so much less far-flung than America's. If there's
good news of a play in Brighton or Bristol, the London producers will see it within a couple of days, if they weren't there,
as they could well have been, on the first night itself.

Suppose, then, an aspiring dramatist has joined a company
with the help of an Arts Council grant, written a play and
seen it produced, and finally managed to interest a London
management in its transfer. What now? Well, his potential
profits won't be as great as on Broadway—unless, of course,
the final result is a move *to* Broadway—but the pressures and
perils will be less, too. Alan Ayckbourn has a story of being
confronted by men with a laugh meter when his *Absurd Person
Singular* came from London to America. They told him there
were forty guffaws and twenty sniggers in the second act, but
thirty sniggers and only ten guffaws in the third. Would he
please transpose the two? He refused, gently pointing out that
there were reasons why he'd shaped the plot as he had, but
he remembers the incident as a sign of the anxiety, the fear,
the hysteria that prevail on Broadway—and as a reason why
writing directly for it doesn't appeal to him at all and even
writing indirectly for it seems a disturbing idea.

Do American producers respect playwrights less as artists,
regard their work more as product to be marketed, than their
British counterparts? That would doubtless be an absurd generalization. But the British seem willing to present riskier
plays, to tinker with them less, and to allow them more time
to establish themselves commercially should they not be well
received. They can afford a degree of failure, as indeed can
the playwrights themselves. "The atmosphere is more relaxed

in Britain," I recall Simon Gray once telling me, "and you do have the right to fail. I've had some absolute stinkers produced, and it hasn't done me much harm. If you have a success in America, there's a terrible burden on you to repeat it, and if you have a failure, you've that aura that Americans dread so much."

Be that as it may, British playwrights do seem to have good reasons for feeling that the conditions in their own country are more helpful, the atmosphere more congenial. Television, for instance, so far from being a lure and a destroyer, quite often allows them to discover and develop their skills. The BBC puts out some 120 hours of original drama a year on TV and between 500 and 600 hours on radio, much of a high standard, and the commercial companies know that they must present at least an hour or two a week or risk losing their licenses to broadcast. Several of Pinter's shorter pieces were broadcast or televised before being seen in the theater. Peter Nichols, Trevor Griffiths, and David Rudkin have done some of their finest work for TV. John Hopkins, author of *Find Your Way Home*, was acclaimed as a serious dramatist on BBC-TV before writing for the theater. In America television sucks playwrights from the stage; in Britain it feeds them to it.

Simon Gray is another example. He was set to become a writer of prose fiction when one of his short stories was bought for television. Because it meant more money, he adapted it himself and, finding the work agreeable, went on to write several TV plays. Then he showed his producers the first draft of *Wise Child*, only to see it rejected because of its homosexual subject matter and dubious language. It was presented on the stage with Alec Guinness in the main part, and a distinguished career was launched. But Gray still writes for TV, as indeed do many established playwrights. That way, it seems, they can make the extra money they need without feeling obliged to compromise their artistic principles.

But congenial professional circumstances can't of themselves produce a flood of playwrights, any more than a warm pool can produce a shoal of fish. Perhaps we have to look to history and sociology to explain the profusion of drama in Britain at the moment. Some would actually invoke Shakespeare at this point, not as a model whom playwrights literally attempt to imitate but as a marker of whom they're always at least subconsciously aware, reminding them that the country's finest literary achievement occurred in the theater. This side of the Atlantic, the Great American Novel is the dream. You don't hear much about the Great American Drama.

But this way of thinking takes too slight account of the ups and downs of the British theater. Little that so much as aspired to be serious was written, for instance, between the years 1914 and 1956, when Osborne's *Look Back in Anger* arrived to sandpaper ears that had become accustomed to imitation velvet. The impact of this play I've mentioned before and it can't be underestimated. Suddenly issues of scorching social moment were being eloquently aired, and in the theater, of all prim ghettos. It brought new audiences to our playhouses, and more to the point here, it encouraged serious writers to turn to the stage. Tom Stoppard reckons he'd now be a literary journalist or maybe a novelist but for *Anger*. It made the theater "the place to be at—if you were in it people paid disproportionate attention to what you wrote." Rudkin, too, aspired to write prose fiction until he felt the impact of Osborne: "The theater was where the excitement was."

The virus spread, infecting more and more, until it became what it now is, virtually endemic in Britain. The theater, for all its unevenness, could still be called "the place to be at." It has an intellectual and cultural status that even the excellence of Shepard and Mamet seems unable to bring it in America. They have their avid admirers, all right, but they've yet to have the same effect as Osborne on society more generally. They don't provoke indignant denunciations on some editorial pages and impassioned endorsement on others. Their heroes haven't become spokespeople for a generation, a class, or anything else. They themselves aren't symbols of anything beyond themselves, as the "angry young man" Osborne managed to make himself. They've done much, very much to improve the American theater, but little, very little to make it less marginal.

For that's what the American theater seems to be: culturally marginal. And much as better conditions and more money for playwrights would help, it could well take something more to give it the centrality it can still cautiously brag of having in England. Perhaps I'm overinfluenced by the example of *Anger*, but it will, I think, take some similar happening, some similar explosion of excitement, some similarly unmissable *proof* that the drama can touch, inspire, and lead, that it's in the very vanguard of the nation's ideas, not shambling along among the camp followers. And where's the play capable of achieving *that?*

Down to Chelsea, there to munch sandwiches and listen to a panel of my new colleagues address themselves to the woes of Broadway. I must say, they looked like a strange and motley crew, perched there behind their plastic table. There was Howard Kissel of *Women's Wear Daily*, long, beaky, and slightly drooping, like a benign heron in glasses, and there was Douglas Watt of the *Daily News*, large and solid and authoritative-looking, a bit like a well-loved character in an English children's book called Mr. Plod the Policeman. There was John Simon of *New York*, a slim, graying, elegant figure, fastidious in appearance and manner, and there was Clive Barnes of the *Post*, bedraggled and uneasily blinking, as if he'd just escaped from a laundry basket and didn't know quite where he was. And there, too, was the amiably rumpled figure of Frank Rich, my colleague and friend from *The Times*.

It wasn't an especially tranquil meeting. John Simon felt

that the critics were to be numbered among Broadway's inadequacies and rounded on two colleagues who he thought had erred when it came to dispensing honors to playwrights last year, labeling them "bums" and "swine" and worse. One of these was apparently Clive Barnes, not the man to take such words lying down or, as was actually the case, slumped worriedly in his chair. He hit boldly back, calling Simon a "Yugoslavian," which in origin he is. Then up jumped the producer David Susskind, to launch an incoherent attack on the platform, while the platform chorused, "Sit *down*, Mr. Susskind." Meanwhile, both my sandwiches and Broadway continued to go their own way—namely, down me and downhill.

Not that the session was altogether without content. Simon took a grimly seigneurial view of the American theater, indeed of America itself, which he declared to have been a "yahoo from the beginning," without culture because without the roots from which culture could grow. Most people, he thought, went to the theater, if at all, mainly to see their favorite TV stars. The only hope for Broadway, as he saw it, was to die, perhaps to be reborn in some new form, and off-Broadway and off-off Broadway were thoroughly unsatisfactory alternatives since insufficiency of funds meant they were murdering new plays and so thoroughly butchering the classics as actually to put people off them. Maybe it was worth fighting for government subsidies and the creation of a National Theater; maybe not. "Why do you stay here?" demanded an incensed patriot from the floor. "Why don't you go back to Europe?" "Ah, well," murmured John, "where things are worst, that is where one is most needed."

After this mandarin jeremiad, all seemed a bit mild and anticlimactic, though others clearly shared at least some of Simon's skepticism. The yeomanly Watt decried the Broadway producers as real estate men who "wouldn't know a play if it hit them"; Frank Rich lamented the spiraling circle of costs and ticket prices and talked of the deterioration of the theater as part of a more general decline in American culture; and Howard Kissel gravely concurred with the feeling of the meeting from behind his thin-rimmed specs. It was left to Barnes to be more optimistic, perhaps more Panglossian, about the situation. Broadway was mainly a shopwindow, he agreed, and nothing new could be expected to happen there; but elsewhere—well, more American plays were being produced than ever before, and of better quality.

But could critics influence things, conceivably even improve them? Watt thought not, as did Barnes. Rich emphasized the importance of reviewers' not letting their standards of judgment decline in a misguided and almost certainly counterproductive attempt to help Broadway out of trouble. I must say, I was glad to hear him say that, since no one could work for *The Times* without being aware of the paper's power at the box office and, if he or she is a halfway decent person, without wanting to temper power with mercy. But excessive or unjustified generosity, however well meant, is a form of lying, patronizing and insulting to the theater and downright criminal as far as one's readers and its audience is concerned. Indulge in that, and one is encouraging people to squander their resources, economic and intellectual and even spiritual, on goods one knows in one's heart to be shoddy. More than that, one is encouraging the theater to *be* shoddy and satisfied with itself for being so.

Myself, I would agree that critics can have little direct or immediate impact on the evolution of the theater as a whole. Our power tends to be specific, not general. I'm told, for instance, that Shaw was little performed in New York when Clive Barnes was chief theater critic at *The Times*, because producers believed, rightly or wrongly, that he disliked his work. More positively, reviewers can generate interest in this author, that performer and ensure that the theatergoing public, or at least some of it, takes a good, hard look at them.

They can, so to speak, put forward candidates for stardom. But even here there are obvious limits to their influence. Every politician knows that you can manipulate the voters only so far and so long. In the end it is they who decide the parameters of the possible. Similarly, a critic who is persistently ahead of his readers' tastes or indeed behind it is going to end by being mistrusted and ignored and perhaps turned out of office as well.

Yet that still leaves room for maneuver. It would be wrong as well as sad to conclude that critics must simply be consumer guides, toadying to the public. They can sometimes stand back, make comparisons, draw attention to the achievements of the past, and wryly note those areas in which the present is less adequate. The critic, Kenneth Tynan once said, is someone who can see the way but cannot drive the car. He can present his readers with possibilities and, perhaps, make them a little more dissatisfied with the theater's failure to fulfill them. That way he may conceivably help create a climate for change or at least do something to ensure that change is accepted, if and when it comes.

Take the most famous review Tynan ever wrote, his one of that play to which I keep returning, Osborne's *Look Back in Anger*. He would never have claimed any direct responsibility for the appearance of that play. On the other hand, he had amply demonstrated its lack and need. Again and again he attacked the coy little comedies, the glib little thrillers, and (for variety) trite little comedy-thrillers that filled London playhouses in the late forties and early fifties, accusing them of being "of no more use to a student of life than a doll's house to a student of town planning." That way perhaps he readied his readers for the eventual arrival of *Anger*. Certainly he was on hand to celebrate with unmatchable eloquence when it did, in fact, burst on Britain out of that more or less empty theatrical sky. Even those who weren't moved to see the play couldn't have missed its significance.

What are my own hopes for my criticism? Well, it would be nice to feel that one might make people here, too, a little more uncomfortably aware of what they don't have, obvious enough though those wants and lacks must be already: companies; classics; a drama more alert to society, nation, world, and yawning cosmos beyond. And if pressed, I'd have to admit that my hopes were even more arrogant than that. I'd like to be part of the evidence when posterity wants to know what it was like to see this performer, that director, this actor, that designer practically at work in the theater of the 1980's. That critical function can never again be as important as it was when Hazlitt reviewed Kean, or Shaw Irving, because we've television and the movies to show us how Olivier moved and sounded and how Gielgud didn't move and sounded, but perhaps their successors can collectively offer something denied to small and large screens alike, a little of the "feel" of such events.

Actually that's less heavy and highfalutin than it may sound. All it means in practice is observing and recording with whatever color one can muster and in whatever detail one can cram into the space available. I'd like to think I was a celebrant and a troublemaker, to be sure, sharing delight and promoting enthusiasm and stirring rebellion, but whatever the particular event onstage, I'd also wish to believe I was a reporter, different from the man or woman who describes a battle or an election rally or a church meeting mainly in that my beat happens to be the living theater. Perhaps I can best bring together these seemingly contradictory aims and aspirations by suggesting that the critic is, or this critic tries to be, a mediator between the stage and the audience.

It's a function that fulfills itself in two ways simultaneously. The critic's face is, so to speak, aimed in two directions at once. He elects himself, unasked and uninvited, as spokesman for the author, the cast, the director, everyone involved in a particular production. He tries to explain to their audiences or potential audiences what it was they were aspiring to achieve, why, how, and, unavoidably, with what degree of success. At the same time, with hardly less hubris, he makes himself a spokesman for those audiences or potential audiences. He informs author, cast, director, everyone involved in that particular production what it felt like to be in that theater that night.

No one is likely to quarrel with the first of these critical aims or purposes, but the second, I find, often causes irritation or even derision in the profession. Who are these critics, elevated to positions of power by no one except the editors of newspapers and sometimes without any qualifications except a certain base journalistic flair? Why should a professional take them seriously in any way or for any reason that goes beyond the tickets they can sell? "If I want to learn something," I've been assured more than once, "I listen to my friends and acquaintances in the theater itself."

Well, no doubt some of those friends and acquaintances are very rigorous and severe when it comes to telling the unvarnished truth about a production, but having been present at more than one postperformance encounter backstage between watcher and watched, I suspect that is rather rarely the case. The aim is usually to reassure, sometimes honestly enough but sometimes not altogether so. Indeed, there are times when the attempt to reconcile candor and kindness, and retain both integrity and a friend, becomes quite comical. Noel Coward's advice to those in such a quandary was to shake the head in an impressed sort of way and say, simply, "Incredible." W. S. Gilbert, slier still, once rapturously informed a performer, "Good *wasn't* the word!"

In any case, actors or actresses who listen only to their friends and fellow professionals are surely guilty of selective deafness. The great majority of their audiences will not, after all, fall into either catagory. Indeed, the critics, in spite and sometimes even because of their failings, are likely to be more representative of the man or woman in the orchestra or balcony. That man or woman can, however, communicate his or her feelings about a performance only by laughing or applauding or fidgeting or, just occasionally, booing, and the trouble with such reactions is that they aren't very precise or detailed. Only the critics are in a position to articulate the feelings of reasonably well-informed spectators, or at least some of them, with genuine frankness, and therefore, a theater professional who ignores the critics is, in effect, ignoring his audience.

Still, as I write, I realize I'm beginning to sound glib and abstract and irrelevant and worse. How often do any of us carry out our principled prescriptions for ourselves? How often am I doing so in this perplexing city? And how much can any critic or critics do to restore Broadway to its onetime importance? To the first two of these questions I'll hope to return; the third leaves me as stumped as it did my colleagues, down in Chelsea.

And another thing the New York theater lacks: anger, outrage, that savage indignation which Juvenal once enjoined on himself and his fellow members of the International Brotherhood of Protesters, Parodists, and Scurrilous Vituperators. To be sure, those family dramas, examples of which *(Levitation, Broken Eggs)* continue to proliferate off-Broadway, sometimes have their ferocious moments. But on the very rare occasions that broader subjects appear over the theatrical horizon, passion seems as absent as those more intellectual qualities whose lack I've been interminably deploring in recent months. The exception, Shirley Lauro's *Open Admissions*, wasn't as exceptional as it should have been. Its fury at what it saw as a gigantic educational swindle was muffled, muted, almost silenced by wholesale recostuming in the domestic apparel so fashionable in the New York theater these days.

All this has been much in my mind just lately because my visiting list has consisted of several American revues and a

couple of imported pieces that might, I suppose, be described
as protest plays. Not that either of the latter was as obviously
explosive as some examples of the genre. No howls of "Abolish
the police," no primal screams about the fundamental human
right to undress in public, none of the hysteria conscientiously
fermented by the Living Theater in its more ebullient, less
dilapidated days. Anger can take more guileful, more insidious
forms, and must do so, if its object is injustice in the same
oppressive nation in which it's first staged. Hence, especially,
Janusz Glowacki's *Cinders* at the Public Theater, a play from
Communist Poland which slyly involves political hypocrisy in
the pre-Solidarity era. It comes in code, assuming an audience
canny enough to know that what they seem to be seeing, a
tale of girl delinquents rehearsing "Cinderella" for the benefit
of a visiting film crew, isn't what they're really seeing at all.

Glowacki is like the boy who kicks the boss in the rear end
and then, when the old tyrant whips around, is smiling and
saying, "Who, me?" His play stings like soap yet seems twice
as slippery when you try to get a firm purchase on it. One
moment it's aiming a more or less explicit gibe at the pretensions of communism; the next, it's innocently about brow-
beaten little actresses in a reformatory. Only in its portrait
of the bully who in practice runs the school, the deputy headmaster, is it consistently and pretty unmissably political. He
thinks of himself as a benign father figure helping construct
the socialist utopia yet doesn't hesitate to expose himself as a
fixer and manipulator, capable of any cruelty when he wants
to advance his ambitions. He hardly bothers to conceal that
the head on his shoulders belongs to Mr. Hyde yet somehow
manages to believe and expects others to believe he's actually
a self-sacrificial Dr. Jekyll. He is, of course, a despotic regime
at its most topsy-turvy.

There's a bile and bitterness here all right, enough to explain why the luckless Glowacki is now an exile in America,
and there's bile and bitterness in *Woza Albert!*, too, more

directly expressed, though often in a comic style. This comes to the Lucille Lortel from Johannesburg's Market Theater, an imaginative account of Jesus' political evolution when he makes a Second Coming to South Africa, there to be plunged into a world of poverty, passbooks, police savagery, and prisons. The Messiah ends, not altogether characteristically, by destroying Cape Town and raising local hero after local hero from the dead: "Woza, Albert!," meaning "Arise, Albert Luthuli!" The show's two performers and cocreators, Percy Mtwa and Mbongeni Ngema, put across this closing call to arms with the same attack and verve that mark their efforts throughout. Mr. Ngema, especially, seems in serious peril of dehydration, losing bucketfuls of sweat as he and his partner mime everything from bongo drums to helicopters and everyone from beggars to Botha. Their satire is, it's true, not very sophisticated and sometimes a bit heavy—but who's complaining, given the inventiveness, energy, and eloquence of those voices, eyes, arms, and unstinting, unstoppable feet? There's always, surely, a place for drama that doesn't argue, doesn't analyze but bangs across a plain case with a conviction that bypasses the appraising intellect and makes a direct assault on the heart.

In any case, such complaints miss the point. *Woza Albert!* was designed for the consumption of a local audience, not for citizens in remote northern climes. So, come to that, was *Cinders*, though its intentions would seem rather subtler, less to denounce and arouse, more to share a rueful recognition of the absurdities of the world immediately outside. Subsidiary differences notwithstanding, both pieces exist to remind spectators of what they already know and thus increase a sense of solidarity, or even of Solidarity. That makes appreciating them difficult for audiences who don't understand their buzz words or hold their grievances. Yet it's right that protest plays, whether they're wily and Polish or downright and African, should be staged abroad. They can bring distant tussles to immediate life, showing the world how at least some of the combatants think and feel. They can inform, conceivably even influence international opinion. And of course, they remind us that such work needn't be artistically crude or intellectually contemptible and could have a use wherever there's cause for resentment, anger, or defiance.

Is there no such cause in America or, for that matter, in New York City? Well, scarcely the cause there is in Poland or South Africa or was here ten, fifteen years ago. To repeat, there's no obvious cause for a *Viet Rock* or a *Macbird* or perhaps even for the most famous segment of *America Hurrah*, the one in which grinning dummies ripped apart a motel room. That sort of intensity of utterance needs intensity of provocation or at least an intensity of alienation among the articulate I don't see anywhere around me. How could it be otherwise, considering that cheerful, beaming President and those H-bombs or that truculent mayor and the multitude of beggars and drug addicts on his battered and scarred streets? If such incongruities aren't likely to provoke the sardonic fury of a *Motel* these days, they would at least seem a fit subject for wry astonishment and maybe something stronger.

After all, remember the Kennedy years. Vietnam was mainly mentioned by people who collected exotic postage stamps when I first lived in New York, twenty-odd years ago, and Watergate probably still had to be built. Yet the New York branch of Camelot was playing host to the Premise, the Second City, Lenny Bruce, and, from my own country, Jonathan Miller and others in *Beyond the Fringe*. Social satire, political satire, every sort of satire seemed to be thriving. And if then, why not now, in a world where the King Arthurs seem weaker, the Mordreds more formidable and dangerous? Why have five months of professional searching on my part yielded so little?

Obviously I've talked about all this to Americans of my acquaintance. Both the United States and Britain have right-wing leaders, we've reminded ourselves, and leaders who seem remarkably like-minded, in economic theory, thinking about defense, everything; yet while Thatcher satire is one of my country's few growth industries, and at times reaches extremes of Thatcher obsession, Thatcher paranoia, Thatcher loathing, President Reagan seems to provoke surprisingly little anguish or ire. Partly, we've agreed, it's a matter of personality. He's everyone's comfortable grandfather; she's too abrasive ever to be mistaken for anyone's dear old granny. He cracks the sort of rueful, self-deprecating jokes Americans adore; she gives remarkably few signs of possessing anything as relaxed and soothing as a sense of humor. Partly it's that she's given a greater wrench to the political tiller than President Reagan. An attempt to move a nation sharply to starboard is, after all, going to prove more uncomfortable and cause wider unease if you've got used to moving gently to port, as we have. Also, this energetic ideological navigation has yet to make Britain a richer or more successful nation, let alone one as rich and successful as America, so the motive for protest is obviously stronger.

Well, maybe President Reagan isn't as inviting a target as Mrs. Thatcher. There are, surely, plenty of other representatives of the American status quo, and (no names named) some of them positively plead to be peppered by the witty and disenchanted. Why, I've asked more than one acquaintance, doesn't this happen when change, renewal, or at least *movement* always seems so much more possible here than in Europe—and certainly easier than in my own island corner? Why aren't a dozen satirists crying, "Off with the old, on with the new," and a score of playwrights echoing that exhortation?

"Perhaps because you see the new in a different way from us," someone suggested the other day, and I saw what he meant. Here change, renewal, movement seem to be seen in personal terms rather than social or political ones, as tends to be the case the other side of the ocean. Talent, determination, energy make for success, their want makes for failure,

and circumstances either congenial or oppressive count for
far less than Europeans like to believe. Altering or even adjusting the existing social and economic system seems pretty
irrelevant to the business of getting on with life. That isn't
everyone's feeling, of course. It wouldn't be the feeling of many
blacks, many Hispanics, and many other members of what
the Reverend Jesse Jackson is calling his rainbow coalition.
But it appears to be fundamentally the feeling of many others,
among them, I suspect, a fair proportion of the relatively
privileged people who are responsible for most plays and most
revues. And that's perhaps partly why their work lacks social
anger, political clout. The notion of raging and railing at
society would seem to some of them as beside the point as for
a marathon man to blame the passing scenery rather than his
lungs, legs, and willpower for failing to achieve his goal.

That individualist philosophy has had its setbacks. It took
a battering in the Depression, a questioning in the early sixties,
and another hammering at the height of the Vietnam War,
but it was deeply enough ingrained in the national character
never to have been very seriously threatened. And now it has
reasserted itself, as we should always have expected. Yet does
that really explain the *extent* to which it has reasserted itself,
in the theater in particular? It may explain why we can't expect
the sweeping and scathing attacks on the consumer society we
were getting in New York fifteen years ago; it doesn't altogether explain why smaller and more localized displays of
subversion are almost entirely missing, too. Why so *thorough-
going* an emphasis on the individual and so little on his context? Why so *widespread* an assumption that our real enemies
are internal, in the psyche or the home, and not external, in
the world outside?

Well, let me not forget the earnest little theories I mooted
earlier in this journal. I tried some of them on a fellow member
of *The Times* staff the other day. Was it that the nation still
had to emerge from the shrugging disgust with public life

generated by Vietnam or Watergate? Or that the issues seemed amorphous, remote, and, were they ever directly to impinge, somehow avoidable? Or that there's greater political consensus here than in other Western countries and therefore less reason for violent wrangling? She listened, cautiously concurred, and then advised me to read Christopher Lasch's *The Culture of Narcissism:* "He goes further and brings a lot of it together." Since she was, in fact, only repeating the advice given me by another friend, a Manhattan psychotherapist, I thought I'd better follow it.

I must say, the book's author is well named. He lasches and lasches America from top to toe. Yet he does also offer serious evidence and arguments for his thesis, which is that after the turmoil of the sixties Americans have despaired of the possibility of change in any area and, at worst, have become almost pathologically preoccupied with the business of massaging their own egos and ids. The picture the flailing Lasch assembles is of a culture where what matters is self-discovery, self-improvement, self-fulfillment, one that feels neither connection with the past nor much relationship with the present nor any responsibility for the future. Its philosophy, insofar as it has one, is not merely that the individual will is all-powerful and totally determines a person's fate but that "fate" should be seen only in terms of material satisfaction and personal happiness.

I didn't stay with Lasch to the bloody end, deciding that he was trying to cram too much complex and unwieldy material into one aggrieved and possibly rather paranoid indictment. Indeed, it began to seem that everything in the United States, from apple pie to the World Trade Center, was in some sinister way a manifestation of what he'd provocatively called narcissism. As an Englishman I felt I was intruding on some peculiarly venomous row within the American family, and yet the book did, of course, help explain some of the trends I've noticed within the American theater. Some; by no means, all.

To say it explains the subject toward which I'm edging, the variegated satire currently on show in New York, would be to do what I've just accused Christopher Lasch of doing. It would be to force too much different material into a single thesis: a somewhat procrustean style of criticism.

Yet there's no denying that the offerings I've seen share one quality, or one negative quality, and that's lack of punch. I've seen *Doonesbury*, the ambling musical entertainment that Garry Trudeau has assembled from his comic strip and found myself thinking nostalgically of the plays that other cartoonist Jules Feiffer brought to the stage a decade and a half ago: *Little Murders* and *God Bless*, two raucous and biting satires of American life. I've seen and enjoyed Charles Ludlam as a parody Callas in *Galas*, a lovely, naughty performance of a posturing diva at her most throbbingly overblown. But the title of the group responsible, the Ridiculous Theater Company, says it all. This is sly, diverting nonsense, derived from reality but hardly very critical of it. In any case, its barbs and darts are aimed at the past, not the present. And that is the case too, with Erik Brogger's *Basement Tapes* and the other burlesque pieces about former President Nixon that have hit town since my arrival. Aiming kicks at the head of someone down on the floor, instead of jabbing at him when he's upright in the ring, is no more useful satire than it's good sport.

And still they come. Something called *Babalooney* arrived from Chicago's Practical Theater the other day, artlessly confident of wowing New York with funny faces, gratuitous acrobatics, tired parodies of TV quizzes ("Can you spot the real Tarzan?") and a slim sub-Pythonesque sketch about a fast-food joint serving "Big Macbeths." It didn't remain long, unlike another and (I suppose) better revue from the Midwest which looks set for a reasonable run at the Village Gate, *Orwell That Ends Well*, presented by the Original Chicago Second City Company. One does indeed hear echoes of Mike Nichols and Elaine May in the company's more agonizedly contemporary moods: "How long have you been sleeping together?" "About six months." "That's almost a *relationship*." Nor would their forebears have been ashamed of a sketch about a salacious talk-show tyrant winkingly interviewing Mother Teresa ("Let me ask you the question that I'm sure is on everyone's lips—how often do you *do* it?") or of a parody reunion of maudlin sixties people ("Oh, that war was a good time") out of place in the Big Chill of today. Yet the show opts rather often and easily for quick, glib laughs. To bring on Margaret Thatcher and then ask her to do nothing but puff marijuana and improbably bop to rock music is schoolboy cheek and chutzpah, not satire. Indeed, only once does political comment intrude to any extent, and that's in a Gilbert and Sullivan pastiche in which warring Chicago potentates are reconciled by Richard Mayor Daley, opining from the hereafter that unity will let them swindle the local citizenry more effectively. But that seems bewilderingly irrelevant. There's a place for insular satire in Manhattan, but only if the island it involves *is* Manhattan.

Being unavoidably and unalterably male, and having more than once been buffeted by drama that seemed to regard that condition as inherently fascist, I approached *A—My Name Is Alice* at the American Place in a rather confused state of mind. My search was and is for revues with attack and clout, but I'm not masochistic enough to like being attacked and clouted for that which I can't really help. Well, for better or worse, this "feminist way to relax" left me pretty relaxed, too. It has no time for hardhats who hoot and whistle at passing breasts. In fact, it recommends an equal but opposite assault on such people's private parts. It thinks that men have an awful tendency to transform themselves into creeps of one sort or another, and it regrets that women are so often and abjectly dependent on them. Yet it's scarcely less funny about its more extreme allies, with their coven mentality, than about male swinishness. From time to time one of the excellent performers comes forward lugubriously clutching a book of poems called *For Women Only*, which turns out to be all leaden accusation and plodding self-pity: "I am a woman, a crippled bird . . . flap, flap, flap."

It's a wise, attractive entertainment but not, of course, especially scathing or Juvenalian. Satire seems a lost art in New York—or is it? The other day I had one kind of bite at a supper club called Palsson's near Lincoln Center and, much to my surprise, found another kind of bite a few yards from my wine and shrimp. On wiggled a travesty Carol Channing, all blubbery red lips, ten-foot tongue, and goggling fatuity, and in trundled a geriatric man-elephant, a creakily trumpeting parody of Anthony Quinn: "Zorba's what he'll do while he's waiting to die; Zorba is his last big try." Julie Andrews, Kevin Kline, Lauren Bacall, *Cats*, "*Screamgirls*," *La Cage*, and "plastic stars who never eat," mechanically strutting through "David Merrick Street"—all get it in the neck and sometimes in more uncomfortable places. Even her recent death didn't save Ethel Merman from a savaging.

Forbidden Broadway, as it's called, is incestuous stuff but scarcely an incestuous love-in. The concept, words, and direction are by Gerald Alessandrini, and though his and his young company's bios aren't unimpressive, neither he nor they have yet to make it in any big way in the Big Apple. Is it tendentious to hear the voice of a hungry new generation in their litany of feeble shows, overpraised stars, inept lyricists, and interminable songs? Maybe. Yet there seemed in the production as a whole a zest for attack not to be explained simply by the fact that a group of professionals were following a formula for burlesque, a recipe for revue. Effective satire probably needs to be personally motivated in some way, whether by feelings of injury and anger or by affronted conscience.

Here one detected resentment at the theatrical establishment, probably not unmixed with envy of those it seems whimsically to favor.

Mark you, it seemed a pity that all that satiric energy should be squandered on what Christopher Lasch would, I suspect, see as a form of embittered narcissim. It may be natural that the subject that should particularly preoccupy the inhabitants of the New York theater should be the New York theater itself. But it's yet another sign of the times, and rather a sad one. There are a lot of potential spectators out there. Surely some of them would like to see other subjects treated with a similar comic passion. There are a lot of writers and performers in Manhattan. You can't tell me that all that exercises them is personal self-fulfillment and career. Surely some feel at odds with establishments, institutions, and systems other than those immediately touching their employment or unemployment. Surely some could bring the same hilarious cruelty to the wider world that *Forbidden Broadway* shows can be brought to a tiny one.

They've rechristened the old Actors and Directors Lab on West Forty-second Street the Samuel Beckett Theater, a suitable switch for at least three reasons. First, it recognizes that there's an audience in New York for work at one time thought dauntingly obscure and severe. After all, what's happening in the auditorium immediately adjoining this? One haggard old man is being readied for public humiliation by a slouched apparatchik, two others are learning to cope with terminal loneliness, and five more are celebrating the coming of decrepitude by solemnly torturing each other to death, and the three plays in which these grim events unroll—*Catastrophe*, *Ohio Impromptu*, and *What Where*—have been running since last summer. Moreover, a new production of *Endgame* is scheduled to hit town before long. Too few seats are involved for one to be able to draw any sweeping conclusions about

the theatergoing public as a whole, but the consistency with
which they're filled suggests that we're talking about a fan
club larger and more dedicated than its counterpart in Britain. No one there has attempted to launch a Beckett theater,
and I doubt if anyone will.

The second reason for welcoming the retitled theater is that
it looks and feels sufficiently somber. You're perched above
a gray carpet, beneath a gray ceiling, between gray-brick
walls, looking down at a black curtain, and you might, with
a little imagination, suppose yourself to be in a long gray coffin
about to slide into the flames of a crematorium. And thirdly,
it's difficult to think of a living dramatist more deserving of
the respect and regard the change of name implies than Beckett, he of the long, stricken face and the short, stricken plays.

Why? Why that respect, that regard, not to mention that
Nobel Prize? Martin Esslin, who has written as well as anyone
about Beckett, tells a nice story of walking through London
with him one morning. The sun was shining, the city looked
beautiful, and ahead were several hours to be spent watching
the playwright's favorite game, cricket. "It's the sort of day
when it feels good to be alive," declared one of the party, at
which there was a long, ruminative pause, and Beckett replied,
"Oh, I wouldn't go as far as *that*." Again and again in his
work he has said much the same. He's looked at the sunlight
and has seen little but the dark. How can the world go on
acclaiming as a master so dedicated a depressive? Isn't there
something masochistic about those critics he impels so eagerly
to forget the comforts and consolations, and sometimes even
the happiness, that most of them feel?

Those aren't altogether Philistine questions, whatever the
more idolatrous loyalists may think. Certainly they flashed
more than once around my own head as I sat watching Billie
Whitelaw, Beckett's favorite actress and the leading exponent
of his work in Britain, go brilliantly about her business. One
moment she was introducing herself, an ample, beaming lady

in a shining white blouse, and humorously warning us of the unhumorous stuff to come. The next, she'd withered and shriveled and started bleakly to claw her way into our imaginations. Up and down she paced, up and down, a bunched and tattered specter, communicating with a mainly unheeding world now in a numb staccato, now in a snatched whisper of awesome intensity, now in a monotonous chant, now in a sort of death rattle. That was *Footfalls*. Then forward and back she went, forward and back, her face much the same yellow-white mask, but black instead of red rims around her eyes, a stately dress of the same hue replacing her green-gray rags, her fingers resting on the arms of a rocking chair instead of scratching and scrabbling at her own shoulders. That was *Rockaby*.

Beckett has asked odd things of Miss Whitelaw in recent years. She's spent his *Play* in a funeral urn and his *Happy Days* buried first up to her waist, then up to her neck in sand. In *Not I* she was reduced to a pair of spotlit lips, writhing, twisting, palpitating like some vermicular sea creature as she told their owner's tormented life history. I met her once, and she described what it was like standing there, intensely babbling in the blackness for twenty minutes, her palms bruised and broken from the ferocity of their grip on the iron bar that had been invisibly placed in front of her, lest she lose her balance. "It was like falling backwards into hell every night," she amiably told me. "I don't think I could do it again." Yes, Beckett asks odd things of his performers, but perhaps nothing odder of this genial, smiling lady than that she should perpetuate his harsh, unsmiling wisdom. What the woman manifestly is seems to contradict what the actress actually says.

Yet who would claim we have to believe an author's every word, whether we're performing or listening to him? It may be enough for him to believe. It's even more likely to be enough if his belief is one of real moment, and he puts it across with passion and logic, as Beckett undeniably does. We're not in the theater to agree, or shouldn't be. Rather, we're there to be disagreed with, challenged, annoyed, upset, forced to defend our thinking, maybe reshape it if it's proved indefensible. The least that can be said for Beckett is that he's a sort of metaphysical *agent provocateur;* the most—well, perhaps that he writes with a scope, a courage, and a beauty unmatched in modern drama.

After all, what is he saying? Roughly this. We've been dumped, for reasons unknown, in a world designed, intentionally or not, to frustrate and hurt us. Love and friendship are evanescent or nonexistent, other names for habit and greed. Feelings and the flesh are sources mainly of pain, and so, above all, is the mind. We retreat into ourselves in our loneliness and distress, only to find we're trapped in a "penny-farthing hell," echoing with guilts, tantalizing memories, regrets, fears, hopeless desires, protests, fixations. Hence the protagonist of *Footfalls,* her legs endlessly ranging one cage and her thoughts another. "Will you never have done," asks her mother from her sickbed upstairs, "revolving it all?" No, not while one brain cell remains to jostle and compulsively to jar another, in hopes of somehow, somewhere, sometime evolving a system that makes sense, a strategy for coping with pain.

But of course, there is no such system, no such strategy. Life is subjectively interminable, objectively the merest flicker in an endless darkness, and either way without sense or purpose. Blindness taught Pozzo to see this with terrible clarity in Beckett's very first play, *Waiting for Godot.* "One day we were born, one day we shall die, the same day, the same second," he cried, "they give birth astride of a grave, the light glimmers an instant, and then it's night once more." In 1969 the celebrated *Breath,* possibly the shortest play ever written, made the identical point without a word's being spoken. A faint cry, then the sight of a stageful of rubble, the sound of lungs slowly inhaling and slowly exhaling, another faint cry, curtain down. And now here's *Rockaby* receiving its New York premiere, Beckett's latest refinement of the same glum vision.

The old woman we see dying in her armchair first tried to avoid the stark truth of existence, as most of us do. She went out seeking "other creatures like herself, a little like." Then she stayed inside but still kept staring out of her window, in hopes of finding someone. "Time she stopped," she repeats in unison with her own recorded voice, which echoes from above, paraphrasing her story, evoking her evolution, describing how she learned her lesson. And "stopping" means abandoning a vain search for love, coming downstairs, sitting alone, enunciating the words "fuck life," consenting to death.

If existence is an illusory gleam in a trash can or a grave-yard, that is the logical conclusion. Beckett regrets the brevity of life yet feels that the briefer it is, the better, because the less painful it must also be. He laments human waste yet sees no point in anything but waste. For him, true wisdom consists of renouncing all wishes, all desires, and becoming as near to a void as possible. He is notably reticent about his creative intentions, but he has advised those seeking enlightenment to bear in mind two quotes. One is from a seventeenth-century Fleming, Arnold Geulincx: *Ubi nihil vales, ibi nihil velis*, ("Where you're worth nothing, you should want nothing"). The other is from the Greek philosopher Democritus: "Nothing is more real than nothing." The fault of old, crazed Hamm, protagonist of *Endgame*, was (Beckett's own words) "to say 'no' to nothingness." The old woman of *Rockaby* isn't so stupid. She says yes to nothingness, and, in her author's opinion, quite rightly, too.

Yet more than two decades separate the two plays. Haven't Beckett's attitudes changed between the two? Little, if at all. His view of man's ontological predicament is still, in the blunt summing-up of the recent *A Piece of Monologue*, that "birth was the death of him," with all that implies about the infinitesimal space between the two events. What has changed is the expression of those attitudes, that view. It's become terser, denser, and, usually, more visually inventive and verbally arresting. Whole lives contract to haunted epigrams, put across by a head grimacing from beneath a flared mane, or a pair of dementedly gabbling lips, or a dour old woman in a rocking chair. Again and again and again Beckett presents us with the evidence for his philosophy of renunciation, and again and again and again he manages to do so in a different way.

That combination of capacities explains why he's valued, and I think rightly valued, as highly as he is. Others, too, would agree that a vast, uncaring universe is our momentary habitat, but how many have looked at it so unblinkingly and so unswervingly faced out the consequences of that stark perception? And still Beckett goes on, a secular monk of austere integrity, picking through his runes, piecing together parable after parable, threnody after threnody, all adding up to a chilling yet exquisite litany of pain and grief, mourning what is, what can't be, and what must therefore be instead.

The revival of Clifford Odets's *Awake and Sing!* at Circle in the Square, apparently the first important one in New York since its original production in 1935, left me with feelings that were decidely mixed, indeed uncomfortably curdled. What a relief to be presented with so masterly a proof that plays can involve the American family yet have horizons considerably larger than the east and west sides of an average-size shoe box. What an irritation to see observation so lively spoiled by the ideological romanticism of the period. What a disappointment to find the standards of performance so uneven. What a shock to find the case for companies, as opposed to ad hoc casts, made with such unintentional persuasiveness at so prestigious an address.

Odets seems to be being rediscovered on both sides of the Atlantic this season: *Rocket to the Moon* and *The Country Girl* in London; *Paradise Lost* as well as *Awake and Sing!* in

New York. It's an enthusiasm to be applauded for several reasons, but perhaps mainly because of what the dramatist's friend, champion, and mentor in the Group Theater Harold Clurman wonderfully called his "tenement tenderness," his "consanguinity with the small fry in the American ferment." He scrutinizes the lower-middle-class anthill with a rare blend of shrewdness and generosity. There's understanding and compassion, discrimination and warmth in his picture of people caught in the cracks, clinging to the splinters of a world which forces beyond their comprehension are yanking apart. Like the great O'Casey, Odets judges yet feels personally. Indeed, he once said that he experienced all his characters' desires, even the most reprehensible, in his own flesh and bones. Another time, walking in a sleazy section of New York, he remarked that there was "not a person in this crowd in whom I don't find a part of myself."

It shows in most of *Paradise Lost*, enterprisingly revived the other day by a new "alternating repertory company" called Mirror Theater. It shows in *Awake and Sing!*—or does so for nine-tenths of its length. The younger Odets was intellectually always more indebted to Jefferson and Thoreau than to Marx or Lenin, but he thought of himself as a socialist, for a time even as a communist, and felt obliged to inject a little Group optimism into the ending of his plays. That way he undeniably distorted, spoiled both *Paradise Lost* and *Awake and Sing!*

In the first, the handbag manufacturer Leo Gordon responds to the killing of one son in a police shoot-out, the impending death by disease of another, the rejection of his daughter by her fiancé, the ruin of his business by a combination of the Depression and a dishonest partner, and the loss of his furniture to the bailiffs. He responds to all that, and more, with a soaring profession of faith in human brotherhood and the happier, less materialistic future waiting to be unfurled. In the second, the young hero, who has hitherto wanted little but his girl and some new shoes, starts grandiloquently declaring that life must no longer be "printed on dollar bills" and that no woman means anything to him "until we can take the world in two hands and polish off the dust." Even his sister's moonlight flit with a cynical gambler, actually a purely personal escape into a tawdry-sounding hedonism, is dignified as part of the new enlightenment, an exemplary determination to "awake and sing."

Yet Odets's attempts to cram his material into "an ideological mold"—his own apologetic self-accusation—doesn't finally matter. The material in both plays is too real, too rich, too interestingly unruly. The language fizzes and crackles, rising at times to a sort of urban poetry, and the people, too, are marvelously quirky and unpredictable. The special character of *Paradise Lost* is to be found not in idealist posture and utopian gesture but in the distinctly earthbound moment when the upright Leo solemnly banishes a German-born canary from his house and his partner refuses the gift with "Am I a Nazi lover?" Similarly, *Awake and Sing!* is most itself when a distraught husband, devastated to learn that his wife has deceived him into thinking another man's child is his own, starts gabbling about how he weighed himself twice on a tell-your-fortune machine in a subway station. Odets had an intuitive understanding of the jumps, twists, and sudden back somersaults of the human mind.

But this isn't the only reason he should be revived and modestly treasured now. His understanding extended from the individual to the society of which he or she was a part. That, apart from his sheer quality, is what distinguishes him from most American playwrights today. Take Bessie Berger, for instance, the matriarch at the center of *Awake and Sing!* She treats her husband with contempt, she successfully prevents her son from marrying the "Miss Nobody" he loves, she dupes a dim but doting immigrant into marrying her pregnant daughter, she breaks the much-loved records of her father, thereby provoking his suicide, and she does all she can to keep his insurance money from the intended beneficiary, his grandson. She's a bully, a liar, a cheat, and very nearly a murderess. Woe betide anyone, spouse, parent, or child, who refuses to be trimmed and chopped in the procrustean bed she has built in her head and keeps invisibly established in the family living room.

And yet to understand her is to forgive her. So often that's a feeble, patronizing philosophy. As applied by Odets to Bessie, it's nothing of the sort. Overlook the odd flash of anger or resentment, and she's a genuinely self-sacrificing woman doing what the world tells her is best for her family. This is a respectable part of America, where it's a sin to fail, be poor, or bear children outside marriage, and this is the Depression, with families and furniture being flung onto the street. Odets's prosecuting brief builds up, but it's not finally directed at personal ruthlessness or family voracity. The true defendant is a society that warps and deforms individuals and their basic relationships, until what was meant for love and nurture becomes a half-crazed mutation, tearing its own flesh and that of others. If any of a dozen contemporary dramatists had managed somehow to create Bessie, she'd simply be an isolated monster, explained, if at all, in Freudian terms, perhaps as the vengeful victim of her own unhappy childhood. Odets would regard that diagnosis as seriously deficient. For him, the "family play" was social, political too.

Since society changes, evolves, conceivably even improves in some ways, does that mean he's a dated writer? Yes, a bit, and then again, no, hardly at all. There's no depression without to explain our depressions within; but fear of failure, if not of actual impoverishment, may actually be stronger these days, and I don't think most Americans would regard their countrymen as a lot less avaricious for material rewards for themselves and their children. If *Awake and Sing!* has dated, then so has *Death of a Salesman*, which is promised for Broad-

way later this month, and *All My Sons*, and much else that
seems quite as eloquent to me as it did to my seniors.

But where was the eloquence I'd confidently expected from
Ted Mann's production? Where we might have had depth, we
got a hectic energy. Where we should have felt the characters
were painfully intertwined at their very roots, we sometimes
wondered if they'd yet been introduced to each other. It was,
in fact, the latest and most convincing of the several performances I've seen demonstrating the need for companies and
company acting. Al Pacino would have been less likely to have
run punctiliously amok in *American Buffalo* if circumstances
had forced him to think of himself less as a star, more as a
key component in a larger machine. Ad hoc casting must also
help explain why *Heartbeak House* was not more extraordinary, or *The Glass Menagerie* more moving, or now *Awake
and Sing!* more consistently powerful.

Of course, a good deal of nonsense is talked about the merits
of companies these days. The word "ensemble" is much and
worshipfully invoked, often by people who have no very clear
idea what it signifies and would wince away from some of its
manifestations in practice. It can mean sectarian content, narrow aims, ossified style. The more limited a company is in
what it does and the way it does it, the more monochrome it
becomes, the more it can accurately call itself an ensemble.

Yet while that may be a proper use of the term, it's obviously
a perversion of the idea. A company, as I understand it, is
simply a group of performers who have worked together long,
hard, thoughtfully, imaginatively, and unselfishly enough to
play as a team, and when the rapport becomes particularly
strong, and everyone is so sure of everyone else's particular
strengths and so responsive to them that pass after pass almost
magically becomes goal after goal, then one can begin to talk
of an ensemble. The Group Theater in Odets's time would
seem sometimes to have been that. So of course was Brecht's

Berliner Ensemble. Though the National Theater in England is too large and unwieldy to be so dignified, and probably has too high a turnover of actors as well, one of its house directors, Bill Bryden, succeeded for a time in evolving a distinctively plain, downbeat style with the help of a subsection of performers. Rightly or wrongly we thought of them as an "ensemble."

The Royal Shakespeare Company has perhaps done more to earn the word partly because it has its own permanent (and very prolific) house dramatist in the Bard, partly because it's managed to keep the same directors and many of the same performers either on its payroll or closely on call, and partly because it goes in for a great deal of offstage training. You're not likely to be trusted with a good part until you've learned much more about the complexities of Elizabethan verse than is taught at any drama school. The style that emerges has its critics, most recently Peter Hall, who founded the company and now runs the National. "There is this slow, over-emphatic, line-breaking delivery of the text," he writes of one production in his recently published and altogether fascinating diaries. "The actors are so busy telling us the ambiguities and the resonances that there is little or no sense of form." Yes, that has happened, but there have been other times when the company's players have succeeded in blending intricacy, subtlety, irony, stealth with momentum, vividness, and a determination to make the play immediately accessible, here and now. That combination is RSC ensemble acting at its best.

Why no U.S. equivalent? I feel its absence more strongly and personally than when I burbled on about the need for a National Theater in New York a few months back. If I were back in Britain, I would be beginning to make regular trips up to Stratford, where this year Roger Rees is doing his Hamlet and new productions of *Richard III* and *Henry V* are about to happen; and I'd also be off to the RSC's London home, the Barbican, to see *Measure for Measure, The Comedy of Errors,* and *Julius Caesar*. Let me admit it: I'm an addict. Sometimes I think it's what keeps me a critic, year after year after year. I mainline on Shakespeare, and I like booster shots of other classic dramatists, and if my craving isn't satisfied, parts of my critical anatomy begin to display distressing withdrawal symptoms. They grumble and snarl and twitch. That's what they did the other day when they heard George C. Scott was coming to Broadway, but as a director, and a director of a modern play, Noel Coward's *Design for Living*. Why (they asked) wasn't he emerging from years of hard slog with an American Shakespeare Company, an American National Theater, to give us his Othello, his Timon, his grizzled and majestic Lear?

Nevertheless, the lack of a big national rep seems to me more explicable than when I wrote about it before. Indeed, no sooner had I put my thoughts on paper in *The Times* than the comedian Bill Cosby sent a telegram to practically every senior member of the arts staff angrily denouncing me for not giving black, Hispanic, and Asian-American playwrights proper prominence in my prescriptions. "The article should be re-titled 'Recipe for a White American National Theater,' " he said, taking particular exception to the faces selected for il-lustration—Williams, Beckett, Miller, Pinter, Shepard, et al.—but not himself nominating additional or alternative minority group candidates. That upset me, since Amiri Baraka, or LeRoi Jones, as he used to be called, did, in fact, figure in my original draft. But the telegram seemed a manifestation of that "Balkanization of American culture" of which Robert Brustein has spoken, itself an indication of why the creation of any homogeneous national theater would be difficult to achieve.

Of course, that doesn't exclude a more heterogeneous na-tional theater or series of national theaters, supposing the money for them could ever be found. Nor is it an argument against smaller initiatives. It amazes me to discover that vir-

tually the only theater groups in New York with any claims
to permanence or even continuity should be the Circle Repertory Company, the Jean Cocteau Company, and the City
Stage Company. The first of these has not been having a good
season, though it has a fairly distinguished record; the second
struck me as unremarkable when I saw it; the third is adventurous and enterprising, as I discovered from its production
of Botho Strauss's *Big and Little Scenes* as much as from its
Hamlet, but can't yet be judged by very exacting standards.
I don't think any of them would be capable of giving an *Awake
and Sing!* the rich company production it really needs if we're
to feel the complexity of its characters' mutual maneuverings
and the sheer depth of their subterranean connections.

The reasons why there are no strong reps in New York are,
I suppose, substantially the same as why there's no national
theater there or anywhere else. Actors come to town in a sort
of gunslinger spirit, to tout their talents and make their names
and fortunes, not to settle into a permanent and probably
penurious theatrical family. Some will have been in one of
those in the regions and have decided, for better or worse,
it's holding back their careers. Even in New York ambitious
young performers aren't prepared to commit themselves for
a year, eight months, six months, or whatever it takes so much
as to begin the process of creating a company. They're looking
for a chance on Broadway or, better, in Hollywood. And what
existing or even imaginable institutional company could compete with *that* when it beckons?

More money would, of course, help. The increased grants
and subsidies Joe Papp wants from city, state, and federal
government would help a lot. It amazes and appalls me to
learn that the National Endowment for the Arts currently gives
the entire American theater only some $9.4 million a year,
plus a little extra in challenge grant projects and so on. That's
less than our Arts Council gives to our National alone, and
less, too, than some German municipalities give to their local

theaters. But it would be silly to suggest that lack of money is the only reason for the absence of a really good rep in New York. Papp himself apparently discovered that a few years ago when he and Meryl Streep tried to set up a company comprising, and handsomely rewarding, the best young talent the country could offer. Time, not money, he told me, was the problem. The company planned to work together for eighteen months, then a year, then six months. At that point the project seemed hardly worthwhile at all and was abandoned, the victim of other offers or hoped-for offers that the performers felt they just couldn't refuse. Papp wouldn't be sorry if his plans for a National Theater on Broadway led to the creation of some permanent company or companies, instead of being a series of plays with ad hoc casts, but he'd be surprised and unlikely himself to be involved. "Someone else would have to do that," he said.

Of course, let's not deny that there are compensations and even advantages in an ad hoc system. There are times when everyone running a company must have wished he were free to approach some particular outside performer, instead of being forced to cast an insider not absolutely suitable for the part. Then again, some producers in New York are able to call on the same performers again and again. They may not have a company, but they've access to a distinct pool of actors, many of whom presumably get to know one another well enough for some of the same strengths sometimes to emerge onstage. Papp himself would fall into that category, along with several other off-Broadway producers, and very good work they've doubtless often presented. But there can be few plays that aren't the better for being performed by a capable, versatile company, and there are some, specially demanding in one way or another, that are obviously the worse for not being so performed. *Awake and Sing!*, as Circle in the Square has unluckily proved, is one of these.

March

The high opinion I formed of David Mamet's *Glengarry Glen Ross* in London last fall seemed triumphantly confirmed at the Golden Theater yesterday. It is a wonderfully lively piece in itself, scabrous, seamy, charmless, funny, and really rather brilliant, and in the context of Broadway it is, let us say, refreshing. It's taken seven long months for me to find a playwright prepared to venture out of the doll's house, toy box, and other places in which his contemporaries are mostly to be found snugly sequestered, and Mamet has done so more decisively than anyone could reasonably have expected. Not only does he take us into the big, bad world where deals are struck, money is made, and men are ruined, but he brings to that tale of dog-eat-dog the snap and bite it needs and deserves.

It's Chicago, a real estate office, a jungle within a jungle where the only unalterable law is grimly Darwinian. Swallow or be swallowed. Sell and survive; fail and be fired. Indeed, the system is such that disaster and dismissal are more or less certain for the weakest of the pack. A Cadillac is the promised prize for the most successful of the four hustling salesmen we see in competition with one another, each trying to chivy, browbeat, and caress gullible locals into buying slices of bare Florida sod or swamp with exotic Scots names. The second gets a pair of steak knives. The last two had better start searching the jungle for some new den or lair from which to launch their hunt for prey.

That explains why the four-letter word most often on their lips, apart from one not often used by nice publishing houses, is "lead." A "good lead" is the name of a promising patsy; a "bad lead" might as well be a one-way sign pointing over a cliff. It also explains the nerves, the fear, the tension, the unscrupulousness, the callousness, the dishonesty, and, finally, a very particular crime.

The first inkling of this, though we can't know it at the time, comes when Robert Prosky's Levene, who is slipping in the steak knife stakes, tries to fast talk J. T. Walsh's Williamson, the office manager, into giving him meatier leads, and his wanglings, maneuverings, bullyings, pleadings, and finally beseechings all come to nothing because he can't produce a large enough bribe in cash. Then James Tolkan's Moss, the most aggressive of the salesmen, is discovered balefully manipulating Mike Nussbaum's Aaronow, the most flustered and forlorn, to break into the real estate office, trash the contents, and steal the good leads. The population of the piranha pool, inured to blood by years of practice on outsiders, don't hesitate to show their teeth to one another or even sink them into one another's necks.

The robbery occurs between Acts I and II and is, as it turns out, committed by Levene, who has presumably been got at by Moss in the intermission. Eventually he admits it, in what's the least convincing encounter in the play, one that depends on an experienced salesman, until then all adept fake innocence, suddenly giving way to a totally uncharacteristic weakness, naïveté, and trust. But that's a small flaw beside the play's abundant merits and strengths. Indeed, most people will probably find that Mamet's gaudy, swaggering idiom sucks them in, carries them along, bounces them over such minor implausibilities like a stream over rusty tin cans. *Glengarry* confirms what *American Buffalo* suggested: that he's the bard of streetwise barbarism, the laureate of the four-letter word, a writer who can create a kind of brazen poetry out of everyday speech—and yet convince you that it *is* everyday speech.

But as in *Buffalo*, that speech isn't just emptily authentic. It's purposeful as well. The salesmen verbally duck, weave, jab, yet feel themselves actually to be up against the ropes and in permanent danger of a knockout. There's pathos in their rhetoric. Often the foulmouthed bravado is only too clearly a desperate bluster, a braggadocio show of power by men well aware of their true powerlessness. Their very speech emphasizes one of the play's principal points: These men live by victimizing others, but the most abject victims of their trade are, of course, themselves.

As this suggests, Mamet writes about the weaker real estate sharks with some sympathy. His attitude toward the stronger might almost be mistaken for grudging admiration. There they are, out in the swim of things, living off their wits, exultant one moment and finished the next. The least likable character in the play is certainly Williamson, a cold bureaucrat cannily calculating from the safety of his desk, and the most is probably the svelte predator played with nice, easy authority by Joe Mantegna from beneath a hairdo seemingly sculpted from black, blow-dried mink. Richard Roma, as he's called, can see a stranger sitting alone at a table in a restaurant, mesmerize him into signing away a fortune before the meal is through, and then, when the victim has second thoughts the next morning, improvise a dazzling, disorienting charade, construct a hologram of lies so solid-seeming, so beguiling that surrender becomes almost inevitable. In former times he would have been a highly successful buccaneer. In better times his intellectual dexterity, imagination, and creativity would qualify him for a calling more elevated and edifying than that of real estate hood. As it is, he's exactly that, the Capone of the Cadillac contest.

Certainly Mamet is as far from sentimentalizing him as any of us would be from sentimentalizing some sleek but hungry lynx that happened to stick its paw in our front door. On the

contrary, the play eloquently, though implicitly, reemphasizes
the very cynical view Mamet has often expressed in interviews:
that his fellow countrymen are to be trusted least when they
put on their business suits, business smiles, and business
selves. He's said that "Three cheers for me, to hell with you"
is the "operative axiom" of their working lives. As I think
I've noted before, he's also suggested that there's a myth abroad
that vicious behavior becomes laudable when committed by
stockbrokers, corporate lawyers, and the "lackeys of business." Actually there's no difference between them and
"crooks."

He said that apropos *American Buffalo*, the main characters of which really were crooks, though they thought of themselves as businessmen and were strangely scrupulous beside
the rather more legitimate businessmen of *Glengarry*. They
had to convince themselves that a burglary was no "shame,"
that its victims deserved to be plundered. The salesmen here
have no such qualms of conscience. They have nothing but
filthy words and contempt for the harmless men and women
they've sweet-talked into swapping their hard-earned savings
for a few square yards never likely to be inhabited by anything
except ants or alligators. Their rationale, insofar as they bother
to have one, seems to be that the working day is or should be
a macho adventure, in which they and they alone are men,
boldly differentiating themselves from the "faggots," "fairies," and "children" all around. Well, had we faggots, fairies,
and children a preference, I think we'd rather be honestly
robbed by the petty hoodlums of *Buffalo* than intricately fleeced
by those fake-friendly slickers.

Glengarry is a less complex, subtle, and resonant play than
Buffalo but packs far greater punch. It's as scathing a picture
of unscrupulous dealing as the American theater can ever have
produced, and maybe more than that. After all, what does it
say? Tantalize them with enough carrots, threaten them with
enough sticks, and the salesmen, the entrepreneurs become

liars, cheats, frauds. Willy Loman becomes what any reasonable person would define as criminal. In other words, crime is only the logic of business, extended. This is not an opinion that scores top marks for tact, and perhaps not for universality either, not unless one believes that Wall Street is to be condemned on account of a few cut-price hucksters in and around Times Square. But whoever thought that it was drama's duty to be either diplomatic or unanswerable? It's enough for it to do what Mamet does: pepper a carefully chosen target with energy and relish and leave us, blinking and boggling, to decide how high and how significant his score is.

There are plenty of obvious differences between being a professional theatergoer in New York and being one in London. Actually getting into a Broadway play is more of a struggle than getting into a West End one since the original architects mostly gave a smaller proportion of the total space to foyers, lobbies, and the like, and the way into a crowded performance can resemble a public enclosure on Derby Day. The programs here are thicker and free, as perhaps they should be since audiences are paying three times more for a good seat, yet tend to contain far less illuminating information about the playwright, the play, and the play's background and subject. The curtain usually goes up more or less on time in London; in New York, never. Here audiences are apter to arrive late, less inclined to imbibe large quantities of liquor in the intermission, and more generous with their applause and their bravos at the end.

Our reviewing industries operate a bit differently, too. We've no regular TV critics, presumably because the BBC is a national, not a London, network, and even the independent stations give less time to local events than their American counterparts. No one in England makes the distinction between the West End and the fringe that the New Yorker still oddly makes between Broadway and off- and off-off Broadway. Again, the principal British critics come to first nights, not to previews, as their New York counterparts now do. And that's important, because it means that those working for daily papers must dash off their reviews in what's often a lamentably short time between the fall of the curtain and an eleven o'clock or eleven-thirty deadline. Their New York cousins can construct more considered, measured critiques.

As for me, I continue to live a more leisurely life than in London thanks to the lack of worthwhile shows and the need to write just one article a week. That means I've been able to get up to Boston, down to Philadelphia, and, of course, all around New York. I hadn't realized that Prospect Park was so marvelously landscaped, or that the Natural History Museum was so large, rich, and interesting, or that the Frick was, well, perhaps the most attractive art gallery in the world. It has an atmosphere, a feel, so wonderfully intimate yet civilized you could imagine yourself personally invited into the private house of some supremely cultivated millionaire—as indeed, you are, since Frick was that, and this is where he lived. And what a selection! Piero della Francesca, Rembrandt, Bellini's St. Francis, Vermeer, Goya, and Holbein's St. Thomas More gazing across an El Greco at Holbein's portrait of the piggy-eyed man who destroyed him, Thomas Cromwell! There's more, much more, too, but not so much as to leave you exhausted and frustrated, as so many great museums do.

With that across Central Park, Lincoln Center up the road, and my new enthusiasm, Thai cuisine, abundantly represented on and around Eighth Avenue, how will I ever bring myself to return to Britain, as the difficulty of transplanting my children to New York schools says I must? Also, I'm feeling less of a foreigner, in as well as out of the theater. It would be absurdly arrogant to claim that I'm yet able to think and feel my way into American minds, American imaginations, American speech patterns, but I don't think I'm as far from doing so as I was just two or three months ago. Take my changing reaction to the oratorio adapted from Saroyan's celebration of small-town life, *The Human Comedy*, by Galt MacDermot and William Dumaresq.

When I saw this in December, I felt I'd been glutinously plunged into a tiny world scarcely more real than J. M. Barrie's Never Land. Indeed, so painfully perfect did virtually all the characters seem to me that I left the Public Theater repeating the words attributed to the novelist Anthony Hope after he'd been immersed for an evening in *Peter Pan:* "Oh, for an hour of Herod!" Yet when I caught *The Human Comedy* on its transfer to Broadway the other day, I began to see what I should have seen before: that Saroyan wrote the original novel at a peculiarly painful time, just when the Second World War was beginning to bite; that he had created his homespun utopia in order, quietly and unpretentiously, to remind his readers what it meant to be American; that it meant or should mean generosity, openness, consideration, a sense of country and community, belonging and sharing; that the present show appeals not to mindless nostalgia but to a craving for half-lost values, half-forgotten decencies, a yearning for shape and order and significance and roots. Not that this awakening of mine mattered to anyone except me. No sooner had I filed my review than *The Human Comedy* closed, the victim (presumably) of its dedicatedly unglitzy production, its absence of star performers, its unusual subject matter, and the Broadway public's mistrust of all these things.

Of course, it's possible that somewhere inside me, without my even knowing it, my critical standards have been gradually slipping on a basic evolutionary principle so that I can mentally and emotionally survive a disappointing season. But I'd rather see my conversion to *The Human Comedy* more positively, as an indication that I'm less and less the tone-deaf alien, blaming American music for the supreme fault of presuming to be American. Indeed, my time here has left me wondering if I didn't understate the case when I wrote a few months back about the need for reviewers to resist the temptation to leap precipitately to judgment. I think we should be reaching for something akin to what Keats called "negative capability." The more we're able to transform ourselves into the human equivalents of slates or pieces of paper, big and blank enough to receive whatever dramatists and performers wish to write on them, the better it seems to me. That way we might more often fulfill what a later nineteenth-century writer, Matthew Arnold, thought the most important duty of criticism: disinterestedly to relay, on those occasions we find it, "the best that is known and thought in the world."

Or maybe I'm just making a merit of a failure of personality, a want of fierce conviction, on my own part. It's one thing to be open-minded and quite another to be indiscriminately tolerant of other people's views, as I sometimes suspect I am. It's one thing to be a good listener and quite another to be pathologically receptive, as I also fear I may be. It's a family joke back in England that I tend to come home from the theater more influenced by what I've seen than anyone should properly be. After immersion in Beckett, I apparently trudge in, steeped in metaphysical gloom, and after an evening with Edward Bond's revolutionary socialism, I'm told I have an embattled, truculent air, as if already waving the red flag over the barricades. Pinter leaves me remote and monosyllabic, or so my wife says. Certainly I can't see one of his plays without feeling afterward that every word I utter is echoing up from some dark and dank well located deep inside me. "Thank you," I intone as some posttheater snack is passed along the table, and what I'm really doing is menacing those around me with strange and sinister revenges if the taste isn't quite right.

Actually all I'm probably talking about is a sensation many theatergoers, and indeed many readers, must have had. You know, you leave a play or put down a book, and suddenly everyone around, up to and including yourself, begins to sound like the characters you've been getting to know. There are some writers who can draw you into an invented world so distinctive and self-sufficient that you begin to feel it's at least as real as the one you normally inhabit, and it seems to me no terrible thing to submit to this process, even if you do happen to be a critic. Better, surely, to open yourself up to a new experience than to impose yourself upon it. Reviewers in both our countries have historically had a tendency to parade their personalities rather than illuminate whatever it was they were supposed to be reviewing. Is it humorless to complain that Dorothy Parker's celebrated quip that Katharine Hepburn "runs the gamut of emotions from A to B" tells one much more about Dorothy Parker than about what Katharine Hepburn was trying, successfully or unsuccessfully, to do onstage? Probably, but it's true all the same.

For better or worse, critics don't write one-liners like that anymore. But there are other, less entertaining ways of being critically overintrusive. One more common in my country than it appears to be in this is ideological. For instance, I've seen writers attacked, subtly or unsubtly, for the crime of being insufficiently aware of Marx or even for that of having lived before him. The careers of Jane Austen, Henry James, and many another since can be reduced to dust by the device of suggesting that their characters are spoiled and self-indulgent people who deserve only to be sent into the factories or paddy fields for reeducation. In fact, you might christen this the paddy-field school of criticism, appealing to its practitioners, like other approaches of different ideological hue, because it shrinks the intricate task of analysis and assessment to one of mechanical measurement.

Yet as I write, I feel a bit uneasy. For all my protestations of receptiveness, for all my claims to be open and boasts of being tolerant, I suspect I've been edging nearer the paddy-field school than I'd wish. I would prefer to believe that I've given the very slightest of those all-American plays about parents and children the chance to work their magic on me, but I would, I suppose, be deceiving myself and everyone else if I suggested that I went to see them without any predilections or beliefs or built-in criteria of judgment whatsoever. Strive as I may to wipe my personal slate clean each time I go to the theater, it has of necessity become furrowed and maybe warped by the million and one messages previously scrawled upon it. Certainly that seems to be what some of my readers feel about my mild animadversions on diaper drama.

Some; not all. I've had a good many letters concurring with my general complaint, not all of them accompanied by bulky scripts which I'm supposed to read in order to reassure myself there are still playwrights writing epic dramas about the history of Freemasonry in the United States and other such broadening subjects. The main respect in which these find my diagnosis inadequate is in the ascribing of blame. One correspondent rails articulately on about television: "That is where our younger and much touted playwrights get their ideas from, and that is the reason their world is small, their language pedestrian, their ideas infantile, and their themes all about self-discovery, self-fulfillment, and relationships." Another waxes somewhat paranoid about playreaders: "graduates of Ivy League colleges, the sons and daughters of the accountants for the producers, and not very accustomed to anything other than family dramas." But the most popular targets would seem to be the producers themselves, who are adjudged narrow and craven, and the critics, who are thought to be conservative and sentimental. "Rats" is the succinct summing-up of someone who keeps sending me long, handwritten, and obscurely sinister letters, signed only "A Playwright."

But others clearly think this phrase, "diaper drama," a bit sneering, a bit cheap, and maybe they're right. As Andre Bishop of Playwrights Horizons says in the latest edition of *Theater Times*, "It's just underestimating these writers, they're not idiots or immature little babies." He goes a bit far, I think, when he proceeds to call some of them "extremely sophisticated, mature artists," but he's quite right to point out that slogans are slogans; propaganda, not criticism. I don't want to be recalled over here as the Dr. Goebbels of theater reviewing, now do I? Still, the phrase has had its effect, insofar as *Theater Times* has been moved to devote its main article to discussing it. Very interesting reading this is to me, too, since nine leading off-Broadway figures are interviewed, and several do attempt to explain and even to justify a phenomenon I still find puzzling. Julia Miles of the American Place argues that American society is so complex, slippery, and confusing that it's difficult to define the problems, let alone an enemy robustly to attack. Hence, presumably, playwrights' preoccupation with personal relationships. "It's such an overwhelming time that we're living in," agrees Robyn Goodman of the Second Stage, "and survival is so tough, that the little problems are all you can really deal with." For her, it's no surprise that the younger playwrights should be especially concerned with the adjustment to adulthood, since they (like she) were brought up in the 1960's, "a very different generation than any generation before us."

Kyle Renick goes so far as to suggest that a playwright who presented fully adult characters would be telling a "lie" since it would imply that the baggage he'd picked up in childhood had been dealt with: "As long as I'm alive, what I feel about my mother and my father and my siblings is going to be with me and govern me. My childhood is the root of who I am." But the dramatists of other countries have also been children, and they don't seem so often to feel that their plays must actually be *about* growing up. Is that because they're less honest or more naïve? Or because their childhoods "govern" Americans more than other peoples? B. Rodney Marriott of Circle Rep argues that they do. Education and therefore dependence tends to go on longer in America; the break from the family comes later and is harder when it happens.

There's no sense of apology in any of these explanations, I should add. Quite the contrary. Several interviewees make the perfectly proper point that family plays can have size, depth, and moment. They can involve an "archetypal, universal journey," illustrate the "dark underside of the psyche, the id, the consciousness," and, of course, have strong social and political implications. Conversely, a dramatist who writes consciously about "issues" is all too likely to produce a dull, abstract play. "Both times I went to Europe I fell asleep at most of the theater because it was didactic and static and dead," declares Curt Dempster, director of the Ensemble Studio Theater. And I know what he means. The man snoring beside him was probably me. But I'd also have to say that I scarcely felt myself on any archetypal journey to any dark psychological underside at the two "family plays" I've so far seen at his playhouse.

Still, at least one of those interviewed in *Theater Times* takes my side or some of my side. What's the difference between certain classic plays, asks Don Marcus, cofounder and codirector of the Ark theater company, and those being written now that makes the latter so unsatisfactory? "The relationships that are being dealt with, and the point of view being taken about them, just don't seem to have the same kind of resonance. What I'm talking about is the problem of immaturity viewed from an immature artistic point of view. It's not far enough removed from the problem to have a really deep and satisfying view of the problem." And he adds, "There's a certain larger dimension to life that these people are not even looking at." He gives no examples and makes no exceptions, but it's not difficult to do so for him. Those "classic" dramatists would presumably be Odets, Miller, and O'Neill, a man who could raise family conflict into something akin to Greek tragedy at its more elemental. The main exception would surely be Sam Shepard, whose *Buried Child* and *The Curse of the Starving Class* are packed with yearnings and dreads and griefs that echo and reecho around the American psyche.

At least I see that more clearly than I did. And even if I've much more to learn about America, my time here has achieved one thing. It's given me a salutory new perspective on my own country. I went off to the Public Theater the other day to see Caryl Churchill's *Fen*, which I'd admired in London, and the impression it left on my internal slate was by no means the same as the one I'd received last year. It was the identical play, that's for sure, and in no way distorted by a sympathetic and able American cast, and yet it was a different one.

It's set in an East Anglian farming village, a semifeudal community most of whose members toil and moil in the fields, as their more obviously serflike great-grandparents did a hundred years ago and their great-grandchildren no doubt will a hundred years hence. It is difficult for these people to change their lives, and their response to that difficulty is to convince themselves that lives cannot be changed. "Nothing's perfect," they repeat to each other. "You expect too much." "What you after, happiness is it?" they sneer. "Bluebird of happiness?" Fatalism, like drink or Valium or born-again religion, is one of the ways they inure themselves to this bleak pastoral world. It allows them to find a kind of contentment in the impossibility of finding contentment.

It all must seem very strange to Americans, living as they do in a country where people don't believe, most of them, that history and geography have thrust rigid, inflexible roles upon them. In fact, the play began to seem pretty strange to me, as I watched it through the new transatlantic spectacles invisibly perched on my nose. Suddenly I realized I was seeing not just some exemplary rural habitat but a microcosm of Britain itself, and a pretty melancholy place the country began to look to me. It was profoundly classbound, lacking in spirit and belief in itself, passive and apathetic and helpless, stuck in a sort of rut of ages, and apparently unable to clamber out of it, whether with the help of Margaret Thatcher and the hard, tough right or of such as Caryl Churchill herself, whom I'd classify among the soft, compassionate left.

Indeed, Miss Churchill's views began to seem strange to me, too. The feeling running through the play is that as long as the economic system is what it is, these people will be what they are. If their land weren't owned by farmers, who are themselves owned by city trusts, which in turn are owned by multinational corporations, maybe that "bluebird of happiness" wouldn't be such a mythic creature. But (I found myself asking) did Adam fancy himself back in Eden because he happened to own the land that hunger forced him to break his back tilling? Would these characters find it so much less paralyzing to their minds and souls if they drudged from sun to sun in potato fields owned by themselves? Is man so absolutely the victim of his material circumstances, so entirely unable to shape his life through the exercise of will? Believing this as she does, Miss Churchill herself would seem to partake of the fatalism she spends the evening lamenting in others.

The play reinforced the opinion I tentatively broached here awhile ago: If some of the better contemporary American dramatists see the world too exclusively in personal terms, some of the better contemporary English ones see it too exclusively in social terms. It also left me feeling decidedly gloomy about my native land. It's odd I had to come 3,000 miles away from it to hear the full mournfulness of its music, but that seems to have become the case.

The German dramatist Peter Handke once wrote a play that substantially consisted of performers confronting the audience and denouncing it as a collection of wet blankets, double-dealers, powder puffs, mafiosi, blubber, cookie pushers, abortionists, hemorrhoid sufferers, and much else. There are times when we all feel that, or something like that, about our fellow creatures in the orchestra and balcony. There are even times when Handke's tirade seems timorously dilute. Is it just misanthropy on my part, or are such times becoming more frequent?

The inappropriate laughers have been especially active in my life of late. Some are to be found at what are supposed to be comedies, laughing longer, louder, and (for some abstruse biological reason) in a different key from everyone else. There was one such at *The Real Thing* when I last saw it, drawing such attention to herself that a great swath of the audience became distracted and more or less stopped laughing itself. It's difficult to be so much as modestly amused when someone is enjoying his or herself so much more than you are. Upstaging can occur in the auditorium as well as on the stage.

But there are laughers who don't require something to be amusing before they start ruining your evening. There's an old Punch cartoon showing the relief of the audience when the hero arrives to rescue the heroine from the villain—and just one spectator, a louche hood in a checked suit, leaning forward in lonely dismay. There was a man rather similarly out of emotional step with those around him at the performance I saw of *Fen*. The worse the sufferings of Caryl Churchill's oppressed serfs, the happier he seemed to be. Cheerful sniggers bubbled from his seat as an embittered wife threatened her stepdaughter, rising to delighted snorts when she made her drink boiling water. And great was his mirth when the protagonists actually began to contemplate suicide. You had the feeling that if only Miss Churchill had introduced something authentically tragic, like the entry of King Lear with his dead daughter, he'd have been rolling in the aisles.

Mark you, those of us who have seen gossamer Lears struggling to carry five-ton Cordelias wouldn't always be unsympathetic to *that*. In fact, I found myself somewhat on the side of the laughers the other night at the American Place, when I saw Maria Irene Fornes's *The Danube*. This was a surreal piece, using wan puppets and droll tape recordings in order to dramatize the slow death, spiritual, emotional, and literal, of most of the characters. "She coughs, I throw up, and you have diarrhea," slowly declaimed one such in a high, wailing monotone, the sort actors adopt when they think they're meant to be symbolic, and a group of young women, who had quietly snickered among themselves when similar solemnities were being exchanged by a half-naked man in goggles and a woman wrapped in a sheet, could contain themselves no longer. They spluttered with helpless laughter, provoking loud sshs and worse from severer citizens. "Be quiet, and you might get something out of it," snapped one. "What are *you* getting out of it?" a young woman managed to answer. "Me? Oh, I get an antinuclear-weapon *thing*" came back the reply. That was perfectly right, as air-raid sirens and the continuing disintegration of the cast proceeded rather heavily to prove, but I have to say I, too, found it hard to take Miss Fornes as earnestly as she evidently wished, even though she was one of the few dramatists I'd found in America tackling a subject of size and moment. There's a point at which the portentous begins to seem pretentious, too, and *The Danube* was well beyond it.

Not that laughter is the only form of disruption I've recently observed in the New York theater. Since most people get most of their entertainment piped or wafted into their houses, I suppose it's inevitable that they should regard the stage set as a three-dimensional television channel and the theater itself as their living room, but it's still irritating to hear them chattering around you. That's been happening a lot recently, most noisily and surprisingly when I saw *Awake and Sing!* at Circle in the Square, not the play or the playhouse one would have expected to attract an audience that cooed and clucked and burst into applause when an old man left the stage to hurl himself off the roof to his death. The explanation for their delight was, it seemed, that he was also taking a cute little dog for a walk, and the creature was happily wagging its tail as it exited. I thought only we British were as sentimental about animals as that.

But dyspeptic impression—which is probably what I'm offering here—is clearly no substitute for scientific observation. What kind of person characteristically visits Broadway? Come to that, who visits off-Broadway? The last big answer to the first of these questions was given by the League of New York Theaters and Producers in 1980, and its survey looked only at local audiences. That's quite a substantial distortion of the total picture, considering that tourists and other spectators from out of the area, estimated at one-third of the total audience some fifteen years ago, must surely account for a higher proportion of seats sold now. Most authoritative observers seem to agree that Broadway has been losing what the survey calls "traditionalist theatergoers," those most interested in "serious theater and not just entertainment," and a very high proportion of those in this category will clearly be local. Indeed, a particularly high proportion of local "traditionalists" must be among the nearly 2 million spectators that Broadway has lost since the year 1980. The league's audience profile is clearly dated as well as incomplete.

Still, four years is only four years, and much of what the survey says about local theatergoers must still be true. Some, indeed, is still very obviously true. In 1980, 85 percent of the Broadway audience was white, while 70 percent lived in Manhattan or the more upscale suburbs. Only 6 percent earned under $10,000 a year, compared with 23 percent of nontheatergoers, and 49 percent earned over $25,000 a year, compared with 10 percent. Of those surveyed, 26 percent proclaimed themselves "not employed," a category one would presume to include a large number of ladies of leisure, and 51 percent fell into the "professional" or "managerial" classes, compared with 21 percent among nontheatergoers. The survey divided its sample into "theater enthusiasts," "entertainment seek-

ers," and "dispassionate theatergoers," as well as "traditionalists," though the samplers themselves admit that these
categories are inadequate and could be misleading. Perhaps
all one can conclude from this is what six months as a New
York critic have made obvious enough to me: that the majority
of Broadway theatergoers are more interested in seeing a musical, or some other piece of light entertainment, than in serious plays.

What else? That "heavy theatergoers"—that is, those who
visit Broadway shows four or more times a year—amount to
32 percent of the sample but account for 70 percent of the
seats sold, and that despite this, birthdays, anniversaries, and
other "special occasions" play a major part in bringing people
to the theater. More than one out of three last visited Broadway for some such celebratory reason. And this is an important finding because here again we've a category of theatergoer
likely to resist serious or demanding drama. Neither "traditionalists" nor anyone else would wish to cap a fun day by
being scorched by Jean Genet or scathed by Eugene O'Neill.
The survey has, incidentally, nothing to say about a type of
theatergoer more likely to be looking for hit musicals and
comedies: the businessman entertaining clients or associates.
A producer I know tells me that this is an important source
of custom only in the first weeks of a show's run, when tickets
still seem glamorously hot. Nevertheless, business entertaining
must still account for a measurable proportion of total Broadway audiences, and it's a pity the survey didn't try to measure it.

Its major surprise is perhaps that the average age of audiences was lower in 1980 than in 1971, when more than half
were over thirty-five. A full 36 percent were between twenty-
five and thirty-four, and 19 percent were between eighteen
and twenty-four. Some 30 percent were categorized as "new
patrons," meaning they'd been visiting Broadway for only one
to five years. This could not wholly have been explained by

the postwar baby boom, which, as the survey concedes, was making itself statistically felt in 1980. It might, therefore, have been regarded as a hopeful sign, reason for optimism about Broadway's future. However, the survey confirmed what I've sometimes suspected, as I've sat and looked at the nattily attired yuppies enjoying this or that musical from the seats around me: The tastes of younger audiences were not significantly different from those of older ones.

I've also seen a survey of the audiences of some twenty-eight off-Broadway and off-off Broadway playhouses, prepared for the Association of Repertory Theaters (ART) a year later. Though my months in New York have long since rid me of any cliché image of such spectators—raggle-taggle young bohemians blinking myopically through knee-length hair as they shamble to their seats in disintegrating sandals—the results did seem in some respects more surprising than those gleaned on Broadway. Maybe one should have expected that these audiences would be, in the pollster's words, "extraordinarily well educated," with 65 percent of their number college graduates, a markedly higher figure than for Broadway, and 39 percent having pursued graduate studies. One might also have predicted that the majority would come from Manhattan and a full 74 percent from the five boroughs. But I for one wouldn't have guessed that 46 percent of those informally attired, youthful-looking people milling in those shabby foyers would be earning $25,000 or more, as well as be on average older than their Broadway counterparts. Of those visiting off-Broadway and off-off Broadway 51 percent are under thirty-four, a figure that falls to 45 percent in the larger playhouses. That compares with 55 percent on the Great White Way.

Many were clearly among the "traditionalists" lost to Broadway. Some 32 percent said they visited its theaters less often than they once did, and the great majority of those explained that this was because it was "too expensive." On the other hand, lower ticket prices, at the time an average of

just $5.93 per seat, were not a prime reason people brought
their custom to off- and off-off Broadway. They were more
interested in "seeing unusual plays" or "sampling innovative,
experimental theater" or "seeing a particular playwright" than
in saving money per se. That would seem to imply that a
cheaper, but not vastly cheaper, and more adventurous
Broadway could tempt back many who have decided that, as
41 percent of the ART sample actually said, the noncommer-
cial theater is currently to be preferred. And since off- and
off-off Broadway are attracting some 2 million spectators a
year, about a quarter of the number now visiting Broadway
itself, that "many" might indeed be many. There is clearly a
large hidden audience waiting for some such initiative as Joe
Papp's low-price, high-caliber National Theater on Broadway.

     And what about those audiences, or potential audiences,
that are still more deeply hidden than that, the ones that find
Broadway too expensive and tend to regard off-Broadway as
a club for the cognoscenti? Neither of these surveys has anything to say about them, but one can hardly be a foreigner
in New York without suspecting that they exist in largish numbers. My accent means people ask me questions in shops and
at lunch counters, in trains and cabs, and in the course of
the conversation they regularly reveal that first, they feel
proud to live at or near the center of the nation's theater;
secondly, that they themselves can't afford the price of those
tickets and wish they could. "I used to go when I was a boy,"
my local launderer typically told me. "I'll start going again
when I win the lottery."

     There's not a lot I can do when confronted with such re-
marks except shake my head, look sympathetic, and mumble
agreement, but Joe Papp, to his credit, has been publicly
addressing the question in the last few months. He believes
that more and more people are growing up without any awareness of the theater at all. As it becomes increasingly remote

to the parents, so it does to the children and, in turn, their children. He wants to see drama taught and performed in school hours and performed and visited out of school hours. He wants to see the public school system more "integrated" into the life of the city's theater. He wants to see subsidized tickets widely distributed in the high schools, and, if and when his National Theater on Broadway appears, he wants to give special morning and afternoon performances for students. Without such a broadening of audiences, that project can't, he thinks, succeed in the long run.

Indeed, he would appear to think that without some such broadening, the future of the New York theater itself must be in doubt. There'll be musicals for the wealthy on Broadway, there'll be more sophisticated entertainments for the cultural elite off-Broadway, and that, more or less, will be that. Ladies in mink coats will dominate one sector of the theater, bright collegiate types the other, and there'll be little or no place for any social or intellectual alternatives. That may sound like a pessimistic scenario, but it's one that seems to me substantially justified by both audience surveys and not contradicted by any event or trend since. Indeed, it squares with my own observation, limited though that obviously is and tetchy though it may have become. The inappropriate laughers will always, one hopes, be exceptional; the chatterboxes, an occasional and unrepresentative nuisance. But surely no impresario, on Broadway and sometimes even off it, can feel entirely comfortable when he looks out into the theater and sees who his audiences are and, more important, who they are not.

No sooner had I got home from seeing Dustin Hoffman in Arthur Miller's *Death of a Salesman* than I jumped into bed with Robert Lewis's entertaining memoirs, *Slings and Arrows*. These two events weren't altogether unconnected. Lewis's thesis, derived from many years of bitter experience and wry observation, is that American acting has yet completely to cast off the residual influence of the dread Method. Performers still have a tendency, among other limitations, to turn characters into their own selves, and sometimes their own mumbling, fidgeting and scratching selves, rather than their own selves into characters. But this has by no means been the overriding impression I've had of American acting since starting to write notices of it, and it seemed most emphatically contradicted by the careful, perhaps overcareful, characterization of Willy Loman that's been thoughtfully, perhaps overthoughtfully, pieced together by Hoffman.

I had gone off to the Broadhurst expecting a lot, and fearing I was risking disappointment by expecting altogether too much, both of the performer and of the play. To say I grew up thinking Arthur Miller *the* American dramatist may only expose my youthful ignorance of O'Neill and Williams, neither of whom has enjoyed the same popularity in Britain, thanks (I fear) to our national mistrust of big, dangerous emotion, our tendency to cry "Melodrama!" when confronted with anything or anyone raw and bleeding. But recent revivals of *All My Sons* and *The Crucible* in London left me convinced that my early enthusiasm hadn't been so wrong. Miller wasn't just the puritan intellectual, the earnest, dogged rerun of Ibsen some of his latter-day detractors have claimed; he brought care and love and dramatic power to subjects that seem never to date. Who else has written so eloquently of the difficulty, the importance, the sheer heroism of maintaining personal integrity, and a sense of responsibility for others, in a bad, bad world?

Death of a Salesman could, I suppose, be seen as a variation on the same rough theme, being about someone who sacrifices everything, including his integrity, to the giddy promises of that world and ends up with ashes—indeed, *as* ashes. But that's a very abstract way of describing a play which, when it was performed at our National Theater a few years ago, struck me as alive, abundantly alive, indeed so alive as finally and unalterably to reestablish Miller as a prominent feature on my mental and emotional map. Nor was I alone in my regard for that revival. Miller himself hugely liked the unusually peppy, punchy performance Warren Mitchell gave as salesman Loman. He also liked the production, which had been staged by an American long resident in Britain, Michael Rudman. And all this added to my expectations last night. Rudman had been imported to redirect the play at the Broadhurst, and rumor said that Hoffman was marking his long-overdue return to the stage by giving a pretty peppy, punchy performance, too.

And so it turned out. When I first saw him, beneath a great looming fretwork of windows and fire escapes, his Loman did admittedly look like a small, dumpy penguin coming home after a losing encounter with whatever fish he'd hoped to eat for dinner. He half trudged, half waddled into the dowdily furnished house that sketchily filled the lower half of the stage, his shoulders sagging with the weight of a sample case so huge you'd suppose he'd been selling tree trunks. But that impression of exhaustion and defeat was quickly and consciously undermined.

The dominant note of Hoffman's performance is, indeed, resilience in adversity. Even in his declining years this Loman cackles loudly and often and retains a bodily bravado, too. He claps his hands for emphasis; he amiably tweaks his wife's breast on the line "You're my foundation and support"; he does a little dance with her and exuberantly brandishes his rump in her direction before making an exit. If one of the signs of the exceptional actor is to suggest what was as well as to show what is, then Hoffman is extraordinary indeed. You can see, in this somewhat run-down replica, the not unsuccessful hustler his Willy was years ago: swapping risqué jokes with the buyers; flirting with the secretaries and occasionally even seducing them; talking more than enough to

make a sale and getting something of a reputation as a loudmouth in the process.

Yet that's not enough, as Hoffman knows and shows. Willy
is slipping, sliding, plummeting out of his American dream
into the American trash can and, self-deceiver though he always was, is dimly aware of his fall. So Hoffman's smiles
become more forced, the laughter increasingly hollow, the
slaps of the palms testier. Even the slick silver hair above his
trim suit—this Willy is walking testimony to the value he
places on appearance and appearances—seems to lose a little
of its shine. Suddenly he's wildly blustering at his uncaring
boss and hammering at his desk, or tearfully clutching and
pummeling at an old friend, or down on all fours, thumping
the floor in an ecstasy of frustration and impotent resentment.

Something may be missing. This Willy seems rather less of
the doomed drudge, rather more of the cocky vulgarian, than
he should be. After all, he's thinking of killing himself, and
may already have tried to do so. Hoffman is faithful enough
to the surface demands of the script when, for instance, he
radiates chirpy enthusiasm at the thought of hundreds of
mourners thronging around his grave. But where's the shiver
in the spine? Where's so much as a touch of the horror that
must sometimes have iced up even a heart so adept at convincing itself that black is white and white gold? When Hoffman's Willy makes his last, fateful exit, it's not with the "gasp
of fear" that one of Miller's stage directions requires but
actually with a great smile on the lips, a skip and bounce of
the feet, another feisty clap of the hands. His "accidental"
death by car crash will, he thinks, bring his son Biff $20,000
in insurance money, enough to transform the young man's
flagging fortunes. Hence his glee as he scampers out, salesman
to the last, to clinch his last big deal.

It's bold, very bold of Hoffman to present suicide, the ul-
itimate manifestation of despair, as an act of optimism, but

lacking any compensating or balancing hint of dread or sorrow, he doesn't quite bring it off. It seems an adventurous but somewhat abstract idea, brilliantly embodied, rather than the expression of nature. In other words, Hoffman proves himself an exception to Robert Lewis's generalizations about American acting by being too thoughtful, too external, too concerned with making clever and revealing points about a character clearly very different from himself. Yet let me not suggest that because his performance at times lacks feeling, or the right kind of feeling, this commodity is altogether lacking throughout. That would ignore what is the most striking encounter of the evening, the center of Hoffman's performance and, perhaps, of Rudman's generally excellent production.

That's when a sobbing Biff and a stunned Willy, alienated from each other for so long and deeply at odds still, manage a stricken, fumbling, but possibly also forgiving embrace. Part of the reason for the moment's impact is John Malkovich's performance as the hapless son. Up to then he'd seemed a somewhat wan and flimsy presence, with a habit of flapping his left hand like a dying flatfish, something that made me itch to jump on stage and pour superglue between his palm and the table; but actually he was biding his time, waiting to show us that inside that willowy frame there was an extraordinary intensity of devotion. And part of the reason was Hoffman's response to that revelation. He cradled Malkovich for longer than one would have dreamed possible, on his face the kind of disbelieving tenderness you expect from fathers when they pick up their newborn children for the first time; he blushed, gulped, inarticulately gurgled in total surrender to what was, one realized, the primary relationship of his life.

Whether or not it justified that somewhat strange ending, it was a remarkable moment in itself, touching and more than touching. I could hear a sniffing around me. In fact, I could hear a sniffing *from* me. It was one of those occasions when the word "magic" wasn't simply a stage-struck cliché but a theatrical truth, there to be felt and remembered. In fact, it left me wondering if Hoffman was not merely an answer to Lewis's animadversions but a living example of that supposedly extinct beast, the complete American actor. He could think and feel at the same time, reconciling the inner and the outer with an absolute plausibility. The trouble was that he wasn't quite that complete throughout the evening.

Still, his performance successfully reminds one how strong and enduring the play itself is. It belongs, and belongs very emphatically in this production, to an all-too-familiar genre since it shows a parent and an overage child wrangling their way to a reconciliation scene. But of course, it's also, and quite emphatically enough in this production, a social critique not a lot less topical for having been penned nearly forty years ago. Indeed, the two are as inextricably interlocked as in Odets's *Awake and Sing!* The reason neither Biff nor his brother Happy has fulfilled Willy's hopes, and Willy himself is in mental and emotional disarray, is that those hopes were absurd as well as tawdry. Their father has allowed himself to be sucked and suckered into a world where reality and realism always take second, third, fourth place to appearance, imaginative expectation, and muddled promises of glory effortlessly achieved. Big ads guarantee a good refrigerator, "personality" success in business, smiles and backslapping words a lasting friendship, cheating a college career, lies and more lies a sound future. That's what Willy believes; that's what he's taught his boys. But daily life is harsh in what he persists in calling "the greatest country in the world," and unsurprisingly, everything breaks down, from those seductive but fragile fantasies to the family itself.

Not that Miller is as radical a social critic as he was originally thought. He'd have us compare Willy, with his huckster ethic, to his long-suffering neighbor Charley, who builds up a business, brings up a son who becomes a high-flying lawyer, and offers the salesman himself a job, all with equal lack of fuss and pretension. If the play has some sharp things to say about American dreams and American dreamers, regarding both as destructive, it takes an approving and rather conservative view of proved achievement within the existing system. Decent, commonsensical, hardworking people can score success, and that success can have substance and merit respect.

These all are thoughts worth airing and hearing, but they don't, of course, finally explain the play's lasting appeal. For that, we must return from macrocosm to microcosm, to the character of Willy himself, with its still-pertinent confusions. His mind may be in thrall to glitter and false gods; his heart is not. What he fundamentally values and what gives him value, in both cases without his really knowing it, is his capacity for love. His trouble, indeed his tragedy, is that his mind mediates what his heart feels. No sooner is he reconciled with Biff than he launches back into the old, murderous make-believe, rapturously announcing, "That boy is going to be magnificent." Even at the play's end and his own, the vainglorious ambitions he's spun from the all-American air are still ruinously at work, misdirecting and misusing his love for his son.

That brings me back to Hoffman because Hoffman brings so much of the play successfully together. The more I think about his performance, the more I find myself thinking of it. Maybe that ending didn't quite work. Maybe you can sometimes see the mental nuts and bolts and rivets of his interpretation. Yet he shows us Willy's energetic wrongheadedness, and more important, he shows us Willy's essential warmheartedness. Indeed, he shows us both at the same time, a choking, hiccuping stammer in the voice revealing his real feelings even when he seems most enslaved to his fantasies. What he means, as he babbles ludicrously on about Biff's imagined "greatness," is that he actually loves him. No ordinary actor could make us see that contradiction and feel its pathos, too.

Certainly this is the most ambitious performance I've seen in my time in New York, but then there haven't been many other opportunities for performers of comparable ambition. I keep feeling I should be drawing some nice, sweeping conclusions about the state of American acting in this journal, and I keep failing to do so, for reasons that aren't altogether my fault. How, for instance, can I endorse or dispute Robert Lewis's doubts and complaints when I've yet to see any very violent demands made on any performer's range and versatility? Come to think of it, how can performers acquire range and versatility unless such demands are from time to time made upon them? The New York theater, offering (as it mainly does) small plays with small characters, doesn't offer much encouragement for an actor or actress who wishes to prove Lewis wrong.

His accusations have to be taken seriously, considering his record as a Group Theater performer, cofounder of the Actors' Studio, and director and teacher of distinction. American actors, he thinks, are still insufficiently prepared to play parts markedly different from themselves. Too many still belong to the "onanistic school of emotion." That is, they play their own feelings, not those of their characters. And too few take account of the overriding demands of the situation and scene. Nor do American performers always see style as something organically related to content, indeed derived from it. They regard both speech and style as something to be tacked onto emotional truth, not fused with it.

I have to say this hasn't been my impression during my time here. Al Pacino's Teach in *American Buffalo* did, it's true, bring to my mind the advice Peter Ustinov once gave a young Method actor: "Don't just do something, stand there." Pacino's was an exorbitantly fussy performance but not self-indulgent in quite the way Lewis describes. Nor were the other actors and actresses that I've disliked objectionable for those reasons. In fact, I realize that my complaints about the New York theater have little to do with performers per se, much more with the material they're playing and the system within which they're working. In any case, I've seen rather a lot of performances that have pleased me, some of which I've already celebrated in this journal, some of which I haven't, some by players I knew from screen or stage, and some not.

The pleasure of an assignment like mine is that it allows me to discover performers who, given Equity's heavy and forbidding hand, would be highly unlikely to be seen on the stage in Britain. For instance, a scrawny-looking actor called Thomas G. Waites turned up in both of New York's recent Odets revivals, making a strong impression first as a venomous and vulnerable young hood in *Paradise Lost*, then as the oppressed hero of *Awake and Sing!*, all frustration, tension, and pug-faced bewilderment. And I was much taken by one Dianne Wiest's performance of a snubbed and rejected wife in the Public Theater's restaging of Lanford Wilson's *Serenading Louie* a week or two later. I can still see her smiling, squinting, desperately burbling out a helter-skelter affection she knew would madden her husband yet was powerless to curb. And her performance lost none of its edginess and emotional truth even when the audience unexpectedly laughed and laughed at one of her wrier lines, and she had to sit and sit and sit, waiting for the seemingly interminable hilarity to end.

What conclusions can I tentatively draw from this and the other evidence I've witnessed? That there seem to be plenty of performers capable of inhabiting the characters they're playing, and inhabiting them pretty thoroughly, from heart and stomach to fidgety feet and gesticulating fingers. That plenty can convince you that their smallest gestures are the outer and visible expression of inner and invisible feeling and, therefore, that content and style are one. That American acting still retains the warmth, the juice, the gumption for which

it's long been admired—witness the unknown Calvin Levels
as the luckless student in *Open Admissions*, achieving an intensity of disappointed rage that few, if any, British actors
could match—but that it is more adept with telling detail than
is sometimes acknowledged. Witness the picture of exhaustion
in defeat sensitively drawn by Robert Prosky in *Glengarry*.
Or Pamela Reed, all restlessness and adenoidal ennui as the
forgivably wicked stepmother in *Fen*. Or, of course, Hoffman's Loman. It would be easy to expand the list.

What else? That maybe I've been mistaken to see the movies
and television solely as satanic temptations, luring talent into
the hell of Hollywood and burning it to ashes. There are some
players who aren't merely surviving the pit but emerging seemingly intact, to give performances of quality in the theater.
Everyone has been noting a marked increase in the number
who have made their names on the screen yet are prepared
to commute between that and the stage, to the benefit of their
art, if not of their bank accounts. Hoffman is again the obvious
example. Al Pacino would be another. Glenn Close, marvelous
in *The Big Chill*, is proving no less marvelous in *The Real
Thing*. Amy Irving and Mandy Patinkin are both currently
to be seen in the movie *Yentl*, yet here's the one in *Heartbreak
House* and the other due soon a few streets south, in the new
Sondheim musical *Sunday in the Park with George*.

Nor is Broadway alone benefiting. Anthony Hopkins, Jane
Alexander, and Marsha Mason all were excellent in Harold
Pinter's *Old Times* at the Roundabout in January. The winter
also brought Elizabeth McGovern to the Lambs in *Painting
Churches* and the Quaid brothers, Randy and Dennis, to the
Cherry Lane in Sam Shepard's *True West*. Kevin Kline will
probably be in Central Park this summer, performing Henry
V in the New York Shakespeare Festival. There'll never be
quite the freedom of movement you get in Britain, where
geography permits an actor appearing at the National Theater
to take part in a television play or even a feature film on the

very same day or at least in the same week. But the mental and emotional distance between Hollywood and New York is less than it was, and lessening.

Mark you, I'm talking of the cream of the profession, the sort everyone notices when it floats back East, because it's up there on the top. There must still be many more who get sucked westward, sink into the television and movie scene, and get no chance to evolve into the first-class stage performers they might have been. When I visited his theater in Cambridge the other day, Robert Brustein told me of a young man he thought quite exceptionally promising. He refused to stay in regional rep, feeling the old pressure to prove himself in New York. But the opportunities didn't come, so off he went to California, where he remains, lucky no doubt to be making a good living from TV serials but scarcely the bravura performer of Chekhov, Pirandello, Genet, et al. he looked like becoming. "Maybe he'll be back," said Brustein, "but . . ." He shrugged a bit hopelessly, knowing from bitter personal experience there's much about America, economically and psychologically, that's still ruinous to tomorrow's potential stage talent.

Still, let's not be too glum. There are now conservatories and university drama schools, like the one Brustein himself used to run at Yale, feeding the legitimate theater with performers whom some claim to be less warm, less passionate, more like journeymen than they once were, but who most agree to be far more versatile. There are now regional reps, like Brustein's own, helping hone their skills. There's the seeming shift of attitude I've mentioned, the new enthusiasm for combining a career on the screen with at least an occasional one on the stage. Yet one has to repeat the question. How can one gauge the quality of American acting, or be altogether optimistic about its future, when it's not being fully challenged in the place where it should still be achieving its most notable triumphs, the theatrical capital of America, New York itself? How can I compare it sensibly with performers in my own country? How argue, for instance, that the best of the Americans still make the best of the British look a bit cerebral, a bit too "thinky," while the best of the British no longer make the best of the Americans seem a bit slapdash when they're asked to deal with mannered language or elaborate style? I've seen inklings of this, but how can I confidently conclude it when virtually every play on offer here is modern and naturalistic?

Looking around the city right now, you'd never dream that the theater evolved on a Greek hillside a full 2,500 years ago. You'd think its history barely went back 50 years. You'd think that almost every dramatist was American or British, and you'd think none had ever written in anything save prose, and in most cases a pretty flat and ordinary prose. You'd think, if you thought of them at all, that the purpose of Sophocles, Shakespeare, Molière, even Ibsen was to be the subject of essays and lectures and theses in schools and universities, not to be brought to life on the stage. That's disappointing for audiences. It's positively damaging to performers.

April

I'm told that the producer Alex Cohen has toilet paper bearing the distinguished visage of my fellow critic John Simon, with whom he's long been feuding. I think I've some way to go before I'm similarly honored, but it would appear I've made a few small strides toward that no doubt magnificent bathroom. I spoke to Cohen the other day, and he wasn't a very happy man. In fact, he informed me that it was my fault that *Carmen*, which he's been presenting at the Vivian Beaumont, was soon to close. My sin, it seemed, was one of omission rather than commission. The Sunday *Times* had published a rather hostile piece about Brook's production by our music critic Donal Henahan; that was followed by an article on the controversy stirred by so unconventional a production, and it was decreed that it was a little late for me to publish yet another review three weeks after opening night. Myself, I was sorry about this since I'd have enjoyed celebrating the show's adventurous excellences, but there it was. I gently suggested to the stricken Cohen that I didn't think my review would have made that much difference. Anyway, wasn't five or six months a pretty good run for such a project? Indeed, didn't it prove an important point: that there is, all appearances to the contrary, an audience prepared to pay steepish prices for something not the least glitzy or soft or bland?

Nevertheless, Cohen and his cohorts have attempted to galvanize business by giving some performances of *Carmen* in English, so I went along to see it again, hoping I could somehow squeeze a piece out of it, even at this late stage. Sadly I found myself less entranced than at any of the three times I'd seen it last fall. Why? So much was still so striking. When that old, bent peasant woman scuttled on and began lighting miniature fires around the pillows and blankets representing the gypsy encampment where José and Carmen were to find a momentary happiness, I once again felt a frisson somewhere on the back of the neck, at a strangely magical piece of atmosphere achieved with stunning simplicity. And James Hoback turned out to be one of the most arresting of the Don Josés, partly because he was superficially one of the less prepossessing: sweaty, plump, maybe even a little piggy of mien. The attentions of Emily Golden's Carmen had clearly hit him the harder for being unaccustomed and unexpected; he wasn't merely obsessed but the pitiable victim of a kind of forlorn monomania.

Yet some of the effects seemed cruder, coarser than I remember them. Lillas Pastia, then as now charged with comic relief, had become openly self-indulgent. He started by speaking French, then jokingly reverted to English and proceeded to make a meal of what had previously been modest nibbles at the audience. He made us all repeat the word "rendezvous," then whipped a pretty girl out of the front row and bundled her across the stage and through a door together with Carmen and Lieutenant Zuniga, who himself had been undressing with a lubriciousness that had graduated from the carefully comic to the openly farcical. It gave the impression that everyone was trying hard to make an overastringent medicine easier to swallow. So, of course, did the use of English.

It seems illogical to complain of this since Sheldon Harnick's translation was clearly as conscientious as it was unpretentious. But I couldn't help thinking that if something sounds less silly sung than spoken, it sounds less silly still if it's sung in a foreign language, even one with which you've some passing acquaintance. "Carmen, I still adore you," sang Don José.

"Carmen, I love you more than ever." "José, what good is this?" she replied. "Your words are pointless now." Somehow it seemed to me more mysterious, more sensual in the original French. Translated, the language of love bustled energetically enough across the earth but simply refused to take wing.

Was that the problem? Or the cast, or the audience, or a simple lack of responsiveness in myself? Whatever the answer, the question dramatizes some of the perennial difficulties of theater criticism. One must allow for so much. There are evenings when audience and performers inexplicably resist each other, like new acquaintances who just can't hit it off, despite cordial introductions and good intentions. There are evenings when you yourself, without even knowing it, simply aren't in a receptive mood. Your mind may be on the business in hand, and the rest of yourself in a perfectly good humor, as I felt I was at *Carmen*. You may think yourself alert and open and simply not be, at any rate that evening. Hard luck on the performers, but unavoidable as long as it remains impossible to program a computer to review their efforts.

Audiences and critics can, of course, have off nights at the cinema, too, but there it scarcely matters so much. The performers don't sag in response or, worse, begin to "push" at their acting in a desperate and invariably counterproductive attempt to win back their spectators' allegiance. They remain impervious to your bad moods and oblivious of your good ones. A critic who feels less than confident of either his enthusiasm or distaste can pay a second visit and be sure of seeing the identical body language, the identical climaxes, the identical everything. What's exhilarating about the theater is that it shifts, changes, dives, soars, and from the stance of the reviewer, that's precisely what's frustrating about it, too. When you recommend a play to your readers, you know that they themselves will see something at least slightly different. It may be better, perhaps because the strains of the press night are over; it may be worse, perhaps because relaxation

has transformed itself into automatic acting; it can never, ever
be quite the same.

How to allow for this as a critic? That's hard to answer.
But at least one can try to distinguish one's own feelings from
those of the audience, struggle to differentiate the production
from the play. The first of these aims is the easier to fulfill,
though not always as easy as it might seem and perhaps not
entirely desirable either. Can one fully resist the emotional
atmosphere gathering around one? *Should* one do so, when
the great strength of the theater is that it's a communal activity, which links spectator and performer in what one hopes
are ever-accelerating circles of shared joy? The critic's duty
is perhaps to be part, yet apart; to surrender, yet hold back;
to ensure that there's at least some tiny, guarded bit of himself
watching himself in his more unguarded moments. And this
seems doubly necessary in New York, where press performances commonly seem packed with people behaving as if they've
been simultaneously confronted with Danny Kaye at his most
hilarious and the spaceship in *Close Encounters*. There was
a man near me at the calamitous *Marilyn* who kept leaping
to his feet, gurgling, whooping, cheering, clapping his hands
over his head, and generally giving the impression of someone
likely either to die of joy or to be launched by it into orbit—
or, I suppose, both at once. As far as I was concerned, all
that display achieved was to double my already intense misery
and make me rethink my pious intention, announced rather
earlier in this journal, to record the reactions of the audience
when they were significantly different from my own. But enthusiasm can, let's agree, take more guileful and insidious
forms and prove more catching than that.

All the same, the tougher task is assessing the extent to
which the director and his cast are doing justice to the play.
This is, of course, less of a problem when you're already
familiar with the text and considerably less so when you're
familiar with that text in performance. Confronted with a

revival of *Hamlet* or *Lear*, you can usually see what's being emphasized and what not, the biases of interpretation, the slant of the production, and so on. If you've seen it well performed before, you can more readily spot the lapses, the omissions, the inadequacies now. In fact, I'd only to compare some aspects of *Carmen* as it was a few months ago with some aspects of it now—that Pastia, that Zuniga—to see where and how it could be better.

But imagine you're seeing *Hamlet* or *Lear* or indeed *Carmen* for the first time. Imagine yourself a critic at its premiere. There you sit, scratching and mumbling and leafing through your playbill and doing all those other things reviewers do before a performance starts, and suddenly the lights go down, the curtain rises, and there is this difficult, fascinating new work being unfurled before your eyes. You'd assuredly find yourself throwing so much of your critical acumen into interpreting the piece's intricacies that unless the oddities or inadequacies of performance were very obvious, you'd be inclined to take its production for granted. You'd be likely to ascribe quirks of interpretation to the text. You'd be likely to attribute to the author what you should be attributing to the director and his performers. And if that would have been the case with a *Hamlet* or a *Lear*, must it not also be so with work that comes fresh to our stages today? If *Hamlet* and *Lear* can be played in a hundred, a thousand different ways, shouldn't we recognize that a new play, too, is not its production?

I'd go so far as to suggest that doing so is as hard a challenge as criticism presents, and I'd certainly accuse myself of having flunked it on occasions. As a cub critic in the sixties I launched pretty venomously into Joe Orton's *Loot*, mistaking the first disastrous production for a farce that subsequent revivals have proved a classic of mischievous subversion. Though I always admired *The Real Thing*, I didn't realize the amount of feeling that could be found in the main part until I saw Jeremy Irons take it over here. I sometimes wonder if the reason that O'Neill is widely regarded as an overblown, melodramatic playwright in Britain is that British performers have rarely been able to achieve the intensity he demands and so have left his work looking hollower than it is.

But how, having distinguished the play from its production and the reactions of its audience, does one proceed to anatomize it in practice? That's a question I've been half raising, then evading throughout this journal, and it's one I'm not at all sure I can answer. I've often asked actors to analyze their craft, and some have given helpful insights in response. To take a random example, I recall Michael Caine saying that if he were asked to produce a dark or melancholy emotion, he would concentrate on the death of his much-loved father, a working-class man who never lived to see his son's success. But quite frequently they shrug and profess ignorance, sometimes telling you that if they allowed themselves to become too self-aware, they might not be able to perform anymore. Well, perhaps critics, too, should remember the story of the centipede that, having analyzed the way it walked, was never able to do anything as elaborate as walk again. And yet isn't that to make a mystique of what many would regard, and perhaps rightly, as a pretty lowly trade?

Again and again I've emphasized the need for reviewers to be open, receptive, even passive, and so perhaps have given the impression they were more vegetable than animal: plants bending to whatever creative wind hits them; leaves rustling in response to the artistic breeze. Though that seems to me a good corrective to the widely held notion that critics are piranhas or carrion crows or slavering hyenas, there is, of course, something disingenuous in so unqualified a claim. What's wanted is an active passivity, a busy and even strenuous openness. Imagine, if you can, being simultaneously run down by a car and explaining the complexities of its inner machinery. Criticism can be a punishing business, not to say hard work.

To say that one's first duty is to discern a playwright's aims

and intentions is, of course, to beg about as big a question as
one could. Who knows what Shakespeare was "trying to do"
when he wrote *Lear?* If you'd asked him, he'd very likely have
talked of writing a good part for Richard Burbage, fulfilling
his obligations to his company, or making a Jacobean buck
or two for himself. Pressed, he might have added something
about moving his audiences, but he would, I suspect, never
have claimed to be "exploring the moral nature of the universe" or some such. Some playwrights are, it's true, more
aware of their intentions than others. Bernard Shaw, with his
view that "all great art is didactic," would certainly fall into
that category. So would Brecht, and maybe even Ibsen, yet
you have only to think of *Mother Courage* or *The Master
Builder* to realize that their characters can acquire lives of
their own, outside their control, beyond conscious planning
and intended meaning. Indeed, it's tempting to say that the
better the playwright, the less deliberate his aims and the
more his reliance on instinct will be. Think of Chekhov, or
of Harold Pinter or Sam Shepard today. To see their better
plays as moral capsules of some sort, there to embody this
idea or that theme, is an obvious absurdity. Not that this has
stopped commentator after commentator from trying so to
shrink and shrivel them.

It's safer, if one wants "meaning" from a play, to look for
its moral thrust, its moral tenor, something of which some
writers will be more conscious than others. David Mamet's
comments on business, which I quoted a few months back,
certainly help one understand *American Buffalo*, as do many
dramatists' comments on their own work, but they aren't sufficient to sum up the play as a whole, as (again) many dramatists' comments aren't. Such remarks should be part of the
reckoning but scarcely regarded as definitive. Similarly, what
we know of a writer's life can help understanding, but only
in the case of very thin, very obviously autobiographical works
can it render understanding complete. We know that the el-

derly Ibsen was a very susceptible old gentleman and that
female moth after female moth danced around his guttering
flame, as Hilda does around that of Solness in *The Master
Builder*, but to equate her too precisely with any of them
would be dreadfully literal-minded. Nothing in the playwright's life can finally account for the richness of his later
art.

Still, what we know of and from a dramatist may not always
be tantamount to disinformation. I've been mugging up on
A. R. Gurney, Jr., for instance, in preparation for what has
turned out to be his rather disappointing updating of Henry
James's *The Aspern Papers*, *The Golden Age*. He's a New
Englander, bred of Brahmin stock, and he's given revealing
interviews in his time. "What seems to obsess me," he once
said, "is the contrast between the world and the values I was
immersed in when I was young, and the nature of the contemporary world. The kind of protected, genteel, in many
ways warm, civilized and fundamentally innocent world in
which I was nurtured didn't seem in any way to prepare me
for the later 20th century. I tend," he went on, "to write
about people who are operating under the old assumptions,
but are confronting an entirely different system of values."
That surely increases, rather than impedes, appreciation of
Gurney's *Children*, his *The Middle Ages*, and perhaps especially his *Dining Room*, that affectionate yet critical elegy to
the finger bowl classes. It helps explain why it's probably
correct to see him as the bard of gentlemanly decay or at least
a sort of dramatic anthropologist, wryly chronicling WASP
culture in its embattled decline.

A writer's published interviews and essays, his background
and history, the nature of his previous work—they all may
provide hints, clues, aids to understanding. But a sharp and
discriminating ear and eye are clearly what a reviewer mainly
requires as he goes about the business of discerning shape,
pattern, and, maybe, significance. The questions one is asking

oneself are not always conscious, but they might, I suppose, include the following.

Why, how, does the play at issue succeed in holding our attention? In what is the playwright particularly interesting us? What's the source of his piece's tension, if it has any? Does that tension derive from conflict, and if so, what sort? If you happen to be reviewing Agatha Christie's *Mousetrap* or some other whodunit, the answers to those questions are painfully simple. The interest is in the identity of a murderer, and tension lies in waiting for his unmasking, and the conflict, insofar as there is any, is between his efforts to escape detection and others' attempts to detect him. But imagine coming innocent to *Hamlet*. The original question—When will the prince kill his uncle?—soon becomes a rather deeper one: Why isn't the prince killing his uncle? What appears at first to be the conflict, that between a wary usurper and his vengeful nephew, evolves into something much subtler. Hamlet the man of action is up against Hamlet's disbelief in action, Hamlet's conscience, Hamlet's scruples, Hamlet's intellectual agonizings, Hamlet's accidie, or whatever you may call it. An outer conflict becomes an internal one of complexity and moment: will versus a fascinating tangle of thought and feeling. The play's dramatic structure begins to reveal what, without too much simplification, one might call its meaning.

On go the critical questions. Which character or characters seem most important, and what aspects of them and their predicament are especially emphasized? Can we sense what the writer thinks, and thinks he feels, about them? Can we sense what he really feels about them? About them as individuals, about them as members of society, about that society, and, perhaps, about the cosmos beyond? Are we being led by the accumulating evidence to see any or all of these ingredients in some particular way, and if so, what way, how and why? Is there perhaps something in the very shape of the fable—successes, disasters—that helps us understand the nature and

significance of the people presented us? In the denouement?
In the tone or mood? In what the seemingly more sympathetic
and more unsympathetic characters say and don't say about
each other? What questions, particular and general, do we
find ourselves asking in response to each or all of these characters and their situation, and what answers do we begin to
give? How representative is that situation, and what, if anything, does it tell us about our own?

That sort of general approach wouldn't be unhelpful if you
were confronted with, say, Ibsen's *A Doll's House*. Before long
we can hardly avoid seeing the emphasis on Nora's child-
ishness, as on Torvald's desire to keep her childish and therefore in subjection. Before much longer we can see that the
husband's self-righteous attitudes are those of his society, his
wife's predicament that of many women in that society, and
it is increasingly clear what Ibsen thinks of each. The big
climax, when Torvald wildly attacks Nora for an act of devotion that's technically criminal, reveals the hollowness likely
to be found at the center of that sort of marriage. The denouement, when Nora leaves Torvald, is an act of exemplary
protest against such marriages and maybe more than that.
The plot, the pattern, the shape of the play leave you asking
still-unsettling questions about the place of women in marriage
and in society more generally.

Of course, this is to make the complex business of analysis
sound like a simple matter of applied mechanics. It can never
quite be that. For one thing, the critic's own experience, his
sense of right and wrong, of what matters and what doesn't
must play at least a minimal part in the process. He can't see
the moral inadequacy of a Torvald unless he has some moral
criteria of his own and uses them to assess him. For another,
not many good plays are as clear in their thrust and tenor as
Doll's House. Try directing the questions I've suggested at
Sam Shepard's better work, and you'll probably get somewhere; but much will still elude you. For yet another thing,

those questions tell you little or nothing about the quality, dramatic or anything else, of the play you're attempting to unravel.

That, of course, involves you in many more questions, increasingly personal in character. How true to life are these characters, their predicament, their world, and if they don't seem especially true to life, what's the reason? There's no point blaming a comedy of manners or a classical French tragedy for failing to be conventionally realistic. Better, perhaps, to ask how vivid and vital the human situation is. Does it touch your heart, stomach, and other organs of feeling, and if so, how and how much? Does whatever it leaves you thinking really matter? How original, how provocative, how challenging is this piece; how searching and profound, how near to the central concerns of us in the audience? How does it relate to the writer's previous work? To that of his contemporaries? To that of the culture as a whole? Does it add to the sum of human joy and enlightenment, or not?

Yet the more the questions I suggest—and there are others where they came from—the more I'm aware I must sound like some insanely zealous diagnostician, applying test after test after test to the patient in his care and all too probably still not coming up with an answer that defines the nature and assesses the health of every sinew and bond, let alone the spirit within. After all my critical toing and froing, I'm not even sure why I admired *Carmen* so much a few months ago and resist it now. It was Rainer Maria Rilke, I think, who said that works of art were "of an infinite loneliness and with nothing so little to be reached as with criticism." I don't like that "so little." I don't like or accept that "nothing." But "loneliness"—well, yes. There, in any work of art, is a secret something, not earth or fire or air or water, which no amount of skilled groping and eager grabbing can ever quite get into the critic's lab, onto his dissecting table and under his knife.

· · ·

The conventional wisdom is that violence is as American as apple pie but found only rather occasionally on the British national menu. This can no doubt be substantiated by the statistics for muggings and other such crimes. Indeed, the murder rate in the United Kingdom as a whole, even counting Ulster, is regularly lower than that for certain American cities. On the other hand, all three of my children have at one time or another been physically assaulted in London, and I myself have sensed, smelled, and even experienced a violence of a rather less direct and obvious kind. More than once, for instance, the car I've been overtaking has deliberately accelerated, in apparent hopes of ensuring collision between myself and the oncoming traffic. Indeed, you only have to look at British driving to see that we're a pretty violent people, but perhaps also a people who prefer to express our violence slyly, not straight on and face-to-face. We inflict injury great and small, bodily or psychological, when seated, so to speak, safely behind a windshield, preferably one made of tinted glass.

Harold Pinter sees this more clearly than any other dramatist. In fact, some such insight explains his special fascination, his distinctiveness of both content and style. People in his plays often neither say what they mean nor mean what they say. They suddenly start talking about bus timetables, or asking for olives, or anxiously wondering whether it's verbally accurate to say "light the kettle," or describing confusing one-way street systems, or repeating the riddle "Why did the chicken cross the road?" But that's all camouflage, code. The message contained in the most innocent of questions, the most irrelevant of anecdotes, the most desultory of repartee is apt to be blunt and even brutish. What Pinter's people tend actually to be expressing are pretty basic needs and greeds, hostilities and terrors. What they may really be saying when they talk offhandedly about the weather is "Get off my turf," "Tread carefully, or I'll destroy you," "Don't hurt me," "Give me that," "Give me yourself." Most dramatists chronicle only that part of the character that breaks the surface; Pinter is interested in the nine-tenths that remain darkly and often dangerously hidden below.

Mark you, this is more apparent from *Old Times*, which I caught at the Roundabout a couple of months ago, than from the trio of playlets now having their American premiere at the Manhattan Theater Club. Two of these I saw at the National Theater last year: *Victoria Station*, an enigmatic trifle about a raging taxi dispatcher and the amiably uncooperative driver at the other end of his airwaves, and the more substantial *A Kind of Alaska*. The other is new to me, a study of political cruelty and oppression called *One for the Road*. All are, I suppose, of interest simply because they're by Pinter. His reputation is so high and his dramatic writings are so few these days that he'd simply have to daub a word or two on his bathroom mirror for the world's scholars to jet in with fingerprint powder and glass-cutting equipment. But none is really top-notch Pinter.

I said somewhere else that British playwrights nowadays risk being called irrelevant and irresponsible if they don't tackle social and political subjects. I might have added that Pinter alone or almost alone has resisted this pressure. True, several of his plays have political implications and reverberations. His first full-length one was *The Birthday Party*, in which the vengeful representatives of an unnamed organization reduced a seemingly harmless young man to a walking vegetable, and his next one was *The Hothouse*, which recorded a similar piece of mental destruction, this time in a Kafkaesque government asylum run by sadists and incompetents. Much of his work, especially his earlier work, involves more or less malign intruders invading more or less private spaces, and as he himself pointed out, the appearance of sinister strangers at the front door, with or without raincoats, oversized dogs, and arrest warrants, hasn't exactly been an unusual experi-

ence in Europe over the past fifty years. But any such implications are, like so much of Pinter, covert and implicit, not
overt and obvious. Besides, for the past twenty or twenty-five
years he's been less a sociologist or a political scientist than
a combination of zoologist and poet, chronicling the guiddities
of the individual human animal with precision and elegance.

One for the Road is surprising both in its subject matter
and in its lack of guile. A burly British apparatchik, exuding
all the genial contempt Kevin Conway can bring to the part,
quizzes a captive family: tortured father, bloodied mother,
and their seven-year-old son, who has committed the only
offense anyone mentions, spitting at some God-fearing dictatorship's glorious legionnaires. Some of what's said is un-
wontedly direct: "How many times have you been raped?"
And even the more oblique and seemingly Pinterish menace—
"I'm terribly pleased to meet you"; "Everyone here has fallen
in love with your wife"; "I trust we will always remain friends"—
should present no difficulties of decoding to anyone who has
seen the sort of movie in which Gestapo sadists smilingly sneer,
"Ve are going to get to know each other very, very vell." By
the end, when it becomes apparent that the little boy won't
be accompanying his ruined parents back to the world outside,
you feel you've been watching a fairly unsubtle, if undoubtedly
impassioned, piece of propaganda for Amnesty International.
The play says more for Pinter's decency than for his art.

A Kind of Alaska is better, but also surprising and perhaps
a little disappointing, though in quite different ways. It was
inspired by Oliver Sacks's marvelous *Awakenings*, a series of
studies of patients struck down by encephalitis lethargica in
earlier decades and reactivated in the late 1960's by the drug
L-dopa. Rose R., for instance, dreamed at age twenty-one she
was a stone statue imprisoned in an inaccessible castle shaped
like herself, became just that for the next forty years, and,
restored to reality one fine day, could never fully accept that
it was no longer 1926. Similarly, Pinter's Deborah has been

mentally incarcerated in a vast series of glass halls where she's alternately listened to faucets dripping and danced "in the most crushing spaces." Now she must accept that her sister is an ample matron, her mother dead, her father blind, the clamor and bustle of a twenties adolescence long ago ended. Dianne Wiest hasn't brought quite the same puckered intensity of disbelieving grief to the part of this gray-haired Sleeping Beauty that Judi Dench did at moments in London. But squinting and blinking from her bed, she certainly makes one feel that hers is an embattled and bewildered sixteen-year-old consciousness and that this consciousness is pluckily, angrily, defiantly getting its bearings in a world way beyond anyone's emotional compass. It's a fine, spiky performance which ensures that the play is more than a bizarre case history from some spidery archive, appealing mainly to those morbidly fascinated by sensational medicine, and much, much more than a lurid horror story from the locked ward.

Actually how could one imagine its being either of those things, Pinter being Pinter? What's surprising about *Alaska* is something else. Throughout his career Pinter has concentrated on the dark intestinal drives, sometimes giving the impression that his fellow creatures are governed exclusively by a triple hunger for territory, power, and sex. Here, and here alone, he acknowledges courage and resilience and generosity, the generosity of others and those who care for us, movingly represented by the doctor who has spent the last twenty-nine years at or near Deborah's bed, watching and tending and cherishing. Nevertheless, there's also something about the play which, I find, leaves me uneasy, dissatisfied, and a trifle disappointed. Pinter has long had a special interest in those shadowy areas of the mind where perception and imagination merge and where memory has its sometimes blurred, sometimes surprisingly sharp existence, and in *Alaska* he has a chance to explore and evoke them as never before. But he takes that opportunity in a somewhat hesitant and cursory

way, telling us less in sum about Deborah's consciousness than
one could gather from two or three pages of one of Dr. Sacks's
more suggestive bios.

This may be an irrelevant and even ungrateful complaint
since the play is, I think, finally about something more than
one strange consciousness. What it offers is a metaphor, admittedly rather an extreme one, for a feeling we all must have
had on occasions. Where did time go? What did I do while it
was passing? Why did I make so little of it? That's true, and
yet, I find, my doubts won't quite go away. Pinter could surely
have told us more about Deborah's weird, frozen adventures
during that interminable twinkling.

Old Times is a more satisfactory demonstration of his quality and class. It involves that favorite figure of his, the predatory intruder, this time a woman coming from abroad to visit
her old roommate, now living alone with her husband in some
provincial English wilderness. This situation allows him both
to investigate that dusky souvenir shop, the human mind, and
to show the avarice, the fear, the hostility fermenting inside
it. *Old Times* is a play of menace, tension, conflict as much
as a study of the complexities of consciousness. In it the past
is the battlefield on which a very Pinterish tussle is being
fought to the emotional death. Memories are among the weapons used by both visitor Anna and husband Deeley as they
struggle to take possession of wife Kate's past, hence Kate's
present, hence Kate herself.

Their private war becomes uglier and uglier until each side
is raring to inflict intimate atrocities on the other. What's
actually being said is "You're a pretentious bitch," "You're
a coarse fool," "You don't really know your own wife," "I
know her in carnal ways denied to you, pervert though you
are," "I own her," "No, *I* own her." Yet the interesting thing
is that the combatant's smiles, though increasingly tight, are
still to be seen, and their language, though increasingly charged,
is still polite. The social niceties are momentarily disturbed

when Deeley blurts, "Am I alone in finding this distasteful?",
only to reassert themselves as he lapses back into aggressive
obliquity. And that's the way it should be. When Luchino
Visconti introduced lesbian gropings and fondlings into his
Italian staging of *Old Times*, the usually reticent Pinter was
sufficiently outraged to ask us London critics to bombard the
director with letters of protest, something we were naturally
glad to do. The play, as decidedly as anything he's written,
is about people who say what they do not quite mean and
mean what they do not quite say. It's full of seething worms
all right, but they remain unseen and mostly unacknowledged,
beneath the fake-civilized skin.

That's very English, yes, but maybe more than English.
Anyone who has found it safer to use sarcasm, hint, or parable
should respond to *Old Times*, as to much of Pinter's work.
So should anyone who has felt got at without quite being able
to explain why. So, for that matter, should anyone who has
talked his way through an emotional minefield, knowing that
a clumsily placed syllable could cause megadeath in the living
room. The fear of being too blunt and provoking situations
you can't control, or handing your enemies information they
might use against you, or revealing your intentions before you
are ready isn't only an English fear. The inhabitants of other
countries, too, are sometimes to be found warily circling each
other. Other nationalities, too, sometimes adopt camouflage
and use code. Others, too, talk about nothing when they mean
everything.

Nor are these the only respects in which *Old Times*, like so
much of Pinter, is perfectly international. It's about how vis-
itors can bring out the tensions in a seemingly stable situation;
how the past merges into the present, defines and threatens
it; how old memories can be exploited for our emotional purposes now. And so one might go on. It's about those areas of
people we love from which we're excluded, those that others
claimed before or after we did, those we can only guess at and

try not to mistrust. It's about the pain of never fully knowing someone.

That comes out very clearly at the play's thoroughly unexpected yet marvelously logical ending. So absorbing has the contest between Anna and Deeley become that we, too, have been lured into sharing their basically crass assumption, which is that Kate is a sort of prize to be won by one or the other. But then Pinter reminds us of what we should have realized before, that human prizes can only award themselves. Kate launches into a long metaphoric speech, obscure in its parts but brutally clear in its message. Neither Deeley nor Anna matters to her. Indeed, she rejects both. Anna lies expressionless on a divan; Deeley sobs, lays his head on Kate's lap, only to remove it when she fails to respond. Their numb despair is all too apparent.

Only Kate seems serene, as she has reason to be. She is, one realizes, the sister of Ruth in *The Homecoming* and Emma in *Betrayal*, one of a long line of Pinter women who tantalize, derange, and even destroy those unfortunate enough to venture into their inviting parlors. There she sits, the svelte spider at the center of her web, scarcely even bothering to glance at the two transfixed victims who misguidedly tried to catch her. It goes without saying that she's the most powerful person in the play, far more so than those who tried to assert their power over her. Indeed, her power is precisely and ironically this, the ability to incite others to frantic displays of power and to remain untouched by them, or, to put it another way, to inspire devotion and not to care herself.

Pinter is, I realize, quite my favorite contemporary dramatist, one I find endlessly puzzling and rewarding. *A Kind of Alaska* is not one of his masterworks, and *One for the Road* far from it. But *Old Times* is a compendium of his peculiar subtleties and strengths. How rich he is, how original, how germane. Seeing such a play is like opening a door the merest crack, glimpsing the long dark passages and musty stairways inside, smelling the dungeons and hearing the hungry dragons beyond, as strange an adventure as one could vicariously enjoy.

There's startling evidence in the current issue of *Playbill* of what I've been hearing: that it's getting painfully hard to raise money for new shows unless your name happens to be Shubert or Nederlander or maybe David Merrick. There, in the copy I was given at the press performance of Joanna Glass's new *Play Memory*, was an advertisement from its producer, Alexander Cohen, asking for money with which to present *Play Memory* itself, among other plays. "Be an angel," it said in big black letters, and went on to point out that though "theater-for-profit theater can be as unprofitable as the not-for-profit theater," those who called their shots carefully would "probably get a run for their money." If there was a loss, well, a tax deduction was always possible.

Play Memory cost $550,000 to stage and apparently was some $160,000 short of that figure within whispering distance of opening night. But since then Cohen's persuasion has done its work. The necessary investors have come forward, and the show is fully financed, for better or, as I fear, for worse. *Play Memory* is about alcoholism and alcoholic violence within the family, not the sort of theme likely to appeal to Broadway audiences in search of comfy entertainment, yet the traumas it describes have been so understated by author, director, and performers alike that it will seem too anodyne to those ready to be more drastically churned. Were I one of the would-be backers Mr. Cohen approached, I would have listened to him with the respect his long record as a producer deserves, but once I'd seen the script, I'd have mumbled something evasive and taken my chance on the New York lottery instead.

Actually who *are* the backers these days? "In the last several years a great deal of theater financing has come from a few large sources," answers Cohen's ad itself, adding that he thinks

"the theater works better with a lot of small investors." The
first of those remarks is clearly incontestable. The early 1980's
have seen big business increasingly replace the old groups of
individual angels. For a time it looked as if big movie business
would be especially important. Paramount funded the successful *Agnes of God*, Warner, *A Doll's Life*, which, as I noted
before, cost and lost $4 million. But unsurprisingly, given such
an experience, most of the film companies have disappeared
as suddenly as they came; most, but not quite all. This season
MCA-Universal financed two shows, *Doonesbury* and *Open
Admissions*. How bullish it feels about Broadway after their
failure remains to be seen.

   Neither of the major producers relies on large numbers of
investors. The Nederlander organization uses its own funds
and those of "certain wealthy individuals." The Shuberts work
in conjunction with ABC and Metromedia, each of the three
partners putting up one-third of the necessary finance. Since
they are about as successful as any producer can reasonably
expect to be these dark days, they'd seem to cast doubt on
Cohen's contention that "the theater works better with a lot
of small investors." In any case, how practicable is it to finance
a show costing $1 million, $2 million, $5 million with units of
$500 or $1,000 or even $10,000? There are producers like
Cohen, who continue to draw on the investors they've accumulated over the years, but they promise to become less and
less in number. Harold Prince himself seems unable and unwilling to work that way anymore. Once he had a regular 175
people putting their $1,000 or $2,000 into his shows, and that
was enough to finance *A Funny Thing Happened on the Way
to the Forum* or whatever he happened to be presenting; but
how could they bankroll *Cats* or *Cage aux Folles?* And how
could he ask a well-off, but not sensationally rich, person to
increase his stake to $10,000 or $20,000, knowing the risks
involved?

   The risks are still, of course, very great. The great majority of shows fail to recover their costs. On the other hand, the gamble can occasionally pay off. Only this week *Variety* reports that David Merrick is earning $500,000 profit a week from his three productions of *42nd Street* and $115,000 from the one on Broadway alone, and since he's the show's sole backer, all that money is currently going into his own piggy bank. *Cats* continues to be a mighty earner for the Shuberts, as does *The Real Thing*, which should recoup its original investment this summer. So, too, should *Cage*, making the Nederlanders' "wealthy individuals" wealthier still. It remains to be seen if any of them will eventually match the more sensationally successful shows of recent years: *A Chorus Line*, currently showing a $25 million profit on a $2.5 million investment; *Annie*, $16.5 million on $800,000; *They're Playing Our Song*, $5.7 million on $800,000; *Deathtrap*, $1.7 million on $200,000.

There's no guarantee that can ever be offered a backer, no obvious formula for success. "Flair, perseverance, and damn good marketing," a producer suggested verbally to me the other day, only to hem and haw when asked to define the first, most elusive, and most important of these commodities. Flair is what Michael Bennett presumably showed when he first evolved the idea of a musical concerning and featuring unknown hoofers and what Joseph Papp demonstrated when he gave him the opportunity to develop it. Flair was what David Merrick displayed when he walked away from the Broadway theater where he was presenting Ruth Gordon in Thornton Wilder's *Matchmaker* and suddenly wondered if it might make a good musical, and flair marked his decision to hand the project over to a little-known tunesmith still in his twenties, Jerry Herman, rather than one of the better-known composers with whom he discussed it. But it was eight or nine years before *Hello, Dolly!* finally ended on the stage, to begin its seven-year run. It all took perseverance, too.

That's clearly exceptional. Something between six months

and two years is the more usual period between the time a producer acquires a "property," which could be a finished script, a few songs, or simply an idea, and transforms it into a "package," ready for rehearsals. Apart from somehow finding financial backing, that means choosing a director, holding discussions with leading performers, appointing a general manager and a press agent, talking to theater operators, going through a long period of auditions, maybe even negotiating with Equity for the import of a British actor, and much, much else. Is it worth paying 10 percent of the gross—a not unusual figure these days—to this particular star? For how long should previews run if, of course, the enterprise progresses to the stage of offering previews at all? Look back at recent issues of the *Theatrical Index*, that compendium of present and upcoming shows, and you'll see how many stumble and fall in the very last straight. Just before arriving in this country last September, I copied down the titles of the shows "set to open through December 31, 1983." Seven of the seventeen, among them four musicals and a "new symbolic drama which takes place in the desert outside of Santa Fe and probes the suicide of a famous American painter," never materialized on Broadway. And of sixty-three more vaguely announced as "plans," just three have reached Broadway to date: *The Real Thing, Death of a Salesman*, and *Beethoven's Tenth*.

But let's assume the show reaches what, since the chief reviewers now mainly come to previews, tends to be the slight anticlimax of opening night. The producer's worries don't vanish with the appearance of *The New York Times* review at around nine-thirty, followed by the talking critics on the major television channels. If all these are hostile, and there's no appreciable advance from ticket sales, he'll probably have to be brave and brutal, accept that those months of hard work were for nothing, and close the show. If they're more enthusiastic or "mixed," all sorts of other decisions will soon be asking to be made.

Are things so promising that he should be thinking of touring companies and foreign companies? Are they so doubtful that he should be asking author, director, stars to accept cuts and waivers, in hope of lowering costs and keeping the show running until word of mouth and clever marketing make it profitable? Indeed, how best is he to promote it? Should he advertise on television, for instance, or not? That has become an increasingly important marketing medium since 1972, when *Pippin* substituted an attractive excerpt from the show itself for the enthusiastically talking mugs usual at that time, reached an audience that did not normally go to the theater, and managed to transform a critical failure into a commercial success, with nearly 2,000 performances to its credit. *Grease*, still more coolly received by the reviewers, made equally effective use of TV and ended up as the second-highest-running show in Broadway history. Mark you, an ad that cost $18,000 to make ten-odd years ago will now set back a producer $100,000; that probably explains why the ones I see most often on TV are for the two shows that would seem least to need such a fillip: *Cats* and *La Cage*. Less resilient shows tend to flaunt their alleged attractions on radio, though rarely, I should parenthetically add, as flamboyantly as Joseph Papp, who continues to celebrate the Public Theater over the airwaves in his absurd tenor chant.

The proportions would obviously vary, but they tell me that nowadays just over 40 percent of a show's advertising budget is likely to end up in the pockets of the TV and radio companies, with newspaper advertising, billboards and so on accounting for the rest. And funnily enough, a recent survey of the audience of *La Cage* reportedly revealed that just 40 percent felt that the ads that most influenced them were those on television, with 35 percent thinking those in newspapers were more important. Unsurprisingly, perhaps, 60 percent of those from the New York area read *The Times*, a figure that was up to 75 percent on Sunday.

Actually four out of every ten analyzed by the survey came from out of town, a surprisingly and suggestively high figure for February, when it was undertaken. Tourists are clearly becoming increasingly important to the New York theater—as they are, incidentally, to the London one—and the advertisers haven't been slow to respond to that either. Every Amtrak station, north and south of New York, seems positively pregnant just now with ads insisting on the desirability of *Baby*. The redoubtable Merrick has gone still farther afield, advertising in newspapers and airports as far away as Miami, in hopes of catching both provincials on their way to New York and New Yorkers on vacations.

Every week, every day new decisions demand to be taken by the producers and their henchmen. Would it be sensible to add extra matinees for Christmas? How many tickets, if any, should be sent to the half-price booth at the north of Times Square? Isn't it time for some bright, attention-grabbing gimmick, such as disguising Jeremy Irons as an Arab Valentino and sending him through Central Park on a camel or, as actually happened last January, holding a well-publicized casting call for a parakeet to understudy the one in *Painting Churches?* When to go on twofers? How and where to concentrate what's probably a dwindling promotional budget? *The Tap Dance Kid,* for instance, has advertised heavily in newspapers with large black readerships and sent some of its cast to talk about the show to black community groups; it's also put together a slick TV commercial, aimed at the rock-loving young; and the tactics appear to be working. A not very well-received musical that seemed to be failing in the dead of winter managed last week to sell no less than 93.4 percent of its seats, taking $345,000 at the box office—a promising accomplishment for a show that, with an original price tag of $2.85 million, has less to earn than most contributions to the genre these days.

I'm no business efficiency expert, but I'm perfectly willing to believe the claim of the League of New York Producers that day-to-day management is more competent and marketing more energetic than ever. All I'd wryly add is that they need to be, because so often the wrong shows are being managed and the price at which they're being marketed is too high. *Play Memory* is by no means the worst thing I've seen on Broadway this year. It's the sort of play that critics tend rather condescendingly to categorize as "worthy," meaning they don't like it but respect its seriousness and integrity. But at $35 a seat it was always going to be a poor deal, and as canny and experienced an operator as Alexander Cohen should have known it. It will, I fear, succeed in encouraging neither new audiences nor new backers to commit themselves to Broadway. In fact, my fear is that it will only succeed in putting off both.

It's beginning to look as if David Mamet's *Glengarry Glen Ross* might actually enjoy a modest run on Broadway. That should be no surprising statement, in view of its quality and the warmth of its reception. *Variety* reported that it got eighteen favorable notices from the critics, one mixed, and just one unfavorable one, by Douglas Watt in the *News*. I myself tend to feel fastidious about banging around the sort of big, guileless adjectives that get pinned onto theater frontages, but this time I quite deliberately did so, calling the play "funny, brilliant and unmissable." Yet those sellout reviews by no means sold out the production. Indeed, *Variety* described business as continuing to be "leisurely," with barely two-thirds of the seats at the little Golden Theater actually filled with flesh. Only now that the play has won Mamet a Pulitzer Prize can one begin to feel a little confidence about its prospects. Last week, after the news had come through, attendance figures suddenly leaped more than twenty percentage points; the theater is now better than nine-tenths full.

The play's faltering start would certainly seem to suggest that the critics are not as powerful as Broadway folklore holds.

If they collectively reject a show, and it has no "advance,"
that show admittedly has very little chance indeed. *Play Memory* has just proved the point by closing almost as soon as it
opened. But a major prize clearly counts at least as much as
our collective rapture. So, of course, does the presence of
stars in the cast. The musical *The Rink* neither deserved nor
got very good notices when it opened in February, but it has
been doing pretty well, thanks presumably to the efforts of
its stars, Liza Minnelli and Chita Rivera. Last week it filled
no less than 86 percent of its seats.

Nearly fifteen years ago William Goldman reported in his
Season that only some 20 percent of New Yorkers (and just
10 percent of out-of-towners) felt they were principally influenced by the critics in their decision to visit a Broadway show,
and the latest survey, the one prepared in 1980 for the League
of New York Producers, suggests that this figure is still correct. Though 57 percent admitted to having seen or heard
reviews, precisely 20 percent considered them a "major influence." Many more, around 32 percent, thought "opinions
of friends" the major influence. In fact, critics are more important than word of mouth only to "traditionalist" theatergoers, the category that, as I've noticed before, seems most
to be dwindling, and then only marginally. All the other categories are considerably more affected by friends than by
reviews. The 1981 off-Broadway survey offers a strikingly
similar picture. There 42 percent said that the main reason
they were attending one of the shows analyzed was that "I
heard about it from a friend," only 24 percent that they'd
read a review of it.

Of course, the situation isn't as clear-cut as this suggests.
Rave reviews can stimulate a rush to the box office that speedily transforms itself into enthusiastic "opinions of friends."
Just occasionally they can stimulate a stampede, leaving
"opinions of friends" irrelevant, at least when a play is at an
off-Broadway theater for a limited time only. The entire run

of Kevin Wade's pleasant little play about love among the bicycling classes, *Key Exchange*, was apparently sold out within six hours of the publication of an enthusiastic notice in *The Times*, although he was an unknown author and the cast contained no one who could conceivably be described as a star. "Nevertheless," I'm told by Jane Moss, who runs ART–New York, which embraces virtually all the important off- and off-off Broadway theaters, "word of mouth is more significant for us even than Frank Rich."

Incidentally, the hottest tickets on Broadway right now are those for *Cats, La Cage, The Real Thing,* and *Death of a Salesman*. According to *Variety*, they're selling every seat up to and including any priest holes that happen to be back of the orchestra seats. It's standing room only at the theaters where they're playing and very nearly as crowded as performances of *A Chorus Line, My One and Only, Dreamgirls,* and *Noises Off*. All had good reviews, if not all quite as good as those for *Glengarry*, but all fall into categories that are more acceptable to Broadway theatergoers and those influential "friends." They're lavish musicals, or bundles of laughs, or star vehicles, or some combination of those things.

That's what succeeds these days, and but for the fillip provided by the Pulitzer committee, *Glengarry* would presumably be continuing to provide negative confirmation of that dismal generalization. Bluntly, it was failing before Mamet's prize came to rescue it, a demonstration that audiences for serious drama are an endangered species as much as proof of the powerlessness of the critics to stop their slow extinction. And what will happen when the glamor of that Pulitzer begins to recede? And what is the prospect for some less prestigiously recognized and rewarded *Glengarry* of the future, when it's put on sale at current Broadway prices?

May

My compatriot Ian Bannen didn't look very happy
when he took his curtain call after playing Jim Tyrone in
O'Neill's *Moon for the Misbegotten* at the Cort last night, or,
rather, he looked too happy to be believed. His smile had a
kind of exaggerated, stricken look, almost as if he were baring
his teeth for a conclave of dentists. "If you decide to jump
onstage and attack me with your pincers," it seemed to be
saying, "I shall bear the attack as cheerfully as possible."
There's a *New Yorker* cartoon in which you can see the cast
still lined up after the curtain has fallen for the last time,
frowning and cocking snooks at the departing audience. You
felt that whatever Bannen's face might be doing after he'd
finally disappeared from view, it wouldn't be smiling.

Things hadn't been easy for him for some time. He'd had
a long, painful battle with a sore throat which had forced the
postponement of opening night. There had also been persistent
rumors that he wasn't the very best of friends with his costar,
the Canadian Kate Nelligan. Unsurprisingly perhaps, there
was something wary and uncertain about his delivery, especially in the first half. He seemed to be scrambling nervously
across sentences, as if afraid that too firm a landing on too
sharp a consonant would puncture his voice box. Nor was
there quite the emotional give-and-take between him and Miss
Nelligan's Josie Hogan there should have been. She blazed,
he guttered; and you could sense the unease and puzzlement
of the audience at this unequal conflagration. It was a pity

259

because Bannen is actually a very able actor, as I've often had opportunity to confirm back in Britain. It was doubly a pity because the producers seemingly had quite a problem persuading American Equity to allow him to appear on Broadway at all.

The current rules are that the only foreigners permitted to perform in the United States are "unit companies," such as the RSC or Comédie Française, or "stars" or "actors providing unique services." Should a producer be looking for someone to play the Cyclops, and a Japanese turns out to be the only eight-foot-tall performer with one eye in the middle of his forehead, then he could be hired—provided a "diligent" search had first been made for an equivalent actor in America. The rules are complex and full of such qualifications. But they've allowed Ben Kingsley, Ian McKellen, and Jeremy Irons to appear on Broadway this season. They also forced its producers to abandon what were very advanced plans to present Peter Nichols's opium-trade musical *Poppy* at the Mark Hellinger. They and Equity agreed that English performers could open the show, but they remained at odds about the length of time they could play before being replaced by Americans.

You can see Equity's point. Were there no restrictions on the trade of actors, British performers would before long be jetting into America by their scores. They are, rightly or wrongly, perceived to be better suited to certain roles and certain plays, ones demanding classical "style" or skill with language or simply English accents. Moreover, New York salaries, especially salaries on Broadway, are far more attractive than London ones. One can easily imagine American performers being excluded from roles they could have handled with perfect success. I can't honestly say that the support Rex Harrison received in *Heartbreak House* this year was significantly weaker than the support he got in the same play in London last year.

I've also discovered that Americans in general are better
at British accents than Britons are at American ones. Our
performers tend to think that if they roll their *r*'s and stretch
their vowels enough, they'll be accepted as authentic New
Yorkers or Californians or whatever it may be. My wife, herself an American, regularly disappears under her seat in winc-
ing embarrassment whenever Miller or O'Neill or Shepard
surfaces in an English theater. There are slips and lapses here
all right—Jeremy Iron's daughter in *The Real Thing* evidently
had a transatlantic nanny—but they're slighter and fewer
than I myself had condescendingly expected. The accents of
the East Anglian villagers in *Fen* for instance, struck me as
just as authentic when delivered by Americans at the Public
as by Britons back home.

Still, the rule must mean that some parts, some plays are
cast less satisfactorily than would be the case if freedom of
trade prevailed. Joseph Papp attributes the relative lack of
success of Trevor Griffiths's *Comedians* in New York to the
presence of Americans in a thoroughly, indeed quintessen-
tially English play about social change and class welfare, and
though its subject matter must also be a major reason for its
failure to attract New York audiences, he's not alone in that
diagnosis. The rule has other unfortunate effects, too. Billie
Whitelaw was prevented from playing *Footfalls* and *Rockaby*
in New York two years ago, even though Beckett wrote the
plays for her and personally begged Equity to allow her to
perform them. She's only on Theater Row now because of a
negotiated swap, under which the American productions of
Ohio Impromptu and *What Where* will be seen in London.

Such swaps seem the best hope of achieving what everyone
should surely want, the audiences of each nation to see strong,
representative stage talent from the other, the actors of each
nation to expand their horizons and maybe their skills by
working in the other. Equity's rulebook talks of maintaining

a "balance" so that "in each country where English is spoken, the number of nonresident aliens from each country admitted to perform shall not exceed the number of U.S. citizens employed in the theater in such foreign country." That's still more of a restriction than a concession because American actors aren't exactly clamoring to cross the Atlantic. London salaries are as offputting to them as New York salaries are onputting to Britons. But at least it's opened the wall a crack and allowed a few performances through. America saw the Royal Court's production of Caryl Churchill's *Top Girls* because Britian saw the Public Theater's production of Thomas Babe's *Buried Inside Extra*. Ian Bannen was permitted to come to New York largely because Frances Sternhagen is to appear in a new play called *The War at Home* on the London fringe.

Actually I saw Bannen in *Moon* in London last year, directed by the same young man who is responsible for the present production at the Cort, David Leveaux. So once again I had that sense of déjà vu I've already had occasion to mention. In fact, let me recap and make a little list. On Broadway, I've rereviewed *Noises Off*, *The Real Thing*, Rex Harrison in *Heartbreak House*, and *Glengarry Glen Ross*; off-Broadway, Whitelaw in Beckett, and plays by Pinter, Christopher Hampton, and Caryl Churchill, among others. New York may be able to manage without British actors, but where would it be without British plays?

There are, I suppose, worrying aspects to this dependence on England, and not only because it can't exactly encourage American writers to turn their attention to the theater. Some of my colleagues back home, I found on my last visit, are worried that London is becoming a tryout town for New York. Why the musical *Jean Seberg* at the National, of all inappropriate theaters? they asked. Because its management hoped it would eventually make them profits on Broadway, they answered. Why has James Nederlander acquired the Adelphi,

if not to test-run doubtful product on the poor London public
at far less risk to his pocketbook than could ever be the case
in America? And what's James Duff's *War at Home* doing in
the government-subsidized Hampstead Theater Club when the
New York *Theatrical Index* announced months ago that the
Shuberts, among others, had cast it, chosen a director, and
were firmly planning to present it on Broadway?

Well, I suspect I, too, would have balked at *Seberg*, but
only because I would have felt it too glitzy for the National
Theater, not because it might eventually have landed up in
America. My mild and moderate view, for what it's worth, is
that there are quite enough theaters and plays in London for
it not to matter very much if their owners or presenters occasionally look across the Atlantic. Who knows, the result
might actually be the odd work of distinction, the sort that
would never otherwise have materialized in the theater, thanks
to the extreme caution of American producers. Maybe *The
War at Home* will fall into that category. Certainly any Lon-
doner would be glad to see his city regarded as a tryout town
if just one out of the fifty tryouts turned out to be a *Glengarry
Glen Ross*.

But London never could be a satisfactory proving ground
for New York, being populated mainly by Londoners, not New
Yorkers. After all, success in Philadelphia or Boston is no
promise of success in the metropolis. Some say, not without
bitterness, that success in Los Angeles is a positive guarantee
of failure here. How much more risky it would be, then, for
Broadway producers to rely on the taste and judgment of
foreign audiences. Apart from anything else, there are plenty
of examples of plays succeeding on one side of the Atlantic
and failing on the other. David Hare's *Plenty* went down better
in New York than in London; Peter Nichols's *Passion*, Ronald
Harwood's *Dresser*, Tom Stoppard's *Night and Day*, worse.
New York critics and audiences even managed to reject C. P.
Taylor's *Good*, which I regarded as one of the most ambitious

and exciting British plays of recent years, attempting as it did
to explain the evolution of a decent, self-respecting man into
a functionary at Auschwitz. It depressed me to see Taylor's
warm but minor war memoir *And a Nightingale Sang . . .*
succeed at the Mitzi Newhouse this season and know that his
masterpiece had been rejected, and several of his better plays
not yet discovered, by New York.

Still, Taylor is another subject, if one close to my heart,
since I knew him, liked him, mourned his recent and pre-
mature death by heart attack, admired his work, and feel that
it should not be forgotten. It's time to return to the discon-
solate Bannen and what, I fear, may be a doomed revival of
Moon. Is the one great strength of Mr. Leveaux's production,
Kate Nelligan's all-electric performance, sufficient to attract
Broadway audiences to a play which somehow manages to
touch greatness without actually bothering to be good?

O'Neill wrote the play in 1943 as a sort of propitiatory
offering to his elder bother, Jamie, who had died, half-blinded
and three-quarters crazed by alcohol, twenty years earlier.
One might have thought that *A Long Day's Journey into Night*
was sufficient memoir, dramatizing as it did the raging love
and loving rage of the tormented young man, but Eugene felt
that it didn't make his affection for their drug-addict mother
clear enough. Above all, he wanted to face, to explain, and
posthumously to forgive Jamie's behavior after the death of
the old lady in California. On the train back east, with Ellen
O'Neill's coffin in the baggage car ahead, he boozed and wal-
lowed and rutted with a "fat pig" of a whore, arriving in New
York in so sottish a state he couldn't walk, let alone go to his
mother's funeral. So *Moon* is a coda to *Long Day's Journey*,
a postmortem written in blood, tears, and bile. It's said that
Eugene wept so much when he penned the play that his wife
Carlotta urged him to abandon it, such a danger did it seem
to both his and his dead brother's repose.

He didn't, of course. In fact, it's those tears and that danger
which make the play so much more extraordinary than it
sometimes threatens to become. Eccentrically O'Neill chose
as his setting a tenant farm owned by Jim Tyrone, alias brother
Jamie, and worked by one Hogan and his daughter, Josie.
That means, believe it or not, that much of the evening is
galumphing rustic comedy. Yet by the end clownishness has
somehow become confession, and pretty painful confession at
that. Under O'Neill's moon Josie, who prefers to present herself to the world as a sluttish virago, reveals her innocence,
warmth, and devotion to Jim; Jim hawks up his guilt, his
anguish, his self-loathing, his longing for the death that's all
but seized him already. Somehow a journey that began among
the bumpkins has ended in the heart, the intestines, the very
bowels of human existence.

David Leveaux stages it all quite as capably as in London,
in front of a rickety gray shanty isolated inside what appears
to be a great piece of broken eggshell, a setting which an-
nounces that the play is naturalistic and more than naturalistic. He gets some sound supporting performances, notably
from Jerome Kilty, who manages to find a little humanity and
even a touch of pathos in the grizzled troglodyte and tyrant
Hogan. But he hasn't been able to correct, camouflage, or
conceal the emotional imbalance at the center of his production, one not apparent last year, when Bannen was playing
opposite Frances de la Tour, an actress with an odd, gawky
magic of her own but by no means as intense as Kate Nelligan.
There must have been times at the Cort when Bannen felt like
a flashlight battery expected to match the voltage of forked
lightning.

Nelligan looks wrong. She's very far from the giant bruiser
O'Neill quaintly specified in his stage directions. Even with
her feet bare, her hair straggling down over a tattered dress,
her cheeks scrupulously begrimed, a pout on her lips, and a

growl in her throat, she can't convince us that she's the "ugly overgrown lump of a woman" she's said to be. But who cares? She has the magnetism and the technique to make us ignore what she isn't and accept what she is, and she's a woman whose surface harshness hides thwarted feelings of great strength and surprising subtlety. Her face can crumple, sobs can rack her body, and the effect seems true. Tenderness can flicker across her forehead or off her tongue, and that seems true, too. How many other actresses can match either her emotional boldness or her discipline, let alone both at once?

Yet her assets paradoxically become limitations when they so thoroughly overshadow those displayed by her partner. It would be unreasonable to expect Bannen, or indeed any performer, to be absolutely faithful to O'Neill's stage directions, which were always apt to expect characters to laugh gaily one sentence and snarl with venomous fury the next. Nevertheless, a debonair smile, fond looks, and an occasional brusqueness of accent and darkness of glance fell rather too short of what's actually demanded, "revulsion," "intense hatred," "guilty loathing," and a sense of horror. They mean that the less important of the two protagonists, Josie, suddenly begins to seem the more important. They mean that her admission that she's really chaste, which is not what impelled O'Neill to write the play, counts for more than Jim's attempts to achieve catharsis by confessing his swinishness, which is. They mean that *Moon* itself is only half-visible.

That's quite a pity, for several reasons. I don't think it's just chauvinism that makes me regret that an English actor didn't demonstrate his undoubted skills to the full. So few are permitted to appear here, one wants them to be the best, at their best. It's also a pity because major productions of America's greatest playwright in America's greatest city seem depressingly rare. All this revival may do is confirm the glum wisdom that prevailed when some idealist tried and failed to bring Jason Robards to Broadway in *The Iceman Cometh* the

other day: that O'Neill just isn't commercial enough for the
contemporary theater.

Last night's audience at Stephen Sondheim's new musical
about Seurat seemed uneasy and restive. No one actually
shouted, "Yes," or, "You said it," when one of the figures in
the painting "A Sunday Afternoon on the Island of La Grande
Jatte" announced, "It's hot and it's monotonous," something
that apparently has happened on the odd occasion during a
noticeably choppy series of previews, with more than the usual
amount of rewriting and reshaping going on behind the scenes
and opening night postponed for nearly two weeks. But at the
end of the first half a woman near me asked if the show was
over, and a man a few seats away cried, "No, *unfortunately*."
This was greeted with a good deal of nodding and hear-hearing
all around. It was always going to be difficult for *Sunday in
the Park with George* to make back its $2.1 million invest-
ment, since it's housed in one of the smaller Broadway theaters, the Booth; last night it looked as if the producers would
have trouble filling even its 750-odd seats for so much as a
couple of weeks.

The enterprise was an improbable one. How could anyone
expect to fashion a musical out of Seurat, who spent his sadly
short life working very hard, saying very little, and doing
practically nothing else at all? But the man mainly responsible
is Sondheim, that laureate of improbability. The next step for
a composer who has forged Broadway shows from dour rec-
ollections of American imperialism in Japan, a sardonic movie
about frigidity by Ingmar Bergman, and a tale of insanity,
mass murder, and cannibalism in Victorian London could
have been anything strange and slippery—a chamber version
of Beckett's *Endgame*, maybe, or even of his *Breath*, which
boasts no characters and no words at all. So there was no
reason to be greatly astonished by the small, intractable subject, the mountainous molehill Sondheim has in fact made his

latest challenge. *Of course* he'd wish to spin a two-and-a-half-hour entertainment out of as personally reclusive a genius as nature has yet managed to produce.

The musical is delightful for at least a quarter of an hour. Mandy Patinkin's Seurat, puckered and furrowed behind a long black beard, sits brooding over a bare canvas on an equally white and vacant stage. To the sound of pointillistic plunks and plonks he begins to furnish both. Trees sweep in from the wings at his beck and slide back at his call. "More boats," he mutters, and on they float, across what is revealed as a river to the left. Cardboard dogs pop up from the ground, and people, both real and two-dimensional, appear from all sides: a sullen boatman; a saucy, scuttling child; a girl with a fishing rod. We're in a Paris park, indeed in the very park where Seurat set the most famous of his paintings. Before long he'll have nudged and prodded the animate and inanimate objects on show into a remarkably precise replica of "Grande Jatte," and the curtain will fall as his hand stretches out and points at the completed masterpiece, a ringmaster presiding over the circus of his own imagination.

It's visually witty, visually daring, visually brilliant. One gasps once, twice, maybe even five or six times, and then, inevitably, one's gasp glands begin to weary and one begins to ask questions. Is visual brilliance enough to sustain the whole act, let alone an evening? Isn't Sondheim's accompanying music more than usually raveled, not to say Raveled, and lacking in melody? Where's the story, the plot, or, more to the point, the human interest? Not in the painting itself, as it turns out. Its population is skimpily characterized, its encounters cursory: the little girl insulting the boatman and being angrily chased by him; dalliance in the long grass, involving a married man and his valet's wife; a more extended amour between one of the two women languidly on the left of Seurat's picture and one of the two soldiers squashed primly together at its back. It would, no doubt, be silly to expect these people to be much more than impressions, since their main function is to end by standing, squatting, or lying in their predetermined positions in a painting of the Impressionist period. Indeed, something is actually added by transforming the second soldier into a wooden cutout symbiotically attached to his living, breathing comrade. That effectively points out the extreme oddity of their joint pose in the original picture. After *Sunday in the Park with George*, one will look much more carefully, much more searchingly, at every last detail in "Grande Jatte."

That's a gain, but a gain to take home with you, not the sort of gain that makes a successful book for a successful musical. So Sondheim and his librettist, James Lapine, have turned from the painting to the painter, only to find themselves confronted with the profound silence that was Georges Seurat. We know little about his external life except that he was rejected by most of his contemporaries; had a mistress named Madeleine Knobloch, who received due homage in the marvelous "Young Girl Powdering Herself"; and was survived by a few days by their illegitimate son, who had probably contracted the same meningitis that killed him. As for his internal life—well, all he'd say about "Grande Jatte" was that it happened to be the subject nearest to hand. We can only guess at his thoughts about anything at all. His supposed radicalism, for instance, is inferred from the fact that his friends were leftish and many of the people in his paintings working-class.

That explains why Lapine and Sondheim have invented a story of sorts for Seurat. It does not, however, excuse the earnest determination with which they've reduced him to that stock mythological creature, the brilliant but misunderstood artist whose earnest dedication to his muse alienates even his nearest and dearest. "Yes, Georges, run to your work, hide behind your painting," characteristically wails Dot, as Madeleine has been rechristened, after he's failed to take her

out for a fun evening at the Folies. "I am not hiding behind
my painting," he equally characteristically replies. "I am living in it—you can't accept me, you can't accept who I am!"
So to adieux in the park as dramatically implausible as they're
historically untrue, she dangling his newborn daughter over
his palette, he reacting with the conscientious brutality traditionally ascribed to genius: "You're blocking my light."

The second half takes us to contemporary America and
involves the reawakening of Seurat's grandson himself, an
aesthetic pioneer weary of his latest creation, a big, bulbous
toy that sends green laser beams crisscrossing round the theater. A trip to Paris, an inspirational encounter with the ghost
of Dot, whom death has apparently converted into an enthu-
siast for the lonely artist, toiling in his garret—and he's left
rapturously contemplating the empty spaces around him and
intoning, "So many possibilities." It's an upbeat ending, but
one sadly lacking in impact, since young George scarcely exists
as a dramatic character. But then the authors don't interest
us very much in old Georges either or at least in old Georges
as a plausible person. It's he as orchestrator of "Grande Jatte"
who matters—that, and perhaps also he as alter ego for Stephen Sondheim. Indeed, the real importance of *Sunday in the
Park* may be that it is camouflaged autobiography and credo,
a tour, with the composer as guide, of the dim and convoluted
passageways of composition.

After all, the two men have much in common. Like his
Seurat, Sondheim is a reformer who hasn't always found the
public at large eager to buy his reforms, an adventurer who
has sometimes found even the critical going rough. Like his
Seurat, he's been accused of being "all mind, no heart," a
cold chronicler of chilling subjects. Like Seurat, he's a perfectionist, laboring with a sort of Herculean delicacy to ensure
that each last adjective or semidemiquaver is absolutely as it
must be—"every minor detail," in young George's words, "a
major decision." Like his Seurat, he can readily be imagined

at the easel, or its musical equivalent, feverishly repeating, "Red, red, orange, orange," or painstakingly thinking his way into the ego of a dog, or bringing all his single-mindedness to the task of re-creating a hat. It's scarcely surprising that notwithstanding some clever patter and the odd soaring chorus, he should have renounced obvious harmony and verbal smartness for songs that obsessively tap, grind, and hammer their way into the spirit of the subject and perhaps into his own spirit, too. Never before can he have offered the world a more introverted score than here. It is a series of furrowed ruminations, restlessly and usually dissonantly evoking the creative process itself. It is, in short, Sondheim.

Maybe *Sunday in the Park* is confession as well as artistic credo, an apologia of sorts on Sondheim's part or at least an answer to such as Leonard Bernstein, who has criticized him for "inhibitedness about self-expression," in other words, for hiding his feelings, and to such as John Lahr, whose recently published *Automatic Vaudeville* wonders if he has any feelings at all. Here are strong emotions, passionate emotions, but they're the emotions of a man whose great love is his vocation, a man who would defiantly explain, with his Seurat, "I am what I do!"

That suspicion is enough in itself to make *Sunday* worth attention. The Sondheim scholars will, I suspect, spend more time poring over its nuances than over larger matters in musicals of more apparent moment. But meanwhile, the theatergoers of today remain to be satisfied, and they can justly complain that artistic manifesto though it may in effect be, *Sunday* fails to meet Sondheim's own artistic criteria, according to which score must be perfectly integrated with character and story, and a musical can't be good "in spite of its book." It's a brave work, an original work, by the standards of Broadway an astoundingly brave and original work; and it's also undramatic and tedious. As a crusading artist Sondheim has my admiration, but as a group of people who seemed often to feel he was crusading against them, the audience last night had my sympathy.

This is becoming a somewhat querulous journal, a litany of moans, beefs, and affronted whimpers, a sort of concerto for solo grouch, and the complaints aren't over yet. I also wish shows would happen when they're supposed to happen instead of happening when they're not supposed to happen or, sometimes, not happening at all. *A Moon for the Misbegotten* postponed its opening night, though for a reason that only a very hard-line Christian Scientist would find difficult to accept, the sickness of the leading man. So did *Sunday in the Park with George,* because after eons spent toiling in the workshops, its presenters felt, with cause then and (I fear) cause even now, that its second half wasn't all it should be. The Manhattan Theater Club isn't apparently confident enough to show the press *Park Your Car in Harvard Yard* by Israel Horovitz, whose *The Indian Wants the Bronx* we all admired back in the 1960's. Nor is the Roundabout Theater officially to open its revival of O'Neill's *Desire Under the Elms.* And Harvey Fierstein's *Spookhouse* has been similarly dickering with us poor critics' diaries.

But now it's taken the plunge, nonplussing me with the flesh-and-blood beastliness supposedly occurring in the rooms above the red-eyed reptiles, fanged devils, and neogothic human dummies of Fierstein's Coney Island spookhouse. The stage machinery, coming as it does with a cart that rolls on rails through the flashing and screeching horrors, is admittedly pretty spectacular. The dramatic and psychological engineering turns out to be more suspect.

Mother is a slatternly palmist; Dad, a helpless, mumbling nothing-very-much. Their younger son is a television-fixated zombie. Their teenage daughter is pregnant, as it turns out by their elder son, who has himself been crippled by a fall sustained after beating, raping, and setting on fire an eight-

year-old girl. It's not the very happiest of families, and it isn't
made happier by the efforts of a well-intentioned psychiatric
social worker, who thinks that all that's needed is a little
"mothering." This the mother in question adamantly refuses
to offer, to the point of sticking a knife in her elder son when
he's foisted on her, a climax that Fierstein fails to make any
less preposterous than the other human spookery that has
preceded it. It's not good melodrama or a vital study of family
conflict or an effective satiric attack on the "caring profes-
sions" or anything else it might want to be.

Nevertheless, Fierstein's *Torch Song Trilogy* is still on
Broadway, still demonstrating how far the American gay theater has come, both emotionally and geographically, since the
Reverend Al Carmines's *Faggot!* ten years ago. At one point
in that then-celebrated revue, two voracious mothers con-
gratulated each other on the fact that their two sons lived
together rather than with any nasty girls: "Did you think that
would happen when they were little?" "No, but I had my
hopes." The implications of that and other moments—that
while gay people should feel free to be as gay as possible, it's
a pity they turned out that way in the first place—wouldn't
be very popular nowadays. Nor, I suspect, would the relentless
cheerfulness with which Carmines preached his swinging theology, a matter, as I recall, of the word made flesh and gleefully
shacking up all over the place, a hunger and thirst after the
"perfect nookie," otherwise defined as "liquid, hairy nice-
ness." That would surely seem a bit unsophisticated, a bit too
purposefully rapturous, to such as Mr. Fierstein.

He knows, for instance, that the gay life can be pretty bleak
and loveless, a matter of furtive, silent encounters in the back
rooms of bars with men you don't even see, and he concedes
that it is a struggle to sustain anything deeper and more permanent. Arnold the queen, unashamedly, flamboyantly and
entertainingly at the center of *Torch Song*, has an on-off affair
with a bisexual named Ed and then a more lasting one with

a young model called Alan, who is killed by red-necks wielding baseball bats. He doesn't disguise his delight in the physical, but he makes it increasingly apparent that his real quest is for security, respect, and love as complete as any heterosexual could claim. The most amusing of the three sections of *Torch Song* is the second, showing as it does, the convoluted emotional algebra of a "civilized" weekend spent together by Arnold, Alan, Ed, and Ed's well-meaning wife, but the most strongly felt is the last, in which Arnold battles to persuade his own impossible mother that he can be a kind of mother, too. He's planning to adopt an adolescent called David and seems to want to do so very much indeed. The love he's seeking is, finally, parental. And why not? Fierstein is careful to cover himself against the obvious charge, that such an arrangement might nudge the boy's sexual preferences in a direction that, society being what it is, might not be for his best. These preferences are already clear. Indeed, it's to reconcile him to them that the social workers have fostered the troubled David with Arnold.

So far, so good—so far, but unluckily no farther. The suspicion grows, hardens, that Fierstein is faking the evidence in order to win a case to which he's passionately committed. "You've taken a punk kid," an impressed Ed tells Arnold, "who's spent the last three years on the streets and in juvenile court and turned him into a home-loving, fun-loving, school-going teenager in all of six months." And David himself, benignly and wisely reorganizing his male mother's life for him, confirms this view with pretty well everything he says and does. I just couldn't believe in this conversion, not (I insist) out of any heterosexual prejudice but because it was so quick and painless. It's sheer wishful thinking on Fierstein's part to suppose that adolescent problems so severe, whether they're afflicting someone gay or straight or both, can simply be magicked away, like stains in a Laundromat.

There's wishful thinking to be found in Fierstein's book for

La Cage aux Folles, too. One can scarcely expect grueling
realism in a Broadway musical, even today, but it takes more
than the usual suspension of disbelief to credit the buoyant
and bouncing heterosexuality of the young hero, who has been
brought up in and around a transvestite nightclub by his
father, its owner, and his "mother," its principal performer.
He's so utterly, so painfully *clean* that you'd think that he,
too, had spent his formative years in a Laundromat, being
whirled around with comfy woolens and cozy cottons.

Torch Song proves that Fierstein is an artist, but it and
Cage leave you wondering if he's clear enough in his mind
about the boundaries between art and propaganda. The one
can dwindle into the other when a playwright allows theory
to determine his picture of life, instead of vice versa. Fierstein
believes that homosexuals can make excellent parents. He
wants the straight world, too, to acknowledge this. What he
seems not yet to have realized is that so contentious a case,
however excellent in itself, can finally prevail only if it's seen
to have been presented with the utmost fairness, down to the
last qualification, caveat, and piece of contradictory evidence.
What *Torch Song* and maybe even *Cage* don't need is the
clutter and confusion of *Spookhouse*, but they could both do
with just a little more of its taste for harsh, unlovely facts.

There are two, maybe three reasons for pondering the case
of Arthur Kopit's *End of the World*, which arrived barely a
few hours before the cutoff date for the Tony nominations
and the close of the official "season." It confutes those of us
who suspect that the American drama is irredeemably dwarf-
ish by tackling no less a subject than the possible annihilation
of the human species, along with most of the animal ones. It
has, however, been rather grudgingly received, some reviewers giving the impression they prefer tiny plays perfectly crafted
to venturesome ones with admitted faults and flaws. Finally,
it turns out to be, with the ill-fated *Brothers*, one of only two

plays that have been produced specifically for Broadway this season.

The other "new" American works, such as they were, all derived from elsewhere: *Open Admissions* from off-Broadway, *Play Memory* from the McCarter Theater in Princeton, *The Golden Age* from Washington, *Glengarry Glen Ross* from London via Chicago. Even the one-woman play that preceded *End of the World* onto Broadway by a few days—Elizabeth Forsyth Hailey's *Woman of Independent Means*, an epistolary saga that would make even Samuel Richardson's *Clarissa* seem short, sharp, and action-packed—originated out in Los Angeles.

One of the sorrows of my American year is that I have ventured out of New York very seldom and reviewed not a single regional production. On the other hand, I can argue that the omission is less grave than it might seem because the regions keep coming both to Broadway and off-Broadway: *Moon for the Misbegotten* from the American Repertory Theater in Cambridge, *Fool for Love* from San Francisco, *The Lady and the Clarinet* from Los Angeles, and *And A Nightingale Sang . . .* from the Steppenwolf Theater in Chicago. Nor is the flow ended. Steppenwolf is bringing Lanford Wilson's early *Balm in Gilead* to Circle Rep. And Chicago's Goodman Theater, which sent us the present production of *Glengarry*, should shortly be dispatching to New York David Rabe's *Spinoff*, now retitled *Hurlyburly*. The Windy City seems a pretty creative place these days, more so, given its size, than the Big Apple.

You can see why some regional producers and directors have their reservations about this flow. They could end up putting on play after play with half an eye, or even a whole eye, on a transfer to Broadway and triumph in the big city. That might lead to soft and safe programming and would certainly be no way to keep a company and repertory system in place. In his *Making Scenes*, Robert Brustein writes of his distress on realizing that some of the best regional theaters were selling their birthrights for a mess of royalties. "Did we," he goes on, "start this movement with the intention of producing plays for the commercial theater? Had we made this effort in order to reproduce the same system we were pledged to reform?"

The same anxieties have sometimes been heard in Britain. Should the National Theater, for instance, really be putting on plays like Peter Shaffer's *Amadeus* or Alan Ayckbourn's *Bedroom Farce*, both of which eventually found their way not merely to the commercial sector but to Broadway itself? It's a situation that clearly needs careful watching in both cities, but perhaps more in America, where the nonprofit-making sector seems weaker and more vulnerable and the commercial managements have more reason to exploit it. West End impresarios still produce new plays with some frequency; their Broadway counterparts, virtually never. To look to new work that has already been successfully market-tested on audiences elsewhere isn't just the norm in New York these days; it's becoming an invariable rule.

You can understand why, considering the costs and risks involved. And it can bring benefits to everyone: the probably penurious company that first put on the play, the commercial management, and, by no means least, the Broadway audiences themselves. New York might not, for instance, have seen Athol Fugard's *Master Harold and . . . the Boys*, had not Lloyd Richards first presented it at Yale. In fact, it wouldn't have seen most of the forty-odd productions that have transferred to Broadway from the regions and off-Broadway in the past three-odd years. In some ways it's a benign parasitism, if one with perils for the vendor and, more subtly, for the vendee, too. It might be argued—mightn't it?—that such swaps and transplants disguise the extent to which Broadway is ailing, camouflage its failure to survive on its own organs. They are, therefore, giving encouragement to those who see no reason for the radical medicine that's really needed.

Meanwhile, *End of the World* is there to be relished, a thoroughly exceptional phenomenon, for all the cavils of my colleagues. Not only was it built for Broadway, not only does it tackle the very last subject you'd expect to appeal to the Broadway crowd, but it's actually a shrewd and lively piece of work. Any season it would surely seem at least refreshing. This one it's an exhilarating rush of oxygen to the brain, restoring cells half-suffocated by the intellectual emptiness of the New York theater. Insofar as it's possible to enjoy a play that fully expects the human species to auto-destruct, and soon, I enjoyed it greatly.

And I enjoyed it even though Arthur Kopit has, I suspect quite unwittingly, borrowed his principal dramatic device from a British writer and handled it less consistently. David Hare's *Knuckle* entertainingly parodied Raymond Chandler's thrillers, using a Bogart-like private eye to unravel a real-estate racket and expose the supposed ugliness of the profit motive itself. Similarly, *End of the World* introduces us to a playwright who is sometimes also a tough-guy tec, a spoof Philip Marlowe interested in creatively answering a still bigger question: Why is Planet Earth doomed to destruction by H-bomb? Off he goes from New York to Washington, informally to hobnob with a suave general, a modern Dr. Strangelove, and the inmates of the local think tank and informatively to explore the paradoxes of the nuclear trade. To be strong (it seems) is perhaps to be strong, but to be too strong is to be weak because it invites preemptive attack by someone who knows that "going first is going best," and thus Armageddon could occur precisely because a country is trying to avoid Armageddon.

When I arrived in this country, I recalled seeing Kopit's *Oh Dad, Poor Dad* here twenty years ago. It now seems to

me that that bravura study of a vulture mum, and the dead
and doomed males in her life, should be revived sometime
soon, just to show how tame most contemporary plays about
parents and children really are. His *Indians*, too, was often
scathingly funny, and that is still more surprising since its
subject was nothing less than genocide. Anyone who admired
that, and most critics did, should surely be able to spot the
ferment beneath the intermittent flippancy of *End of the World*,
the tense nerves behind the caricature. In any case, isn't
"caricature" a pretty wishful word for some of its characters?

Life is more inclined to cartoon itself than we like to pretend, especially when power turns men's heads, making other
people abstractions to them and ideas fixations. In a world of
newspeak and nukespeak, it isn't impossible to imagine an
eminent policy maker hankering for "anticipatory retalia-
tion," which means destroying a country that may possibly
be thinking of destroying you, over noodles in a Japanese-
American restaurant. Several times Kopit slyly juxtaposes the
ordinary, the banal, with the inconceivable. Several times he
suggests that planetary war has become an armchair sport, a
sort of apocalyptic blend of chess and chicken, played by men
too obsessed or cerebral or scared to face what it would actually be. So far the result is a draw, but can draws be infinitely extended, even by two expert combatants? When doom
comes, perhaps it will be as a result of political brinkmanship
practiced by smiling intellectuals in aprons in a Georgetown
kitchen.

Or perhaps it will be because there's a glitter about nuclear
weapons, an excitement we can't expect our species endlessly
to deny itself, given its curiosity, its thirst for thrills, its sudden, mad impulses. You can hold peace conferences, sign
treaties, put hot line telephones and fail-safe devices conscientiously in place, but nothing can finally allow for the sen-
sation-hungry lunatic who lives at the back of the human head
and yearns to find out what the ultimate catastrophe is like.

That's the final fruit of the dramatist-sleuth's researches and the conclusion of *End of the World,* which may and may not be the play he writes—and I have to say it seems to me horribly plausible. I would agree that Kopit's attempts to reconcile instruction and fun aren't always successful. In fact, I'd agree he's written better. But I don't think he's ever written more devastatingly to the point, and to greet the play with strictures on its structure strikes me as a bit like condemning Paul Revere for his posture in the saddle.

You can't help feeling sorry for Ted Tally. His *Terra Nova* was first produced eight long years ago in New Haven and has since been well received in almost every part of the world, on two separate occasions in my own island corner. But until it appeared at the American Place two weeks ago, it had never been done in New York, and so quickly is it disappearing from the American Place it must seem to poor Tally it *still* has not really been done there.

I went along a day or two ago, encouraged by some warm reviews from my colleagues and hoping maybe to spin one of my review essays out of the experience, only to discover that it was about to close. I have, as it happens, a friend in the cast, an English actor married to an American. He tells me that the play's producers had exhausted their guaranteed audiences, the theater's subscribers, and had therefore come to the point of deciding whether or not they could rely on a more general public to keep the play running. But that would mean advertising and promotion amounting to maybe $30,000, and they'd concluded the expenditure would be too risky.

No, you can't help feeling sorry for Tally, and for New York audiences, and for off-Broadway, and maybe for the American theater itself, for being in such a wretched fiscal predicament. *Terra Nova* itself wouldn't, I suppose, rate among the masterworks of our era. Tally wrote it when he was still a student at Yale Drama School, and it does sometimes suffer from youthful solemnity and other such awkwardness. But there is also skill and tension and technical adventurousness in his version of a story every British child knows from about the time he learns to say the names Winston Churchill or Baden-Powell: Robert Scott's heroic attempt to be the first to the South Pole in 1911. The very first prize I won at school— for being the best-behaved eleven-year-old, alias the class creep—was an account of that doomed expedition.

Tally, being an American and a realist, is not enslaved by the myth. He knows, for instance, that somewhere near his core Scott was a disappointed man, somewhat embittered by his lack of advancement in the navy, compulsively seeking some grander memorial than "a bloody little plaque in the fifth-floor lavatory at the Admiralty." He wanted glory, but glory achieved through struggle, self-sacrifice, principle, and fair play. Not for him the expediency of the Norwegian Roald Amundsen, who systematically devoured the dogs driving his sledges and won the race to the Pole; Scott and his men trudged there on foot, made foolish, if high-minded, errors, lost, and died. It's a tale of an idealist destroyed but idealism itself somehow undefeated and, as such, of interest to spectators other than the more unthinkingly blimpish sort of Brit. It deserved better than three weeks in a cellar-theater on Forty-fifth Street, especially since there are some good, strong performances to be found in the interminable whiteness of Douglas Stein's set.

Still, its failure is instructive. This journal has largely concentrated on Broadway and its slow destruction by market forces. It's some time since I've said anything about the scarcely more inspiriting achievements and circumstances of off-Broadway. Some of its problems would seem to be similar: ever-increasing costs; fear of failure; a caution in program choice that's encouraged by the current public preference for small, inward-looking and usually naturalistic plays. Some of its problems are its own: forms of finance that tend to discourage danger, experiment. The result, at any rate, is an off-Broadway that's less and less the creative, exciting alternative it was twenty, even ten years ago. As Joseph Papp remarked to me a few months ago, "the avant-garde, daring theater of the sixties and seventies seems to have gone. It's become more conservative, more institutional, and its eye is much more on Broadway."

His own Public Theater, he agreed, is as institutional as any and has become a prolific source of Broadway successes—isn't *A Chorus Line* still flourishing at the Shubert, the most triumphant transfer of all time? But Papp's tastes are broader and less predictable than most, so it seems quirkier and more stimulating in its product than the other major off-Broadway theaters. This season it's staged Václav Havel's protest plays, and Janusz Glowacki's highly original *Cinders*, and a fine revival of Lanford Wilson's *Serenading Louie*, and short pieces by David Henry Hwang, and *The Human Comedy*, and Caryl Churchill's *Fen*. But that record is exceptional. I've been a pretty regular visitor at the major off-Broadway theaters and a not infrequent one at some of the minor ones, too. And apart from Charles Ludlam's *Galas*, the revivals of Pinter's *Old Times*, and *Other Places*, at the Roundabout and the Manhattan Theater Club respectively, and Durang's *Baby with the Bath Water* at Playwrights Horizons, there isn't a lot that sticks in my mind—except, I'm afraid, as signs and symptoms of what's thin and limited about the American theater.

Maybe this just means that the 1983 to 84 season wasn't a vintage one. Maybe the theatrical sun will shine and the crop improve next year. But I can't help wondering if there's something more permanently wrong with the soil underneath.

First, let me make a necessary distinction. Off-Broadway theaters must have at least a hundred seats to merit the title; anything less, and they're off-off Broadway theaters, with considerably less demanding rules governing wages and employment. Off-off Broadway, the average salary for an artistic director is apparently just $8,000, and actors get paid as little as $45 and rarely more than $650 for an eight-week engagement. Off-Broadway, payments fall far short of what Equity has won for those appearing on Broadway, but are considerably better than that, from $200 to $350 a week. Normally everyone in the cast, however large or small his part, is paid the same. That, or perhaps a bit more, may be enough to attract the occasional performer of renown or excellence or even both—after all, it can mean a juicy part, not too long a run, attention from the critics and from fellow members of the profession, and considerably less pressure than obtains on Broadway itself—but it is clearly not enough to keep them on the same boards for production after production. Off-Broadway tends to make do with the promising, the sound, the solid, reserving the really exciting and accomplished actor for occasions which, if more common than they were, are still obviously exceptional.

The cost of production is surprisingly high. It's not, of course, as steep as for an equivalent show on Broadway, but steeper than for the West End of London: $250,000 for an average straight play; $500,000 or more for a musical. That means that off-Broadway has become biggish business. The major theaters are now spending more than $1 million a year and therefore are having to find $1 million from their various customers and supporters.

At least 50 percent of total income normally comes from the sale of seats, presently a $24 top off-Broadway and $10 off-off Broadway. Grants and subsidies from public sources, which means the National Endowment for the Arts or New York State, could bring the luckier theaters up another 15 percent of their total costs, leaving a shortfall of perhaps 35 percent. Of this, one-third is likely to come from wealthy individual donors, one-third from corporations, one-third from foundations.

That means, of course, that a large part of the theater's

efforts, as well as a fair proportion of its budget, will go into the business of raising funds. It's said that it takes roughly the same effort to cajole $2,000 from a corporation as it does to strike lucky and get a foundation grant of $35,000, and either way the amount of wooing is considerable in itself and has to be repeated, year after year after year. Manhattan Theater Club, one of the most prestigious and successful outfits, has no fewer than three full-time "development people." Yet it recently had to drop a production it had planned because disaster suddenly struck on another front. New York State cut its grant by $30,000. Circle Rep was similarly let down by a foundation which said that it was a question of giving money to it or to the Newark Fire Department and that the latter was the needier.

As this suggests, theaters are having to compete more and more seriously for a diminishing amount of public money and for private funds that are themselves subject to constantly increasing demands, and at a time of relentlessly rising costs. It is difficult, doubly difficult, because both the philanthropists and the legislators seem unable to comprehend why drama should need support at all. Jane Moss, who runs the alliance of eighty-seven off-Broadway and off-off Broadway theaters collectively known as ART–New York, finds it quite a struggle to explain the difference between the Lucille Lortel, which often plays host to commercial ventures, and Circle Rep, a nonprofit-making resident playhouse. It can, she says, even be hard explaining the difference between Circle Rep and Broadway.

"They say, if the Shuberts can make it pay, why can't we? It doesn't help when we point out that our members have a higher earnings ratio than symphony orchestras and many other arts organizations. They think us less necessary, less of an art form. Part of the trouble is a puritan thing. They think the theater is slightly illicit, or at least people just having a good time, not a serious matter. And part of the trouble is that we're terribly young. We stumbled very late into an arena that was started as a commercial operation, and we never cried poor enough, never argued the need for grants strongly enough. So they were able to keep us quiet by throwing us a little bit of subsidy, like welfare. Or, of course, give us nothing at all."

So what hope for serious, challenging, even difficult drama off-Broadway? What hope for classics with big casts? Not a lot; not without putting up seat prices to levels that would risk alienating too many of the 2 million who presently attend the off-Broadway and off-off Broadway theaters each year or without chivying those theaters' supporters to new and astonishing displays of generosity. But even if this last achievement were possible, would it be altogether desirable? What the foundations and corporations are said all too often to want are good notices, public fuss, maybe a transfer to Broadway. The form it finally takes may be emotional gratification rather than hard currency, but what they're looking for is pretty much what investors and speculators are looking for: conspicuous critical and commercial success, not artistic achievement. The theater which interestingly and worthily fails risks losing its grants; the one that sells out the morning after a new play has opened is likely to be showered with money it scarcely needs.

That's bad, especially at the present time, when the margin between success and failure is so small, and one flop can cancel a production, a series of them quickly put a nonprofit-making theater out of business. Their dependence on private charity encourages artistic directors to play safe, and so, some will privately admit, does their dependence on subscribers. You can see why theaters are keen to enroll these. In return for guaranteed seats at bargain prices, they give money "up front," at the beginning of a season, making it possible to plan ahead more confidently and safely. Subscribers will probably account for from 50 to 70 percent of the seats sold during a play's showing, which is likely to be from four to six weeks. The management may then extend that run, moving the production to a different theater or postponing its next offering; or, like the American Place with *Terra Nova*, it may decide to close. But either way it means that the first and overwhelming obligation is to keep the subscribers happy, and those subscribers tend to be older and wealthier, people with more conservative tastes, and liable to cancel their membership if Genet or Edward Bond or even Sam Shepard suddenly appears on the bill.

Let me not suggest that there aren't also theaters eager to put on Shepard in particular. Haven't *Fool for Love* and the revival of *True West* given the past off-Broadway season such small distinction as it's enjoyed? That's for sure. Nevertheless, it's increasingly being left to the more marginal off-Broadway theaters, the ones less richly endowed with resources both financial and human, to put on the riskier, quirkier work. The more mainstream institutions should perhaps remember the example of New York's own Theater Guild, which came into being in the early 1930's as a nonprofit-making alternative to Broadway and eventually became indistinguishable from it. Considering what Broadway is in 1984, that would be a melancholy fate.

There would always have been reasons why Beth Henley, whose *Miss Firecracker Contest* has just surfaced at the Manhattan Theater Club, was and is an exceptional talent, but one at least has a lot less validity than it did only five, ten years ago. This, of course, is her gender. That very useful encyclopedia *Contemporary Dramatists*, published back in 1977, contains essays on nearly 300 American, British, and Irish people writing for the stage. Of these only 27—14 of them working this side of the Atlantic—are women. And that number includes Iris Murdoch, Doris Lessing, Brigid Brophy, and others for whom the theater is a relatively unimportant

means of expression; a few, notably Elaine May, Shelagh Delaney, and Ann Jellicoe, who would appear to have renounced
it; several others, among them Agatha Christie, Enid Bagnold,
and (most sadly and recently) Lillian Hellman, who have abandoned it more irretrievably, by dying; and more still who
aren't exactly household names. How many Americans have
heard of Jane Arden? How many English people, of Nancy
Walter?

One may reach into history and pick out a Susan Glaspell
here, a Dodie Smith there, but the difficulty of doing even
that seems only to emphasize that compared with what women
have done and continue to do for the novel, their contribution
to the drama until very recently has been not merely slim but
anorexic. What's the reason for this, to me, very puzzling
silence? Is it the one sometimes given by women themselves:
that theater managements have historically been, or seemed
to be, more aggressive than publishing houses?

Perhaps. Write a book, and you can remain at home exchanging letters with your editor or maybe taking the occasional trip into town for lunch and a chat. Write a play, and
you're liable to be sucked into a sweaty male world of tele-
grams and anger, with auditions, readings, meetings, wran-
gles, triumphs at Sardi's, disasters at Sardi's, and the rest of
it. It's difficult to imagine a Charlotte Brontë or an Emily
Dickinson having a furious row with some actor-manager in
his theater's pit. Yet this explanation overlooks not only the
few women who *did* turn their talents to the drama in former
times but the many more who would have been perfectly capable of standing up to the male establishment in more recent
ones. You can't tell me that Lillian Hellman's personality was
uniquely pugnacious. Nor, incidentally, can you tell me that
the most dedicatedly swinish of male chauvinist producers
would have failed to take an interest and display a little di-
plomacy if (say) a Virginia Woolf or a Eudora Welty had
started to write for the theater.

Could, then, there be something in the female temperament innately alien to the dramatic form or at least to the form it has so often taken? Plays have traditionally been too external, too rectilinear, too rigidly structured a means of expression for creative minds that tend to be subtler, more curvilinear, and therefore perhaps better suited to the novel. The reason that more women seem now to be beginning to write for the stage may be that the old, mechanical "well-made play" is in decline and more elastic and flexible styles of drama are on the rise. Yet this is a theory that could be accused of propagating sexist attitudes in a fake-flattering way and in any case is challenged by theatrical history. Did Chekhov, say, write more "rectilinear" plays than Susan Glaspell or Lillian Hellman? There were women who were comfortable enough with conventional forms, and there are women comfortable with them still.

Marsha Norman has suggested that since plays mostly involve action, playwrights need to see themselves as active, effective, and influential, as women historically haven't. That's an interesting theory, but maybe the practical explanation is simpler. Maybe it is that until very recently the theater, without excluding female writers de jure, was de facto a sort of no-go area, a club whose leather armchairs had so long been occupied by male buttocks that most women did not seriously consider entering it. For a long time it also had a rather risqué reputation, a hangover from the mid-nineteenth century and before, so it was double intimidating to the socially more orthodox. Tradition brainwashed, rather than positively browbeat, would-be dramatists into writing novels or staying mum, and only a few, and those not necessarily the most talented, broke the unwritten rules.

However, all that seems to be undergoing an overdue, a long-overdue change. I don't know whether something has happened to the theater establishment, to the drama, to women themselves, or to all three, but something *has* at last happened. Back in Britain I've found myself reviewing more and more work by female dramatists in the last two or three years, some by writers accomplished enough to make their way across the Atlantic before long. If America hasn't yet heard of Louise Page, Sue Townsend, and Catherine Hayes, it surely will soon. And over here, I've been much preoccupied with the talents of Tina Howe, Wendy Wasserstein, Marsha Norman, Maria Irene Fornes, and most recently, the novelist Joyce Carol Oates. Her *Presque Isle,* presented somewhere on the Upper East Side, was yet another combat drama involving parents and children, but more vigorous than most examples of the genre.

You can't say that women are responsible for the present profusion of "family plays." You can't even say that they're writing more of them than men. Indeed, generalizations about their qualities and capacities seem no easier than about those of the opposite sex. What, for instance, has Wendy Wasserstein's nervy wit in common with Rosalyn Drexler's aggressive high jinks or Marsha Norman's mordant anguishings about the purpose of life? What has Pam Gems, author of *Piaf* in common with Ann Jellicoe, author of that delightful study of male sexual mores *The Knack?* What has the American Beth Henley in common with the Englishwoman Caryl Churchill? Nothing, except merit and originality.

Churchill I take to be one of the top five or six British playwrights currently producing work, and that's not a judgment I would primarily base on *Fen,* strong, bold, compassionate stuff though its recent New York revival confirmed it to be. Her *Cloud Nine* was a marvelously inventive reminder that our sexual identities are mostly too intricate, too unruly ever to be neatly categorized and compartmentalized. Her *Top Girls* seemed to me to combine the same incisiveness with still greater imaginative verve, starting (as it did) with a social gathering of some of the more extraordinary women history has produced, then launching into a debate about the ways their descendants are using the liberties they have so painfully won. Does freedom consist of mutilating the self in order to slot into a male world? Does it mean aggressively adopting the very values that have for centuries been oppressing your sex? What use is it if it transforms the clever women into predators and does nothing for the stupid, weak, and helpless? The English thought those good questions, and so, if we're to judge by the enthusiasm for *Top Girls* in New York, did the Americans.

Though *Top Girls* concentrated on one career woman, *Cloud Nine* on one family, *Fen* on one community, they all displayed an interest in big social issues. In that Caryl Churchill is, of course, at one with many of her fellow playwrights in Britain, male and female, and at odds with many over here, not least Beth Henley. The latter is interested in people for people's sake, not because they're evidence in some larger thesis, in families as families, and in communities as communities, not as case studies for the social scientist. Indeed, what makes her special is the wise and healing humor with which she chronicles the oddities and incongruities of personality, relationship, and, of course, habitat. Her characters tend to be fidgety and sometimes footloose, but they're southerners, so they have deeper roots than most of their fellow countrymen; they belong even when they chafe at belonging. Not many dramatists have created a world so distinctively and decidedly their own that you could recognize it if you accidentally blundered into one of their plays in mid-performance, stayed long enough to apologize to an usher, and then scrambled embarrassedly out of the auditorium into the street; but Beth Henley is certainly to be numbered among them.

Crimes of the Heart left one with that unmissable, irresistible feeling: reason enough, I'd have thought, for its success on Broadway and the Pulitzer Prize it won in 1981. *The Miss Firecracker Contest* does so, too. You need only a moment

with the lumpish seamstress Popeye, so called because someone once put eardrops into the wrong part of her head, somewhat impairing her ability to make pink pajamas for bullfrogs
but leaving her eyeballs able to hear voices. You need hear
only a word or two about old Mother Williams, who used to
torment the dogs by feeding them lemon rind and herself grew
black ape fur after a course of rejuvenating injections. You
know at once where you are.

But where, precisely, are you? In *Crimes of the Heart* it
was called Hazlehurst, in the underrated *The Wake of Jamey
Foster* it was Canton, and now it is Brookhaven. But it seems
to me that its name should properly be Henley, Miss., after
its affectionate annalist. One imagines her on a wisteria-
covered porch, surrounded by listeners sobbing with glee as
she relates story after story, remembers hilarious calamity
after hilarious calamity, all involving the same tiny southern
town. That evening when Jamey Foster lay in his coffin in
yellow tweed, with one sister-in-law absently dropping a ham
sandwich on his face, another cutely expostulating "honey
child" and "poppa sweet potato," his widow refusing to go to
his funeral in protest against his affair with the fat woman
down the road, a girl arsonist loose in the kitchen, and good
old Brocker Slade, the farmer whose hogs exploded of over-
eating combined with constipation, inappropriately singing
"Nick nack, paddy wack, give the dog a bone." Or that awful
time when Babe Bottrell—you know, the one with the sister
with deformed ovaries and the mother who hanged first her
pet cat, then herself—shot her husband, the state sena-
tor. . . .

Henley, Miss., is a sort of living folklore factory, and *Miss
Firecracker* as beguiling a tale as any that has emerged from
that rich source. It's all about the ritual held in the town every
fifth of July—a beauty contest for which the main character,
Carnelle Scott, has been shortlisted. If only she could become

the local equivalent of Miss Universe, everyone would, she believes, forget the years she spent contracting the clap inside the cars of a fair proportion of the local citizenry. But as it turns out, she trips over her ludicrous dress and lands on her rump, to cries of "Miss Hot Tamale" from the chortling onlookers. Even a tap dance routine to the accompaniment of "The Star-Spangled Banner" can't prevent her from losing to the yellow-toothed Caroline Jeffers and even to Sapphire Mendoza, who is there with her hula-hoop only to show how integrated the town is these days.

The play displays the same sly delight in the quirky, the bizarre, the drolly disastrous that marked Miss Henley's previous town reports, and it introduces us to some characteristically entertaining citizens. There is, for instance, Carnelle's cousin Delmount, one of those flowers of southern chivalry who go early to seed, a Lancelot who has picked up some dubious habits from Mordred. He's done time in a New Orleans sanitorium after attempting to strangle someone who "was boring me to death." Not long ago he fought a duel for a woman with "classically beautiful features," but with broken bottles. Now he's lost his job sweeping rotting dogs from the sidewalk and dreams of returning South, there to study philosophy and "let everyone know why we're living."

Are examples of southern eccentricity being paraded around the stage for the amusement of Yankee audiences? If one sometimes suspects so at the MTC, it's the fault of Stephen Tobolowsky's production, which grabs for laughter instead of letting laughter emerge from carefully prepared characters and atmosphere. There is, to be sure, an element of caricature in Miss Henley's work, but it's by no means the crude, monochrome sort one associates with the parodist or theatrical puppeteer. Her people aren't painted marionettes, nor is the South a gaudy gothic showcase for their antics. She herself once said she felt "close to all her characters," and

one believes her. They're grotesque, yet they have feelings;
they're exorbitant, yet they're vulnerable. Indeed, what makes
them absurd and sometimes even outrageous may also be what
gives them their poignancy and sometimes even their pathos.

As Miss Henley has also said, their lives are difficult and
occasionally terrifying, but as she might have added, they have
the knack of surviving and surviving with a flourish. They
have curiosity, natural resourcefulness, and imaginative resilience, positive virtues that help them cope with their constantly disappointed dreams and the much that's bleak and
desolate in their lives. You never can be quite sure of what
they'll say or do next. Quite suddenly they'll be interjecting
irrelevant information into the conversation, or delivering
themselves of wise little sentiments, or earnestly reminiscing
about this or that. They tend to be jealous and can suddenly
become bitter and rancorous at family sins of commission and
omission suffered long ago. Yet they tend to underreact to
greater and more obvious disasters, giving the impression that
a suicide, a murder are as ordinary as apple pie. Appalling
events become cozy anecdotes, experiences remembered and
consigned to history as examples of the everyday ups and
downs of life in Henley, Miss.

This unpredictability says something about the people of
Miss Firecracker and adds to its undoubted sense of life. At
any moment someone may start puffing out smoke rings and
demonstrating how to eat lighted cigarettes, or someone else
counter by doggedly trying to waggle his ears. Or someone
may describe how she almost strangled to death on the um-
bilical cord, or announce how much she likes the phrase "host
of whales," or relate the sad story of a midget called Sweet
Pea, or plonkingly opine that "the abundance of treasure
serves only to underline the desperate futility of life," or start
blowing on her heart to cool the unrequited passion it feels.

As this last incident suggests, the helpless, hopeless yearnings that afflict so many of the characters may suddenly and unexpectedly bubble to the surface, giving us tiny climaxes like the one involving Popeye, Carnelle, and Carnelle's sister, Elaine, the ex-beauty queen who has left home and children because her husband wears sweet cologne and "makes me ill." A cry of "I hate my hair" follows a wail of "He doesn't care about me" and a howl of "My life is over" as the three women whip each other up to a joint hysteria you feel they half enjoy. It's a scene Chekhov himself wouldn't have been ashamed of writing.

Not that you'd know it at the MTC, where the climaxes have the clatter of farce, not the watchfulness of comedy. Belita Moreno's Popeye, with her forlorn grin and big-boned diffidence, has her moments, and so does Mark Linn-Baker's Delmount, a nice blend of the raffish and the shabby. So, too, does Holly Hunter's tense, scrawny Carnelle, though she's apt to become unnecessarily strenuous, like the evening as a whole. The production's veins are packed with adrenaline, its heartbeat veers from 130 to 150 a minute, and its nerves are the nerves of New York, not those of long, slow afternoons in midsummer Mississippi. Too often it's funny and energetic and nothing much else.

That's a pity, because it means we hear the tune but miss the harmonic texture, the haunting chords beneath. Those should be especially apparent at an ending markedly similar to that of *Crimes of the Heart*. There the main characters, three sisters, forgot their angers and fears in a long, golden moment of togetherness over a birthday cake. Here Carnelle squats with Delmount and Popeye on the roof of the tent where she's endured public humiliation, raptly watching zooming firework after zooming firework, proof after proof that, as Beth Henley once said, "everything doesn't have to be wonderful for it to be wonderful." But even if the production can't catch the subtle magic that's needed, it can't hide the quality of the writing, which remains impressively idiosyncratic. Just three full-length plays into her career, Miss Henley has given us so strong a sense of Henley, Miss., that you simply wouldn't believe any cartographer, travel agent, or realtor who pretended it didn't really exist.

June

*B*alm in Gilead, which has just been lavishly revived at Circle Rep, is an act of documentary homage to the Lower Depths of the Upper West Side, and if that sounds a bit contradictory, then it accurately reflects some of the more obvious qualities of its author. Lanford Wilson has spent his career communicating what he once called "one of my primary concerns, the *sound* of American speech," and his search for an absolute authenticity has extended from that to setting and atmosphere. He's camera, he's tape recorder—but the circuitry inside is powered by blood, and good, warm blood at that. He writes with almost too great charity of the dispossessed, the deviant, the desperate, the defeated.

That blend of detachment and sympathy is particularly apparent in *Balm*, the play that established him as a fresh and lively theatrical voice way back in 1965. The stage at Circle Rep has been transformed into an all-night coffee shop of dreadfully plausible seediness, and it's populated by hookers, bums, hustlers, and drifters who don't hesitate to add reality to realism by holding two overlapping conversations at once, neither one about anything of any great moment. We are, it seems, being taken on an anthropological field trip into the jungles of New York. But our group leader, Lanford Wilson, doesn't want us simply to observe and analyze the local population, like scientists; he expects us to involve ourselves in their small disasters, like members of the human family we're also supposed to be.

In those twin aims he's considerably assisted by his present director, John Malkovich. As the audience enters the auditorium, it has to step on the squashed beer cans, the cigarette butts, and the other insalubrious detritus that has spilled off the stage, and once there, it's waylaid by actors in full period costume. Some were accosted by an importunate hippie in dark glasses, a peace symbol hanging below the beard and free-flowing hair; I myself was feverishly invited by a huckster in black to buy a curious red garment, which appeared to have been custom-designed for an Amazon seven feet tall and three feet wide. "What *is* that?" I asked. "A slip," he improbably claimed.

In other words, the cast stakes its claim to our camaraderie with a more generous helping of what used to be called audience participation than the original script demanded and then and thereafter devotes itself to the main business of the evening, which is bringing the coffee shop lovingly to life. Here an aging tramp, his face blackened by winter and foul living, repeatedly slaps his brow and gravely addresses the empty air on the subject of women's greed. There a white-faced drug addict, twenty going on ninety, slumps onto the counter, coughing and coughing. Over there a pinched, cropped lesbian balefully fidgets as another woman tries to hijack her drunken, blundering lover. The snoozy chatter eddies, rushes, briefly explodes into excitement, then recedes, dies, to begin the process all over again.

The performers, members of Circle Rep augmented by imports from Chicago's Steppenwolf Theater Company, total twenty-nine in all, an astonishing number to find together on a New York stage in these tightwad times. Moreover, Malkovich has somehow managed to orchestrate them into something nearer an ensemble than anything I've seen in my time here. Every piece and part of this desultory human whirlpool matter, the two characters at the center no more and no less than they should. One is an amateur pusher played by Danton Stone, a gray, fungoid-faced ditherer, helplessly wondering how to renege on a promise to sell heroin for the meanest hood in town. The other is the amateur prostitute he off-handedly befriends, a gawky, guileless chatterbox beautifully played by Laurie Metcalf. A hit man with a cattle syringe brutally ends their brief affair but only momentarily disturbs the arguments and complaints and gibes and jokes that look likely to continue rippling across those tacky booths and cracked counters into the next millennium.

That's surely quintessential Lanford Wilson. *Balm* is, admittedly, very much the play of a very young man. It chronicles the ferment inside the human garbage can with bounce and fizz and glee; its mood is wide-eyed and ingenuous, one of artless excitement at the big, bad city; it is packed with a callow *nostalgie de la boue*. Yet it's also a seminal work, worth discovering by anyone interested in what Wilson went on to write, and not only the more obviously similar pieces such as *The Hot l Baltimore*, set (as it is) in a stately flophouse teeming with tarts and transients. Many of his more interesting characters—the male queen, Lady Bright, or the incestuous couple at the center of *Home Free*—have been the sort that right-minded citizens would piously reject. Many have suffered in some way and to some extent from the national sickness: rootlessness. They tend to be displaced both internally and externally, cut off from the society around them and, more often than not, marooned between a past that has failed to live up to their expectations and a future that looks at best uncertain, at worst very forbidding indeed.

Much of Wilson's work could almost be dubbed crossroads drama, so persistently does it present us with characters at crucial turning points in their lives. What's to happen to the residents of the Hot l Baltimore, now it's to be demolished? Or to Lady Bright, now the disappearance of his beauty and his lovers can no longer be ignored? Or to Ken Talley in *Fifth of July*, faced as he is with such contradictory options as returning to teaching, selling his house, despair, suicide? Or to Sally Talley of *Talley's Folly*, faced as *she* is with the chance of emotional salvation in the form of a gangling Jewish wooer? Or to the uneasily married couples of *Serenading Louie*? Or to the representatives of art, religion, medicine, teaching, and so on whose collective arrival at the crossroads of *Angels Fall* Wilson somewhat overcarefully contrives?

There they all are, disoriented by their very American predicament: Where to find somewhere to belong? For some, there's hope if only they can see and seize it. For others, the way ahead is painfully unclear and painfully painful, too. The signposts at the crossroads are plastered with vague promises of disaster or, at best, a dogged survival. At the end of *Serenading Louie* one forlorn and floundering husband actually kills his wife and children. After the climactic murder of *Gilead* the coffee shop is like a nest of cockroaches adjusting after a visit by the exterminator: Individually they may be destroyed, but collectively they'll always be found in the cracks of the city, sustaining a kind of life with the help of street savvy, cussedness, and sheer biological adaptability.

Lanford Wilson is a tricky writer to assess because his merits sometimes seem to be his faults, and his faults his merits. He can be marvelously truthful; he can fuss truth itself half to death, getting absurdly preoccupied with quirks of speech, niceties of naturalism. He's an agreeably good-natured writer, justly celebrated for the sympathy he shows the least lovely of his characters; he's an excessively good-natured writer, apt to get sentimental about his outsiders and outcasts. All this is embryonically apparent in *Balm in Gilead*, as are some of the themes that have continued to absorb him. At the very start of his dramatic career his people were alone though together, lost though on familiar ground, marooned between that irrecoverable past and that uncertain future—and that, if one thinks about it, is pretty much the way they are still.

. . .

It certainly had its moments, that exotic tribal ritual which calls itself the Tony Awards. Was it my imagination, or did I really see Dorothy Loudon dressed in white fur, sitting on top of a car which was being dragged across the great Gershwin stage by dancers dressed as huntsmen and mugging even more outrageously than she sometimes does in the farce *Noises Off?* Did I really see the cartoonist Al Hirschfeld, a worried-looking gnome with a white beard, entwined around Carol Channing, herself wearing a green dress and a purple hat with a green feather in it, and looking more like one of his caricatures than one of his caricatures? Did I hear the two of them join in a hit song from *La Cage aux Folles?* No, I didn't. Yes, I did. And it seemed a most improbable climax to what, for me, and I imagine many others, was a certain amount of agonizing about which Tony nominees were the most deserving, which winners best for the health of the American theater.

I take awards seriously, maybe too seriously. I like to believe they draw the world's attention to the most remarkable achievements in the writing, directing, performing of drama and musicals; I like to believe they set standards, both for the public and for theater people, now and in the future; and I like to believe that in a small way I myself have contributed to those highfalutin ends. Indeed, one of the things I've most missed while on critical safari over here has been helping choose the *London Evening Standard*'s annual theater awards.

Its winners are picked in a way that's enjoyably conspiratorial and, I suppose, less democratic than are the Tonys. Just before Christmas six or seven of us, critics and theater-mad literati, huddle with brandy and cigars in the upstairs room of a Soho restaurant and bicker and barter until we've chosen what are, I think, the most important honors of their kind in Britain. Here it's much more complicated. A committee of twelve, mainly critics and academics, nominates four candidates in each of nineteen categories; some 670 voters, comprising producers, "media people," actors, directors, members of theater service organizations, and heaven knows who, then select the winners. Whether this produces more satisfactory results I wouldn't dare say. The tough arguing at our judging sessions in London helps exclude some of the more common failings of awards. You don't, for instance, get votes cast out of softheartedness and sentimentality, the feeling that it's actress X's or actor Y's turn to win. You have rationally to justify your choice as articulately as you can. But it could, of course, be argued that with so small a number of judges, you need only one or two to react eccentrically to a play or performer for a prize to go the wrong way. On the other hand, our decisions have been pretty well received over the years by the theater community at large.

Actually the American system doesn't seem to exclude controversy and ill feeling. Quite the contrary. The reason is presumably that the Tonys have more impact on the box office than the *Standard* awards would claim. They can make fortunes, let alone reputations. Even a nomination can increase ticket sales by 30 percent, and victory can transform, in the curiously violent jargon of the trade, a hit into a smash—or, of course, a miss into a hit. Hence the rows and recriminations without which, they tell me, the Tonys just wouldn't be the Tonys.

This year some of these have been about general issues. Several groups of theater professionals, including the Dramatists Guild and Actors' Equity, wanted to be represented on an expanded nominating committee and more heavily represented on the voters' roll itself. The Tony administration committee, which consists of thirteen prominent members of the League of New York Producers and oversees most aspects of the awards, is willing to talk with the would-be reformers but not, it seems, to institute any reforms. They think more professionals would mean more "politics," by which they would appear to mean bias in favor of Americans, especially Americans known to them, and against foreign plays and performers. The reformers think that more professionals would mean more professionalism and point to the example of the Oscars, for which only practitioners and specialists can make nominations in any given field.

Myself, I feel it might be fairer, juster if the profession itself took rather greater part in the nominating and voting process. It is perhaps a bit absurd that "media people" account for nearly one-third of the 670 ultimate arbiters, Actors' Equity and the Dramatists Guild for just over one-sixth. But I have to say I'm not vastly impressed by the arguments adduced either for or against that change. It's surely slanderous to suggest that theater professionals would be totally unbalanced by favoritism and xenophobia. I also find it difficult to idealize the Oscars, which regularly seem to me to reward the safe, bland middlebrow choice. Nor am I convinced by the reformers' other big argument: that the expertise they'd introduce would prevent the more specific rows and recriminations that manage to afflict the Tonys year after year.

Last season Neil Simon's *Brighton Beach Memoirs* failed to get nominated, to some a disgraceful omission. This one, neither Dustin Hoffman nor Michael Rudman appeared on the ballot, though everyone assumed that the skills they displayed as (respectively) leading man and director of *Death of a Salesman* would automatically place them there. The absence of the former has been darkly explained as punishment for his presumption in insisting on playing seven instead of the regular eight performances a week in Miller's play if its initial season is extended. That's a ridiculously paranoid notion—isn't it?

Surely so. There were, after all, perfectly proper objections to Hoffman's performance. He was a bit too young for the part, though that seems more his mother's fault than his own, and perhaps too perky, an error for which he must take responsibility. As I've said before, he sometimes seemed a bit cerebral and calculating, an actor who had spent hours poring over the algebra of his gestures and the mathematics of his movements. Yet that was proof of enterprise, invention, ambition, commodities I myself prefer to reward rather than reject. In any case, he consistently managed to seem spontaneous and sentient and sometimes managed to seem more. I personally deplored his absence, especially when Ian McKellen was nominated for a lecture recitation that I'm sure he himself would have regarded as ineligible for any best actor award, but it made my task easier. I'd expected to anguish between Hoffman and Jeremy Irons in *The Real Thing*. Instead, I was able to plump confidently for Irons.

Actually there were other omissions that struck me as almost worse, suggesting as they did the need for reforms more fundamental than those advocated by the theater professionals. How silly, in view of the decline of Broadway and particularly the decline of Broadway as a forum for straight plays, to limit eligibility for the Tonys as vigorously as the organizers do. Earlier in the year there was a dispute about whether productions at the Lambs and the Mitzi Newhouse—*Painting Churches* and *And a Nightingale Sang . . .* —should qualify, and the narrower argument prevailed, on the grounds that though the performers were paid something akin to Broadway wages, the auditoriums themselves were too small to be considered Broadway theaters. I found and find this hard to understand, but then I don't really see why work in playhouses that confess themselves to be off-Broadway should be excluded from consideration. The *Standard* asks its judges to choose the best that London offers, whether it's to be found in the West End, the National, Hampstead Theater Club, an attic in Canning Town, or a hayloft on Richmond Common. True, that has caused problems since not everyone has always been able to see everything everywhere. But it's meant that the winners have, so to speak, triumphed in an open race, not in one closed to everyone except thoroughbreds from a few stables of long but fading repute. The *Standard* awards may not come with as much swank and swagger as the Tonys, but they recognize more hard-earned accomplishment. They are, genuinely, the Derby.

For instance, it's perfectly possible that the most important, most admirable play to have hit New York this season was *Fool for Love*. But not only was I precluded from considering it as candidate for the best play, I was asked instead to weigh the merits of *Play Memory*, an infinitely less interesting piece and one that ran only a few days. Limiting the Tonys to Broadway productions, yet insisting that four contestants must be put forward in every category, might have been all very well when Broadway overshadowed off-Broadway in quantity and quality of offering. But in the season just finished there were only thirty-six new productions, and the straight plays among them mostly fared very, very badly. If we discount *End of the World*, a commercial failure that I was one of the few to admire, there weren't as many as four genuine candidates in that particular slot. Hence the makeweight appearance of the doomed *Play Memory* on my ballot, along with *Noises Off, Glengarry Glen Ross*, and *The Real Thing*.

The *Standard* has a slot for best comedy as well as best play. That meant that the hilarity of *Noises Off* could be rewarded and, to my delight, was rewarded back in 1982. But though the Tonys have a bewildering number of categories, they have none for best comedy, thus obliging Michael Frayn's bravura farce to compete with two plays of more evident moment. Let me not suggest that a comedy, whatever that is, can't sometimes be more serious, more memorable, and better, whatever that means, than a straight play, whatever that may be. To believe anything else would be to prefer some doleful and dreary neoclassical tragedy to the work of William Wycherley, John Vanbrugh, William Congreve, and George Farquhar. But I suspect that Frayn himself, who has produced more important work than *Noises Off*, would defer to the

higher aspirations and undoubted achievement of Stoppard
and Mamet.

Even before my nice white ballot turned up at *The Times*
theater desk, it was evident that one or other of these would
be proclaimed best playwright. The majority view in the office
was that Stoppard would probably edge it, since *The Real
Thing* was more amusing, more obviously commercial, and
therefore more appealing to the majority of those 670 voters:
a view, I have to say, that still further reconciled me to the
Standard system, where more rigorous tests than mere entertainment value normally get applied to a work. Everyone
at *The Times* also seemed to agree that Jeremy Irons would
be best actor, and Glenn Close best actress, for their performances in the same play. It was when we started to talk of the
musical categories that doubts became apparent. Which would
prevail, *Sunday in the Park with George*, which had ten
nominations, or *La Cage aux Folles*, with nine? No one at
The Times seemed sure.

Well, I ended by voting for neither, for reasons that should
be clear from this journal, but instead allowed the decent, if
unremarkable, *Baby* to sweep my personal board. In the straight
drama slot I chose *Glengarry*, feeling that, while there might
have been some chauvinist pleasure in supporting my fellow
Brit Tom Stoppard, it was much more important to rally
around an American play that will surely be provoking argument ten, twenty, fifty years from now. I also found myself
opting for Kate Nelligan (*Moon for the Misbegotten*) over Glenn
Close, George Hearn (*Cage*) as best actor in a musical, Mike
Nichols (*Real Thing*) as best director—and, oh, so many others that I've not the breath to record them all here. Not that
any or all of my choices mattered greatly to anyone save
myself. The little ticks I scratched onto my ballot might as
well have been on the neck of an elephant, so little effect can
they have had on whatever direction the Tony Awards took.
As it was, I scored with Irons and Nichols and Hearn and a

few others; but *The Real Thing* beat *Glengarry*, Close beat Nelligan, and *Cage* beat *Sunday* as well as *Baby* in practically every category, including best musical.

All that took time to emerge, however. First, we gathered in the Gershwin and were readied for the awards ceremony by the producer Alex Cohen, who perched at a lectern center stage looking and sounding like a crusty but kindly headmaster at the lower school prizegiving. Off came his spectacles as he genially bade the winners to be "witty, intelligent, charming, and, above all, brief" in their acceptances. On they went as he more severely, if bewilderingly, went on to insist there be no "posthumous speeches." Off they came again as he slowly and carefully explained the procedure to be followed by any little boy or girl lucky enough to be called onstage: He or she should exit right, hand over the award for engraving—"and you'll get it back if you've spoken under thirty seconds." And on they went again as he began to check that no one had been silly enough to sit in the wrong seat ("Chita! Chita!") and started shifting about those who turned up in places he didn't like. Why the fuss? Was Sir separating known troublemakers in order to avoid embarrassing displays of school unruliness once the parents had arrived and the proceedings started? Well, sort of. Soon the great American public would switch in, and it would expect the cameras to be on the right faces at the right time, and the whole occasion to be over by 11:00 P.M.

Already one was getting the feeling that the prime object of the evening was to keep the television audience and the television moguls happy, and what happened afterward, when Cohen had retired to the wings to watch, listen, and take the names of malefactors, managed only to reinforce that impression. Increasingly it became apparent that the awards themselves were somewhat irritating interruptions in a show dedicated to demonstrating that Broadway was still Broadway and that even this season has been (as everyone was informed at the

beginning of the telecast) "exciting, productive, and rewarding."

Well-known artist after well-known artist appeared in number after number by Kander and Ebb, Stephen Sondheim,
and Jerry Herman. Shirley MacLaine was there, and Anthony
Quinn in his Zorba outfit, and Raquel Welch, and, strangely
surrounded by men in boaters and draped across what appeared to be a statue of Ebb and Kander, Liza Minnelli. With
all that and more bubbling about them, no wonder the Tonys
themselves seemed a bit bathetic. Still, they happened. Suddenly Al Hirschfeld was onstage to get a special award for his
super drawings. And what followed had, as I say, its curious
and amusing moments.

Up went Jerry Herman, composer of *Cage*, to indulge in
what sounded like gratuitous gloating over the defeat of his
rival, the resolutely dissonant Sondheim: "There's been a
myth abroad that the simple, hummable tune is no longer
alive on Broadway—well!" Then the identity of the winning
librettist was revealed to strange whooping and gurgling sounds
from the row just behind me. It was the noise of the gentleman
who had written the book of *Cage*, Harvey Fierstein triumphant. Up he leaped, weaved and wobbled in high delight
down the aisle, hugging assorted people as he went, clambered
happily onstage, and proceeded to thank all his colleagues,
ending with "my lover, Scott, who typed everything late at
night."

That caused a small sensation. The Gershwin audience nervously buzzed as the television people took a no doubt very
relieved break for ads, though one that must have come too
late for some viewers. One could almost hear the sound of the
sets being indignantly switched off in Iowa and Nebraska and
other places inclined to see New York as a huge fleshpot run
by a mayor with a suspiciously phallic name. Nor can the
viewers have been greatly reassured when Christine Baranski,
best featured actress in a play, came onstage to thank "my

three darling husbands." That was a reference to her supporting role in *The Real Thing*, but one which, since it went
unexplained, must finally have convinced Kansas and Idaho
that Broadway was under the control of the emperor Nero.

The great Dustin Hoffman controversy then decided to make
itself felt. First, Jeremy Irons came up to say some graceful
and pointed things about the excellent performances he'd seen
in New York, "both those nominated and unnominated." And
then who should appear to present the best play award but
Hoffman himself? He stood there, squat and unkempt and
generally looking as if he'd just returned from a clothes-buying
spree on Devils Island, and the audience rose to him as he
explained he'd "come from the *Salesman* company, and they
join me in congratulating the performers honored tonight."
It was a nice, conciliatory gesture, but there was something
about his appearance that seemed to contradict it. The body
language proclaimed that someone, conceivably that nominating committee, had tipped a trash can over his head.

With the news that *The Real Thing* had beaten *Glengarry*
to the bays, there hurried onstage a great gaggle of men in
suits, presumably producers, backers, and one or two of those
people who always join lines when they see them, just to discover what's on offer the other end. At the front was Stoppard,
whom I know from the *Standard* awards in London to be a
good speaker, but here conscientiously incoherent. He muttered something about thirty seconds, rattled out a few dozen
acknowledgments, and disappeared, along with his entourage.
The television audience must have wondered not only who
they were but who the hell he was, this Speedy Gonzales with
the quick-fire British delivery. What it didn't know was that
Cohen's edict against garrulity was being enforced by a monster machine on the balcony, a great circle of red bulbs which
lit up one by one and then flashed out in unison the message
that the allotted half minute was over.

Its impact on the next winner was quite different. "Lila
Kedrova," announced the presenter of the award for the best
featured actress in a musical, and all at once there was an
extraordinary fluttering in a seat near me, as if a thousand
butterflies had been whipped up to frenzy and then released
en masse. Surely so flabbergasted a lady could never make it
to the stage, I thought. But somehow Miss Kedrova did so, to
launch into a long, garbled, and disconcertingly complete list
of those to whom she felt indebted. The audience began to
fidget and nervously giggle, not out of unkindness, but because
that invisible time clock was matching her excitement and
distraction. It flashed, it throbbed, it bulged, it did everything
but explode; and still Miss Kedrova kept on, thanking distant
uncles, long-lost great-aunts, and third cousins twice removed.
Surely there could be no one else, either in the Kedrova clan
or in show business, to acknowledge. But there was. "And I
thank God because He is my producer," gasped Lila, and
came breathless to a halt.

Soon afterward Julie Andrews, who had cohosted the evening with Robert Preston, jubilantly opined that "the lights
of Broadway are shining brighter than ever"; Al Hirschfeld,
Carol Channing, and all the other prizewinners and participants clustered together to sway and kick and sing "The best
of times is now, is now, is now"; and just a quarter of an
hour late, the evening came to its end, leaving me, for one,
somewhat befogged.

Is the best of times really now, at least as far as Broadway
is concerned? Are its lights burning brighter than ever? I
enjoyed voting in the Tony Awards. I was glad when my choices
won, sorry when they lost. I was glad to be at the ceremony
itself. But all the ado couldn't really conceal what the Tonys
seem to have become, a big propaganda exercise, which tries
and perhaps even manages to convince the rest of the world
that the Fabulous Invalid is still fabulous and not really an

invalid at all. And as such maybe they're a way of perpetuating his sickness.

It's about time I sought out some inside views about the health of Broadway, and where better to start than at the offices of the Shuberts and the Nederlanders, who between them own twenty-eight of its theaters and so more or less *are* Broadway? They've wrangled about the management and control of playhouses, they've been reconciled, they've warred again, and now they seem to be observing an uneasy truce. But to meet their top executives is to know that they're never likely to be toasting each other's birthdays over dinner. That's not only because of their professional differences but because they're such a personal contrast. You can easily imagine Bernie Jacobs, of the Shubert Organization, sipping good, dry champagne at Sardi's. James Nederlander, Sr., seems the sort of fellow who'd be happy with a convivial Bud in the bar next door.

The Shuberts themselves, Lee and Sam and J.J., were brought to Syracuse, New York, by their father, a Lithuanian peddler, back in 1882 and proceeded to live out the sort of dream Broadway musicals are wont to celebrate. They began by taking odd jobs in local theaters and rose to success by leasing the flagging Herald Square Theater and booking in the stage western generally credited with popularizing its genre, *Arizona*. Before the present century was more than a few years old, the Shuberts had broken the virtual monopoly of A. L. Erlanger's Theater Syndicate over the nation's playhouses; by 1953 they'd produced no fewer than 520 plays on Broadway, building up an empire itself so large and powerful that the government invoked the antitrust laws and forced its shrinkage. One of the lawyers in that case was Gerald Schoenfeld, who joined the organization and brought in a fellow attorney and family friend called Bernard Jacobs. In the twenty-odd years since the death of the last founding brother, J.J., these two have themselves become synonymous with "the Shuberts." Schoenfeld is the organization's chairman; Jacobs, its president.

James Nederlander is indisputed head of the family empire his father, David, founded in a small way in Detroit and has expanded it greatly. He bought his first New York theater, the Palace, back in 1965 and now has eight in the city, another seventeen out of town, and two in London. In fact, he's clearly a very able businessman, in spite of his aw-shucks manner and country-cousin modesty. Had it not been for his father, he's said, he would very likely be a plumber. You can't imagine Bernie Jacobs, droopy-eyed, silver-haired, and altogether somewhat seigneurial, making any equivalent claim.

Their very offices seem to proclaim their differences. When I saw him, Jacobs sat discreetly enthroned behind a majestic desk in what one might have supposed to be a receiving room in the Élysée Palace were it not for the wonderfully patterned ceiling, which looked as if it belonged to a cardinal or princeling in Renaissance Florence. James Nederlander ("call me Jimmy") slumped amiably backward in his chair in what, were someone to tidy it, might almost have passed muster as a junk shop on Ninth Avenue. Jacobs and I pleasantly conferred about matters theatrical in a comfortable corner of that exquisite room, while he took important phone calls or, more disconcertingly, made them: "Give him five hundred dollars," "Give him air conditioning," "Give him anything he wants." Nederlander mumbled in earnest, homespun tones while rumpled figures shambled inexplicably in and out, genially shaking my hand as they went, "Hi, I'm James, Junior," "Hi, I'm Arthur."

Of the two, the Shuberts are generally regarded as the more interested in artistic quality and have proved it this season by presenting both *Glengarry Glen Ross* and *Sunday in the Park with George*, neither of which can have seemed a likely commercial success. Jacobs is a naturally cautious man—"the problem with Broadway is people trying to raise money for shows that should never be done," he told me. "Most shows that close in a week should never have been done in the first place"—but is himself prepared to take calculated, considered risks. Indeed, he went so far as to claim that the Shuberts put on some of their more obviously commercial offerings "in order to be able to afford to do other things. You've got to remember that the theater is an art form as well as a commercial business. We Shuberts do what we can to keep it alive and creative."

Nederlander's view would probably be that it's easy for Jacobs to talk like that since the Shubert Organization is in a financially privileged position because it's a subsidiary of the nonprofit-making Shubert Foundation and has no mortgages on its theaters. Moreover, didn't he bring the Royal Shakespeare Company's nine-hour adaptation of *Nicholas Nickleby* to New York, and hasn't he taken risks on other upscale British imports, such as Simon Gray's *Otherwise Engaged*, Harold Pinter's *Betrayal*, and Tom Stoppard's *Night and Day?* Nevertheless, his organization's reputation is less for cultural distinction, more for broad entertainment, and he certainly tended to talk in a more down-to-earth way than Jacobs when I met him. "I'd rather be lucky than smart," he characteristically declared. "There isn't a man alive who can pick a hit from a flop, and don't you believe anyone who says he can."

The more I listened to them, the more different the two men seemed, in opinion as in style. For instance, Nederlander told me he'd bought his two theaters in London not because he saw it as a tryout town but because—aw, he loved England, liked to be involved in the English scene, and might transfer the odd production one or the other way. I told him of Jacobs's more mandarin view—"if we want a play in London, we don't need to own any theaters to have it"—and it seemed somewhat to irk him. "The Shuberts," he muttered wearily.

Again, the two men diverged in their diagnoses of the principal troubles afflicting Broadway. Jacobs spoke with feeling against what he called "unreal critical standards—and double critical standards. The critics aren't so rigorous in their judgment of off-Broadway, they expect more of Broadway, and if they don't get it, they complain. I'd like to see an atmosphere where the name of the game wasn't to see how quickly plays can be closed and to tell you how many flaws they have. There never was a piece of theater without flaws. If there was more recognition of this, a more receptive critical attitude, we'd have more straight plays, more serious plays; we would encourage more people to write and more actors to appear in their work."

Was it my imagination, or did Nederlander take a certain relish in demurring? "I think the critics are right about a lot of plays, even if some of them are my own," he rather piously declared. "You can't ask them to subordinate their integrity." He preferred instead to talk of lack of suitable product ("we get so many scripts we feel are so inadequate, it's unbelievable"); of the competition from film, TV, and especially film on cable TV; and of overstringent union rules and featherbedding ("that's a curse of the industry—in my view everything that's nonproductive should be eliminated; you can't go on driving a Model T forever").

Jacobs, too, felt that some sorts of "special deals" would have to be negotiated if the smaller theaters were to become profitable again or, indeed, to survive. New York, he added, had built its last playhouse and might eventually lose some of its existing ones: "If a theater is no longer capable of functioning, there's no point in treating it as the Holy Grail. After all, the important thing is what's on the stage." He also thought that rising costs meant that even fewer works would be produced directly on and for Broadway. Not only would straight plays more and more often be first tried out elsewhere; but more and more musicals would originate off-Broadway, out of town, or in workshops.

Does that sound depressing? Actually Jacobs proclaimed himself "comfortable" with the prospects for Broadway, and Nederlander clearly felt much the same way. Both have good short-term reasons. Nederlander's production of *Noises Off* had, he said, "just about" paid off, and *Cage aux Folles* was on the brink of what must surely be a long, fat period of profit. "All the other things would fall into place if only more of the right product happened to be around," said Nederlander. "All we need is a few more hits, and everyone agrees the Fabulous Invalid would be back to life."

Meanwhile, four of the five musicals in the big Shubert houses—"the primary source of our income"—look set to continue for the foreseeable future. Only *Zorba* at the Broadway will have to be replaced, and, said Jacobs, "there are plenty of candidates for that." *The Real Thing* has already recouped its costs, and somewhat more surprisingly, *Glengarry Glen Ross* is now confidently expected to do so too. *Cats* is still selling out and even continuing to attract the ticket touts. "People in the theater worry about prices more than the purchasers," said Jacobs. "If you've a show they want to see, that doesn't deter them. With hit shows you find the average ticket being sold for substantially more than the cover price."

Indeed, only one thing seemed to make the Shubert president happier than the current offerings on his professional menu, and that was the toy he then proceeded to show me, a computer he keeps secreted in an anteroom. Suddenly there was an adolescent glint in the eye of the high-powered producer, and his fingers began to summon up the bookings for *The Real Thing:* "Look, every seat sold in every section, except four. Four. And I can tell you exactly where they are—"

Was every mainstream voice in the Broadway swim as con-

tent as these two? You couldn't meet the next producer on
my visiting list, Hal Prince, and still think so. There he sat,
in an office that might more accurately have been described
as a closet since it barely had room for a desk, a few books,
some of his many trophies and awards, and his own shiny,
smiling self. But it was soon clear that he was less than sunny
about Broadway, and not only because the two plays he'd
personally directed last season, *Play Memory* and *End of the
World*, both turned out to be flops. He was worried about the
future of straight drama in New York but even more about
that of the genre in which he's long been preeminent, the
musical.

Prince is fifty-six, the son of a stockbroker, an avid theatergoer from boyhood, and from his student days someone
with much more than the usual quota of initiative. At the
University of Pennsylvania he wrote and directed plays and
started a radio station; he used his military service to publish
a *GI Guide to Europe*; at age twenty-six he coproduced *The
Pajama Game*, and two years later *West Side Story*. Since
the death in 1961 of his original partner, Robert Griffith, he's
personally produced and directed some of the most original
and important shows to have hit Broadway, among them *Cabaret*, *Follies*, *Company*, and *Sweeney Todd*. With Stephen
Sondheim, he's been the principal proponent of the so-called
concept musical, with text, score, staging, everything seen
from the start as interdependent parts of an organic whole.
He's had his failures—recently *A Doll's Life*—but they're still
heavily outweighed by proof after proof of his zest, flair, and
enterprising imagination.

But what chance of a similarly fruitful career for a twenty-
six-year-old Prince or Prince clone these days? "Very little,"
he answered. "I have to tell you I'm real glad I'm not starting
in the theater now." He's often produced musicals that have
provoked skepticism in the profession. People thought him
crazy to assay *West Side Story*. They pooh-poohed *Cabaret*.

They took a look at *Fiddler on the Roof* and said, well, they supposed he could afford a flop. Later they dismissed *Evita* as a song album. But reasonable production costs combined with Prince's growing reputation to ensure that those and other doubtful-seeming shows made it to Broadway. You can't easily imagine some tyro finding finance for them now or, indeed, for the genial *Pajama Game*, which cost $169,000 to stage in 1954 but would be more than twenty times that price now.

As I've noted before, Prince accumulated a list of 175 investors, each of whom he'd ask for $1,000 or $2,000. The successes and profits greatly outmatched the failures and losses—"but in any case, no one got hurt, no one *could* get hurt, because if the worst came to the worst, you spent a couple of thousand dollars and you had a marvelous experience." But that system couldn't finance a show that cost $4 million or $5 million, "and even if it could, there's a part of me that would think it obscene." For Prince, the days of the small investor are sadly over. In the future shows will be financed "not for the adventure, the experience, the future of the form, the stature of art but for the return." A *Follies*, a *Pacific Overtures*, a *Company* will, he thinks, stand little or no chance; more and more musicals will be imitations of successful musicals, with any *Raiders of the Lost Ark* of the future inevitably followed by its *Indiana Jones*.

"There'll always be a Broadway, but what sort of Broadway?" asked Prince. "The terrible escalation of costs and prices has narrowed the audience, reduced risk taking, and trivialized the serious theater. What we'll see is the occasional big event like *Cage aux Folles*, and one or two can't-miss plays because they've Dustin Hoffman in them or have proved themselves in England, plus maybe the odd lucky piece from Louisville that got the Pulitzer Prize. And everything will open two weeks before the Tony Awards, and those that win will run.

"What the Shuberts say is perfectly true. People will prob-

ably pay sixty dollars or more for a show. The question is,
What people? I feel terribly worried about the present Broadway audience. They're no longer the sort of people you see
lining up at the Whitney and the Met, people who really care
about the theater. When *Death of a Salesman* was revived
this season, I wondered how it would have done if it were
opening for the first time, cold, without a star. I honestly
don't think it would have made it."

Prince found more creativity in the regional theater than
off-Broadway, which he regarded as "becoming quite like
Broadway, very, very conservative," but he saw its limitations, too. It was more a forum for drama than for musicals
and, either way, was far from being able to boast the professional importance New York still possessed. "The paradox is
that your chances of getting to Broadway with anything sophisticated is very slim, but if you don't get there, you don't
get the attention we managed to get with *Company* and *Follies*
and *Pacific Overtures*. You don't make an international reputation unless you're in this unattainable, absurdly expensive
shopwindow called Broadway."

What, then, of Prince's own future? Well, he'd like the sort
of relationship with some theater that David Mamet has with
the Goodman in Chicago, one that didn't involve him in its
management but gave him houseroom to try out the riskier
sort of musical. "Not a conventional theater, not somewhere
antiseptic like the Kennedy Center, but a place whose masonry
lends itself to the sort of work I like, a great, grimy, grungy
space, maybe a broken-down burlesque house. There's a need,
a need for a musical theater like that, and Broadway is just
not fulfilling it."

I'm nearing the time when I must make my farewells, some
fond, some frustrated. I've at long last learned how to distinguish between an E train and an F train, how correctly to fill
in a New York lottery ticket, how to bargain with those um-

brella salesmen who appear from nowhere when showers strike, and how to get a smile out of the ladies who sit behind the counter in my local post office, severely ensconced as they are beneath a poster reading, "Courtesy is catching, let's start a plague." I've a considerably fuller address book than when I arrived and feel there are plenty of people I'll be seeing again when they or I decide to hop the pond. But I've also an uneasy feeling that after a year spent looking for it, I never quite managed to find the New York theater. It often seemed to be out when I called.

That was a pity, because I'm ending my year as a resident maggot in the Big Apple with a still stronger feeling, which is of possibility waiting to be fulfilled. There's talent; there's skill; there's enthusiasm, vast enthusiasm. There are performers in profusion, itching for a chance to prove themselves; there are theaters in abundance, ready to receive them; and in a conurbation as enormous as this there are more than enough spectators to keep the former busy, the latter filled. There's wealth, both private and public, around, too. The problem is finding the algebra that will bring all these elements together in a nice, satisfying equation.

The productions I've recently seen all seemed to me to reinforce some general point. There's been yet more evidence that the stars of the silver screen are increasingly prepared to go three-dimensional. We've had Kevin Kline as an earnest, pious, and occasionally sanctimonious king in Shakespeare's *Henry V* in Central Park. We've seen Jill Clayburgh with Raul Julia and Frank Langella in George Scott's revival of *Design for Living*. Most important, we've seen the theatrical equivalent if not quite of the Milky Way, at least of one of those dense, bright constellations with names borrowed from Greek myth, in David Rabe's *Hurlyburly:* William Hurt, Christopher Walken, Harvey Keitel, Sigourney Weaver, Judith Ivey.

Wilford Leach's production of *Henry V*, though offering some good individual performances, was pretty uneven as a whole and seemed to reemphasize the lack of, and need for, companies and company acting in Manhattan. So perhaps did *Design for Living*, which was performed in so brash and bulldozing a style that one wondered if its eminent director had got his roles mixed, and the play been staged by General Patton. But Mike Nichols was responsible for the production of *Hurlyburly*, and though one sometimes wished he'd manage to cut a clearer, quicker path through the play's undergrowth, he and his cast succeeded in bringing to collective life the human jungle that was its subject. They made the point that enthusiasm for companies shouldn't mean contempt for ad hoc casts, especially when their members are primarily committed to the movies and so scarcely have time, opportunity or inclination to be anything except ad hoc.

In fact, *Hurlyburly* made several other points, too. It reinforced the current reputation of Chicago as the most theatrically creative of American cities, coming as it did from the Goodman. It reemphasized that big names are increasingly happy to appear off-Broadway, staged as it was at the Promenade Theater. It showed how worryingly expensive off-Broadway production is getting since it was capitalized at $400,000, much the same cost as a Broadway play three or four years ago. It also confirmed that David Rabe is that relatively rare creature, an American dramatist who would regard it as a moral duty to bring his diagnostic and perhaps even remedial skills to the ailing organs of America itself.

By way of putting Rabe's achievement in context, and summing up much that has troubled me about the drama here, let me briefly recall the most striking instance of social and emotional insularity I came across during my stint as a *Times* reviewer. *A Hell of a Town*, as it was called, postulated the destruction by neutron bomb of every inhabitant of Manhattan except a single couple, a workaholic publisher and a workaholic advertising executive. That allowed the author, one Monte Merrick, to crack chirpy jokes about *A Chorus Line*'s

closing and make other in references cumulatively suggesting
that though New York no longer existed, New York was still
the center of the universe. Unsurprisingly it also led to a
certain awkwardness of tone. You could almost hear the question rattling around Merrick's brain box as he contemplated
the corpses piled in the streets outside, the strenuous psyches
intertwined in the apartment where the action was set: What
to take seriously, what to treat frivolously?

Eventually he made up his mind. Megadeath was trivial;
personal relationships were important. He continued gently
to satirize the characters' mental and emotional contortions,
as they earnestly analyzed each other's conscious and uncon-
scious motives and wondered whether their real problem was
that "we don't hurt each other enough." He also seemed to
expect us to care about their feelings, one for another. Their
apparent happiness, they decided, had long been a brittle
sham. Perhaps they should break up. But as the young wife
prepared to leave the young husband for a lonely bed in
Bloomingdale's, he yelled, "Don't leave me!": an agonizing
cry, the climax of the play, and a devastating demonstration
of the priorities of more than a few dramatists these inward-
looking days. There are those who would walk through the
Valley of the Shadow of Death itself with their faces buried
in me-generation propaganda.

But there are those who most decidedly wouldn't, David
Rabe prominent among them. *Hurlyburly*, unlike *Streamers*,
Sticks and Bones, and *The Basic Training of Pavlo Hummel*,
has no connection with Vietnam, but its foray into sleazy-
smart California leaves you feeling you've been dropped by
parachute into a subtropical war zone mainly populated by
the lost, the fearful, the callous, the vicious, and the frankly
reptilian. Its people are mostly members of the movie sub-
culture and almost always high on something, whether it's
booze, drugs, sex, jargon, self-absorption, or paranoia. They
inhabit the Californian jungle, the Californian jungle inhabits

them; and if the result sometimes seems cluttered and confusing, it's also dense and disturbing. With Rabe, Mamet, Shepard, Norman, Durang, Henley, and the long-established Kopit still about, perhaps one needn't be as pessimistic about the future of the American drama as everyday immersion in the New York theater tempts one to become.

All the same, I can't recant or disguise my belief that both that theater and that drama could and should be far more productive and rewarding. That's a conclusion one would base on comparisons, not so much with the achievements of Britain, as with those of America itself. When my country had little to offer except the brittle wit of Noel Coward and Frederick Lonsdale and the slow, didactic plod of J. B. Priestley, this country could point to the towering figure of Eugene O'Neill. When the British theater was, in the words of Arthur Miller, "hermetically sealed off from reality," the American theater could boast Miller himself, not to mention Tennessee Williams and William Inge and the aging Clifford Odets. The American drama, the American theater have been great in the not-so-distant past and, given the right conditions and a little luck in the lottery of talent, could surely be great in the not-so-distant future.

Given the right conditions. That's perhaps where the comparisons with Britain begin to be helpful. As I've said before, the renaissance that has occurred in our theater over the past thirty years owes much to factors that can't be produced to order. There's no formula which can be guaranteed to create a considerable playwright, a remarkable play. But that renaissance would never have happened, or been sustained, without an ingredient which, as it happens, is within the control of the politicians, not of the theatrical muses. This is, of course, the regular injection of public money in grants and subsidies.

They've bought new and renovated theater buildings, and they've brought and continue to bring theater companies. Virtually every British city of any size now has its own permanent rep, many doing work of a good standard. At their head is the National, with its three auditoriums on the South Bank of the Thames, and the Royal Shakespeare Company, with two in London and two (soon to be three) in Stratford-on-Avon. Touring companies bring the regular clients of the principal grant-giving body, the government funded Arts Council of Great Britain, up to a total of eighty-odd, and all its theatrical clients, including those receiving less regular grants, to over a hundred. No one can say precisely how many productions they collectively offer each year or the size of their total audience, but the first figure must well exceed 500 and the second be in the millions. Yet by American standards of national wealth, or even by German standards of public generosity to the arts, the sums involved are pitifully small. In the present financial year the Arts Council is giving some $140 million to all its English clients and about $30 million to its theatrical ones, of which roughly $14 million is going to the National and RSC.

It isn't much, and the theater managements themselves persistently complain that it isn't nearly enough. Yet the relative certainty of receiving the same sum each year, plus whatever it takes to keep pace with inflation, means that they can budget and plan and offer actors regular employment, all with some confidence. It means they can play less safe than if they had to rely on the box office alone, can take the occasional risk and sometimes more than the occasional risk on unknown writers and unusual dramatic subjects, and, at least in some cases, have that right so seriously undervalued in America: the right to fail and fail again. It means that seats can be offered to the public at prices lower than their free-market value by a quarter, a third, a half, sometimes more. Someone sitting in a nice, central position in the National Theater's great Olivier auditorium will pay roughly $14; were all subsidies to be suddenly taken away, and the box office obliged to charge its full cost, the sum on that ticket would be nearer

$30. It's a common complaint in Britain that the social spread
of audiences is narrower than it should be, but subsidies de-
monstrably make it much wider than that currently to be
found on Broadway.

The commercial London managers have sometimes complained of unfair competition, but there's no doubt that the
subsidized theater has been a great help to them at a time
when they've been suffering some of the same economic difficulties as their American counterparts. It has transferred
production after production to the West End, and some offerings have eventually found their way onto Broadway: Harold Pinter's *Betrayal*, David Hare's *Plenty*, and of course,
Peter Shaffer's *Amadeus*, all of which began at the National;
Peter Nichols's *Passion*, C. P. Taylor's *Good*, Pam Gems's
Piaf, which were first produced by the RSC; Ronald Harwood's *The Dresser*, which began in subsidized Manchester;
Trevor Griffiths's *Comedians*, which opened at subsidized
Nottingham; any Alan Ayckbourn play you care to name, since
it would first have been seen in the subsidized theater the
author runs in Scarborough; Bernard Pomerance's *Elephant
Man*, which began at the subsidized Hampstead Theater Club.
This last season the little Lyric Theater in West London, which
relies mainly on local, municipal sources for its subsidies, has
fed both *Noises Off* and *Kean* to New York via Shaftesbury
Avenue.

Some new plays originate in the commercial West End, of
course; but most of the better ones owe a debt to the subsidized
sector. Take *The Real Thing*, for instance. Michael Codron,
who first presented it, is the most creative of commercial managers and, indeed, was described to me by James Nederlander
as the "best dramatic producer in the world." But I'm sure
he would agree that *The Real Thing* would probably never
have existed had not the National Theater and the RSC made
Tom Stoppard's name by performing his important and difficult *Rosencrantz and Guildenstern Are Dead*, *Jumpers*, and

Travesties. Moreover, the actor who originally took the main part in London was Roger Rees, whose reputation rests entirely on his work for the RSC. Indeed, there can hardly be a leading British performer who hasn't been a member of one or the other national companies, and few who haven't appeared at other subsidized theaters, too. Directly, indirectly, the British theater these days *is* the subsidized theater. Had the government and the municipalities never given it the money they have, it would doubtless be at least as deep in the doldrums as it was in the early 1950's; were they to withdraw their help, it would effectively collapse.

That degree of dependence on government generosity often troubles even those Americans with no ideological objection to subsidy, and to some extent their anxieties are shared by the British. We've been worried, for instance, by the coming to power of a Conservative administration dedicated to promoting financial self-reliance in as many areas of life as they can and reducing public expenditure wherever possible. This year the Arts Council has not received the increases it wanted and needed and, partly for that reason and partly because it thinks it should divert more of its resources from relatively privileged London to the relatively underprivileged regions, has left some theaters seriously concerned for their future. The metropolis's first and best known pub-playhouse, the King's Head, is where Hugh Leonard's *Da* proved itself before triumphing on Broadway, but that and other achievements haven't prevented the theater from losing its entire grant. Menacing noises have also been directed at the Royal Court, where Osborne, Arnold Wesker, David Storey, Edward Bond, Caryl Churchill, and many another playwright first made their names, but they seem likely to result not in the withdrawal of grants but in a debilitating financial standstill. And yet the Thatcher government, probably the most right-wing administration I've seen in Britain in my lifetime, still accepts the idea of theatrical subsidy in principle, whatever the economies it's made in practice. It knows that without subsidy an industry which has done much for our national prestige, brought tourists to Britain, and earned yet more foreign currency abroad cannot simply be permitted to die.

The other worry Americans often express about government subsidy is that it could lead to government censorship. So far it doesn't seem to have done so. True, politicians occasionally gripe to find public money spent on artistic projects they find strange or unlikable, but the Arts Council is a government-sponsored and not a government body and over the years has managed to resist such pressures. Its ruling council consists of nineteen people of eminence in public life or the arts or both, reflecting a variety of political attitudes and cultural persuasions, and behind them are specialist advisory panels, consisting of professionals in various artistic fields. I myself sat for some years on the Drama Panel and was there when it voted funds to the socialist Joint Stock Company, the feminist Monstrous Regiment, the revolutionary Marxist Red Ladder company. Of course, the fact that these and others of more or less unorthodox political hue are still Arts Council clients doesn't necessarily mean that their counterparts would find similar tolerance in America. But which, I ask, is the worse: the danger of old-fashioned censorship or the kind of censorship currently inflicted by American dependence on private philanthropy and the box office? The latter, so it seems, tends to censor out of existence the odd, the risky, the controversial, the dangerous quite as inexorably as some puritan ideologue with a blue pencil.

Off-Broadway has continued to seem pretty conservative to me, notwithstanding the sudden appearance in New York of the Mabou Mines, with a rather drab and dull play about the gay life, *Pretty Boy*, and the seasonal figures for Broadway itself tell their own melancholy story. The thirty-six new productions in 1983–84 were easily the lowest total since records properly began in 1899–1900, and fourteen fewer than in the

previous year, which themselves were seventeen less than in
the last good year, 1980–81. Of these just fourteen were new
plays—a category that would include Ian McKellen talking
about Shakespeare and three other one-person shows—compared with twenty-four in 1982–83, and of those ten have
already been proclaimed commercial failures by *Variety*. Total
"playing weeks" were also down, from 1,259 the previous year
to 1,119, and so were audiences, from 8,102,000 to 7,899,000,
even though the 1983–84 season ran one week longer.

There was just one piece of good news. That was that receipts at the Broadway box offices were a record, a total of
$226,508,000 compared with the previous high of $221,235,000,
achieved in 1981–82. That reflected the astonishing success
of, especially, *Cats, La Cage, 42nd Street, A Chorus Line*,
and, to a lesser extent, *The Real Thing* and therefore was not
perhaps such unrelievedly and unmixedly good news. It emphasized the extent to which Broadway is dependent on the
big, exotic musical happening for its financial health. It emphasized how much its name is now synonymous with show
business, and how little with theater, let alone the sort of
theater it stood for twenty, thirty, forty years ago.

And to judge by my recent conversations with them, the
principal producers seem content for that trend to continue
or even to accelerate. It troubled me that Bernie Jacobs,
undeniably a man of sophistication and taste, should have
told me, as he did, that New York was "the place where the
creativity of theater has reached its highest zenith point"—
and then justified that judgment by talking of its technical
excellence. On Shaftesbury Avenue, he no doubt correctly
noted, a total of 150 lamps is considered a large number for
a play; on Broadway, the same production would be illumi-
nated by 350 to 400. I felt like pointing out that a healthy
drama wasn't the same thing as a brilliantly lit one. A finely
written and performed play can hold its audience even if the
lighting is a couple of neon tubes borrowed from the local

mortuary, and conversely, a million lamps and all the technical expertise in the world can't transform a poor piece into a good one. But I sensed that Jacobs was reading the collective mind of his audience correctly. The more you pay, the more technical excellence you expect; so up go costs, the more you pay, up goes the pressure for more wizardry; and so the circle continues. It seems to me a recipe for more flash, more glitz, less content; some would say, precisely the way Broadway is going.

What hope, then, for the smaller Broadway theaters and, therefore, for the straight drama in New York? That still seems the problem. The Lyceum, the Belasco, and the Ambassador haven't opened at all during my time here, and the Royale, the Ritz, the O'Neill, the Cort, the Biltmore, the Nederlander, the Longacre, and the Music Box are among those cheerfully advertising shows that have closed and in some cases closed months ago. Indeed, no fewer than nineteen of the thirty-eight functioning Broadway theaters are currently dark, and the prospects for many of them can't be good. It's not only Jacobs who is darkly hinting at possible demolition to come. His fellow Shubert, Gerald Schoenfeld, recently estimated that 50 percent of Broadway theaters were "either economically obsolete or obsolescent—they can be counted upon to generate greater and greater losses." It may only be a question of time, he added, "before their demolition will occur, or government will face the prospect of subsidy or government operation in order to ensure their continuance—a prospect no one in a free society and a free theater would even wish to contemplate."

The warning is obviously well informed, but the apprehension about one of the possible solutions seems curious. Is subsidy really to be equated with demolition as something too horrible to contemplate? Can it really not be reconciled with a "free society"? Isn't Britain a pretty free country, and hasn't it a theater as free as most people would wish a theater to be? The truth is that some sort of government, state, or city help may be the only way of ensuring that Broadway remains even slightly hospitable to straight drama and, indeed, that the rest of the New York theater flourishes as it could and should flourish. That's not just the view, let me reemphasize, of some dreamer from a European social democracy. That's the view of very many people over here, starting with the inevitable Joe Papp, who was (incidentally) even more emphatic, decided, and articulate about the matter when I ran into him the other day.

Not that he seems to have been able to do much about it. There has been progress in some of those areas that have preoccupied me in the past months. Those trying to create a National Theater at the Kennedy Center in Washington have made a bold choice for its first director in Peter Sellars, but it is, of course, far too early to discover if he'll be able to justify the enterprise's grandiose title. Again, the board of Lincoln Center appears to have prevailed in its conflict with the board of the Vivian Beaumont, news that means that the theater itself could be more or less permanently open before long. However, there seems to be nothing encouraging to report about Papp's plan to create a National Theater on Broadway with funds derived either from the sale by theater owners of their air rights or from the coffers of local and national government, or both.

Yet surely this is the way forward, not just for Broadway but for the American theater as a whole. This isn't to say it ever could or should become as exclusively reliant on public sources as its British counterpart. The sanest, most balanced voices—a Papp, a Prince—would like to see a mixed theatrical economy, with more public funding but no decrease of private philanthropy either. That would mean a theater totally vulnerable neither to shifts of sympathy in national and local government nor to the vagaries of foundations, the whims of sponsors, the sort of mass revolt by well-to-do subscribers that brought about the end of the Irving-Blau regime at the Vivian Beaumont.

Hope of more money from city and state sources doesn't seem wholly unrealistic. Federal funding is considerably less likely, considering the economic convictions of the present administration, which has been doing its best to cut the National Endowment for the Arts's already slim budget to still paltrier levels. But who knows? President Reagan cannot hold power forever, and while he does, there are forums in which the Papps and their followers can wage their crusade for more public money for the theater and, as important, for more public acceptance of the *idea* of public money for the theater. And here let me interject a curious fact which I've just discovered and perhaps isn't as widely appreciated as it might be: That is that the American government is already much more generous to the arts than its British counterpart. It is just that it displays it in a different way and in my respectful view a less satisfactory one.

Its system of tax relief makes it far easier and less financially painful for both individuals and businesses to support the arts, and of course, every dollar thus lost to the IRS is one that the U.S. government could be said to have donated. If one takes that into account, one finds that public spending in the field in the United States was recently running at an annual $14 a head, compared with about $7.50 in Britain. Indeed, my country shows up very poorly in a table of Western generosity to the arts. Sweden is at the top, with a per capita expenditure of over $30, followed by France, and Britain is at or near the bottom. There is, I should add, no equivalent table devoted to the theater alone, but the proportions would probably be much the same.

Why, then, has public expenditure achieved so much more for the theater in Britain than would appear to have been the case in America? The reasons are obvious. Individual and business charity doesn't always respond strictly to need or rigorously reward desert, and when it does, it has little sense of the picture as a whole. A disinterested organization of national standing, able to draw on every kind of professional expertise, is more likely both to take the large cultural view and successfully to balance application for funds against application for funds. In other words, an Arts Council or a properly funded NEA is more likely to lead to a thriving theater than hit-or-miss philanthropy.

But is it somehow less "free"? I can't see that it's freer for the American government to allow a minority to disburse tax revenue that would otherwise belong to the nation than to find some democratic way of using the same money to advance the cultural interests of the majority. At least it seems a matter worth considering and debating, coming down (as it does) to this question: Are the funds that the U.S. government is giving the theater really helping it as much as they might? Might not, let's say, half the present amount achieve twice as much if it were sagely administered?

To repeat: Public money can't achieve much of and by itself. I've heard it unkindly suggested that the heavily subsidized German theater, that temple to boredom, is a proof of that. But more subsidy in America would give a fillip, and maybe more than a fillip, to the underused, underdeveloped talent already here, waiting, and ready to go. One might even see it as a possible answer to the narrow horizons of so much American drama, that emotional insularity of which I've so often complained. Make more money available to more theaters, and they'll rapidly start looking more energetically for new work and new writers, and the more playwrights there are, the more pressure there'll be on them to range and diversify in their choice of subject. Those familiar, familial obsessions simply won't seem enough.

But it's hard to forecast the precise effects of more public subsidy for the theater. It's a lot easier to wax oracular about the effects of its dearth or absence. Without it, New York can't expect any "national theater" or, indeed, any repertory company of stature. Without it, it can't expect classic revivals, plays with large or largish casts, or even much in the way of serious or original drama. Without it, it can expect to see more dark theaters on Broadway and more cautious theaters off it. Without it, the Fabulous Invalid will increasingly resemble a gaudily painted clown, crazedly singing and dancing in a terminal ward, and off-Broadway will increasingly be thought of as an invalid, too, only not a very fabulous one. Without it—but why go on? All that energy and expertise, all those beautiful buildings, all that tradition, all that possibility—what a sad, sad waste that would be!

Index